COMPARATIVE POLITICS TODAY

FIFTH EDITION

COMPARATIVE POLITICS TODAY
A THEORETICAL FRAMEWORK

Gabriel A. Almond
Late, Stanford University

G. Bingham Powell, Jr.
University of Rochester

Russell J. Dalton
University of California, Irvine

Kaare Strøm
University of California, San Diego

PEARSON
Longman

New York   San Francisco   Boston
London   Toronto   Sydney   Tokyo   Singapore   Madrid
Mexico City   Munich   Paris   Cape Town   Hong Kong   Montreal

Acquisitions Editor: Vikram Mukhija
Supplements Editor: Brian Belardi
Executive Marketing Manager: Ann Stypuloski
Production Manager: Eric Jorgensen
Project Coordination, Text Design, and Electronic Page Makeup: GGS Book Services
Cover Design/Manager: Wendy Ann Fredericks
Cover Photo: Rubberball/Photolibrary
Senior Manufacturing Buyer: Dennis J. Para
Printer and Binder: Courier Corp.
Cover Printer: Coral Graphic Services, Inc.

Library of Congress Cataloging-in-Publication Data

Comparative politics today: a theoretical framework/Gabriel A. Almond . . . [et al.].—5th ed.
   p. cm.
  Includes bibliographical references and index.
  ISBN 978-0-205-57656-2
  1. Comparative government.   I. Almond, Gabriel A. (Gabriel Abraham), 1911–2002.
  JF51.C6149 2008
  320.3—dc22

                                     2007023991

Please visit us at www.ablongman.com

ISBN-10: 0-205-57656-7
ISBN-13: 978-0-205-57656-2

1 2 3 4 5 6 7 8 9 10—CRW—10 09 08 07

BRIEF CONTENTS

DETAILED CONTENTS

PART TWO
System, Process, and Policy

C H A P T E R   6

Government and Policymaking   133

C H A P T E R   7

Public Policy   168

Comparative Politics Today: A Theoretical Framework, Fifth Edition, presents in the form of a separate book Parts One and Two of *Comparative Politics Today: A World View*, Ninth Edition (2008). As a text, *Comparative Politics Today: A Theoretical Framework* is ideally suited for courses that seek to provide a broad and comprehensive thematic overview of comparative politics, which instructors may then combine with their own selection of reading materials from the literature of country and analytic studies.

For the past three decades, *Comparative Politics Today: A Theoretical Framework* and its "cousins" have been among the most influential textbooks in comparative politics. Our book traces back to the original Almond and Powell, *Comparative Politics: A Developmental Approach* (Little, Brown 1966), as revised and expanded in *Comparative Politics: System, Process and Policy* (Little, Brown 1978), by the same authors. The framework these books developed was incorporated into the *Comparative Politics Today* texts and supplemented with analyses of specific countries by leading specialists. Earlier editions of this book in the 1970s pioneered the teaching of systematic comparison of the political cultures, structures, processes, and policy performances of the world's political systems. Later editions have explored the impact of enormous changes—such as democratization, the breakup of the Soviet empire, and intensified threats from ethnic conflict—that have shaped politics in many nations. Throughout, these editions reflect Gabriel Almond's creativity and the applicability of his framework to the changing concerns of students of political science.

FEATURES

This Fifth Edition, like the previous one, begins by explaining why governments exist, what functions they serve, and how they create political problems as well as solutions. Chapter 1 also introduces the three great challenges facing most states in the world today: building a common identity and sense of community; fostering economic and social development; and securing democracy, human rights, and civil liberties. Chapter 2 sketches the concepts needed to compare politics in very different societies: political systems and their environments, structures and functions, policy performance and its consequences. Jointly, these two chapters constitute Part One, which spells out the unique framework that our book employs.

Part Two elaborates on important components of the system, process, and policy framework, discussing the causes and consequences of political cultures, interest groups, parties and other aggregation structures, constitutions, key policymaking structures, and public policies. The continuing and unprecedented spread of democracy is not only a development to be celebrated, but also a reason that the issues of democratic representation, as discussed in Chapters 4 through 6, are becoming increasingly relevant to an ever larger share of the world's population. Growing prosperity in many parts of the world means that the issues of development and public policy (Chapters 1 and 7) are changing. While the global incidence and intensity of war has happily declined in recent years, conflicts still devastate or threaten communities in areas such as Iraq, Afghanistan, Lebanon, South Asia, Sudan, and other parts of Africa. And the world faces enormous challenges, new as well as old, in such areas as climate change, migration, economic globalization, epidemic disease, international terrorism, and nuclear proliferation. All of these developments make it more important than ever to understand how political decisions are made, and what their consequences might be, in the very different political systems that make up our political world.

The tables, figures, and boxes in *Comparative Politics Today: A Theoretical Framework* provide examples, compare systems, and discuss important trends, such as globalization, democratization and backsliding, the rise of fundamentalism, the challenges to the rule of law, and the recruitment of women into leadership roles in politics. These comparative tables, figures, and examples draw systematically from the same set of countries: Britain, France, Germany, Japan, Russia, China, Mexico, Brazil, Iran, India, Nigeria, and the United States. Our book can therefore be conveniently supplemented with case studies on any or all of these twelve countries. The Ninth Edition of *Comparative Politics Today: A World View* contains a separate chapter on each of these countries.

NEW TO THIS EDITION

This Fifth Edition of *Comparative Politics Today: A Theoretical Framework* contains a substantially revised set of chapters that now include review questions as well as a guide to the key themes in each chapter. The chapters have also been shortened and revised for greater readability, and we have expanded the number of illustrative example boxes.

Also, this new edition is now accompanied by MyPoliSciKit, a premium online supplement that offers book-specific learning objectives, chapter summaries, weblinks, flashcards, and practice tests, as well as case studies with streaming video, comparative exercises, mapping exercises, and country studies to aid comprehension and critical thinking. To also help students make connections between concepts and country knowledge, MyPoliSciKit includes an hourly *New York Times* newsfeed and access to popular and academic journals through Research Navigator. With the Instructor Gradebook, instructors can easily track student work on the site and student progress on each activity. MyPoliSciKit is available at no additional charge when bundled with a copy of this text. To learn more, please visit www.mypoliscikit.com or contact your Longman representative.

ACKNOWLEDGMENTS

The Acknowledgments in the Ninth Edition of *Comparative Politics Today: A World View* express our debts and appreciation to those who helped us prepare that edition, which is the basis of this volume also. We reiterate our gratitude to the authors of the twelve country studies in that volume—Richard Rose (Britain); Martin A. Schain (France); Russell J. Dalton (Germany); Frances Rosenbluth and Michael F. Thies (Japan); Thomas F. Remington (Russia); Melanie Manion (China); Wayne A. Cornelius and Jeffery A. Weldon (Mexico); Frances Hagopian (Brazil); Subrata K. Mitra (India); Robert J. Mundt, Oladimeji Aborisade, and A. Carl LeVan (Nigeria); Houchang E. Chehabi and Arang Keshavarzian (Iran); and Austin Ranney and Thad Kousser (United States)—who added once more, as they and their predecessors have many times over the years, essential contents and interpretative insights to our basic theoretical framework. We are also grateful to Farhat Popal for research assistance and to Sonal R. Desai for assistance in developing the index for this edition. Finally, we wish to thank the reviewers of both volumes—Jim Peterson, Valdosta State; Michael Brittingham, University of Louisville; and Jon Jonassen, Brigham Young University-Hawaii; Maria Hsia Chang, University of Nevada-Reno; James Sperling, University of Akron; James Warhola, The University of Maine; and Dwayne Woods, Purdue University-West Lafayette—and the team at Longman and GGS Book Services: Eric Stano, Vikram Mukhija, Lucy Silberman, Eric Jorgensen, Dennis Para, Wendy Fredericks, Ann Stypuloski, Liz Hoens, and Doug Bell.

Gabriel Almond, from whose innovative work this book derives, had enormous influence on the study and teaching of comparative politics. He wrote at length about many important political topics, including political culture, interest groups, fundamentalism, and the history of political science. One of his greatest achievements was his continuing commitment to finding ways to understand, compare, and explain the most diverse aspects of political life. This text is deeply shaped by that commitment, both through Gabriel Almond's own involvement in writing it and through his influence upon each of us. And one of his greatest legacies is the generations of students who have learned about comparative politics and our world through the insights he provided.

G. BINGHAM POWELL, JR.
RUSSELL J. DALTON
KAARE STRØM

ISSUES IN COMPARATIVE POLITICS

WHAT IS POLITICS?

Some people love politics. They relish the excitement of political events, such as a presidential election, as they would an exciting athletic contest (the World Series of baseball or the World Cup of soccer, perhaps). Others are fascinated with politics because they care about the issues and their consequences for people in their own communities and around the world. Still others hate politics, either because it sets groups and individuals against each other, or because it involves abuse of power, deceit, manipulation, and violence. Finally, some people are indifferent to politics because it has little to do with the things that matter most to them. All of these reactions involve kernels of truth about politics. Indeed, most of us react to politics with a mixture of these sentiments. Politics has many faces and can be a force for good as well as evil. The core of politics, however, is about human beings making important decisions for themselves and for others.

This book is about the comparative study of politics. In order to make political comparisons, we need to understand what politics is as well as what it means to study politics comparatively. Comparative politics thus involves two separate elements:

- It is a subject of study—comparing the nature of politics and the political process across different political systems.
- It is a method of study—involving how and why we make such comparisons.

We address the first point in this chapter; Chapter 2 discusses the second.

Politics deals with human decisions, and political science is the study of such decisions. Yet, not all decisions are political, and many of the social sciences study decisions that are of little interest to political scientists. For example, consider when you go with a friend to an event, such as a concert or a soccer match. You can spend your money on the tickets (to get the best seats possible) or on food and drink, or you can save your money for the future. Economists study the sorts of spending decisions people make, and perhaps how they reach them. Psychologists, on the other hand, might study why you went to the event with this friend and not another, or who suggested going in the first place.

Political scientists seldom examine such personal experiences, unless they have political consequences. Instead, we examine the political process and its impact on the citizens. Political decisions constantly touch our lives in many ways, our careers, and our families. Our jobs are structured by government regulations, our homes are built to conform to government housing codes, our public schools are funded and managed by the government, and even when we go to a concert or sporting event, we travel on roads maintained by the government and monitored by the police. We might not think of politics as omnipresent in our lives, but it affects us in many important ways. Therefore, it is important to study how political decisions are made and what their consequences are.

Political decisions are *public* and *authoritative*. There is no such thing as political solitaire, playing politics by yourself. Political decisions take place within some community that we call a *political system*, which we describe below. Yet, not all social decisions are public. Most of what happens within families, among friends, or in social groups belongs to the *private sphere*. Actions within this sphere do not bind anyone outside that group. In most societies, your choice of concert partners and food are private decisions.

The *public sphere* deals with collective decisions that extend beyond the individual, typically involving government action. In totalitarian societies, like Hitler's Third Reich and some communist nations, the public sphere is very large and the private sphere is very limited. The state tries to dominate the life of its people, even intruding into family life. On the other hand, in some less developed nations the private domain may almost crowd out the public one. People in many African nations, for instance, may be unaware of what happens in the capital city and untouched by the decisions made there. Western democracies have a more balanced mix of private and public spheres. However, the boundaries between the two spheres get redrawn all the time. A couple of decades ago, the sex lives of U.S. presidents or members of the British royal family were considered private matters, not to be discussed in public. These norms are changing in Britain and the United States, but the traditional standards remain in other countries. Similarly, at one time in British history certain religious beliefs were considered treasonous. Today, religious beliefs are considered private matters in most modern democracies, but not in many other parts of the world. Even though politics may be influenced by what happens in the private domain, it deals directly with only those decisions that are public.

Politics is also *authoritative*. Authority means that formal power rests in individuals or groups whose decisions are expected to be carried out and respected. Thus, political decisions are binding for members of that political system. Governments may use force to ensure compliance, although authority is not always backed up by force. For instance, a religious authority, such as the Pope, has few coercive powers. He can persuade, but rarely compel, the Catholic Church's followers. In contrast, tax authorities, such as the U.S. Internal Revenue Service, can both exhort and compel people to follow their rules.

Thus, politics refers to activities associated with the control of public decisions among a given people and in a given territory, where this control may be backed up by authoritative means. Politics involves the crafting of these authoritative decisions—who gets to make them and for what purposes.

We live in one of the most exciting times to study politics. The end of the Cold War created a new international order, although its shape is still uncertain. The democratic transitions in Eastern Europe and many developing nations have transformed the world, although it is unclear whether these new democracies will endure and what forms they might take. In Western nations, new challenges and choices have arisen that divide their citizens. Some of these problems—such as confronting global warming and achieving international peace—are transnational. Part of their solutions, we hope, lies in the political choices that people make about their collective future. Our goal in this book is to give you a sense of how governments and politics function to address these challenges.

GOVERNMENTS AND THE STATE OF NATURE

Governments are organizations of individuals who have the power to make binding decisions on behalf of a particular community. Governments thus have authoritative and coercive powers. Governments do many things. They can wage war or encourage peace; cultivate or restrict international trade; open their borders to the exchange of ideas and art or close them; tax their populations heavily or lightly and through different means; allocate resources for education, health, and welfare or leave such matters to others. People who are affected by such decisions may well agree with them and indeed welcome them, but there is also often heated disagreement about the proper role of government decisions.

Debates over the nature and appropriate role of government are far from new. They reflect a classic polemic in political philosophy. For centuries, philosophers have debated whether governments are a force for good or evil. In the seventeenth and eighteenth centuries—the time of the English, French, and American revolutions—much of this debate was couched in arguments concerning the **state of nature.**

Philosophers thought about the state of nature as the condition of humankind if no government existed. In some cases, they thought that such a situation existed before the first governments were formed. These philosophers used their ideas about the state of nature to identify an ideal social contract (agreement) on which to build a political system. Even today, many philosophers find it useful to make such a mental experiment to consider the consequences of having governments.

These debates have shaped our images of government, even to the present. The contrast between Thomas Hobbes' and Jean-Jacques Rousseau's ideas about the state of nature is most striking. Hobbes was the ultimate pessimist. He thought of the state of nature as mercilessly inhospitable, a situation of eternal conflict of all against all, and a source of barbarism and continuous fear. He pessimistically argued that "[i]n such condition, there is no place for Industry; because the fruit thereof is uncertain: and consequently no Culture of the Earth; no Navigation, nor use of the commodities that may be imported by Sea; no commodious Building, . . . no Arts; no Letters; no Society; and which is worst of all, continuall feare, and danger of violent death; And the life of man, solitary, poor, nasty, brutish, and short."[1]

Rousseau, in contrast, was more optimistic. For him, the state of nature represented humanity before its fall from grace, without all the corruptions that governments have introduced. "Man is born free," Rousseau observed in *The Social Contract*, "and yet everywhere he is in chains." Rousseau saw governments as the source of power and inequality, and these conditions in turn as the causes of human alienation and corruption. "The extreme inequality in our way of life," he argued, "excess of idleness in some, excess of labor in others; . . . late nights, excesses of all kinds, immoderate ecstasies of all the passions; fatigues and exhaustion of mind, numberless sorrows and afflictions . . . that most of our ills are our own work; that we would have avoided almost all of them by preserving the simple, uniform, and solitary way of life prescribed to us by nature."[2]

John Locke's ideas have been particularly important for the development of Western democracies. He took a position between those of Hobbes and Rousseau. Compared with Hobbes, Locke thought of human beings as more businesslike and less war prone. Yet, like Hobbes he proposed a social contract to replace the state of nature with a system of government. While Hobbes thought the main task for government is to quell disorder and protect against violence and war, Locke saw the state's main role as protecting property and commerce and promoting economic growth. He believed government would do this by establishing and enforcing property rights and rules of economic exchange. Whereas Hobbes thought government needed to be a Leviathan—a benevolent dictator to whom the citizens would yield all their power—Locke favored a limited government.[3]

Although these debates began centuries ago, they still underlie current discussions on the appropriate role of government. To some, government is the solution to many human needs and problems—a theme that former U.S. President Bill Clinton often advocated. To others, the government is often part of the problem—a theme that former U.S. President Ronald Reagan articulately argued. To some, government exists to create the social order that protects its citizens; to others, the government's rules limit our freedoms. This tension is part of the political discourse in many contemporary nations, including the United States. We explore these contrasting views and different examples of government structures in this book.

WHY GOVERNMENTS?

A recent libertarian science fiction book begins with the scenario of a group of travelers landing at an airport after a long overseas flight. As they disembark from the plane, they notice there are no police checking passports, no customs officers scanning baggage, and no officials applying immigration rules.[4] They had landed in a

U.S. Government's Top Ten List	**BOX 1.1**

Paul Light surveyed 450 historians and political scientists to assess the U.S. government's greatest achievements in the past half century. Their top ten list is as follows:

- Help rebuild Europe after World War II
- Expand the right to vote for minorities
- Promote equal access to public accommodations
- Reduce disease
- Reduce workplace discrimination
- Ensure safe food and drinking water
- Strengthen the nation's highway system
- Increase older Americans' access to health care
- Reduce the federal deficit
- Promote financial security in retirement

Source: Paul Light, *Government's Greatest Achievements of the Past Half-Century* (Washington, DC: Brookings Institution, 2000) (www.brookings.edu/comm/reformwatch/rw02.pdf).

society without government, and the puzzle was what having no government would mean for the citizenry. The answer is a lot (see Box 1.1). As philosophers have pointed out, there are many reasons why people create governments and prefer to live under such a social order. We shall discuss some of these, beginning with activities that help generate a stable community in the first place and then those that help this community prosper.

Community- and Nation-Building

One of the first purposes of governments is to create and maintain a community in which people can feel safe and comfortable. While humans may be social beings, it is not always easy to build a community in which large numbers of people can communicate, feel at home, and interact constructively. Governments can help generate such communities in many different ways, for example, by teaching a common language, instilling common norms and values, creating common myths and symbols, and supporting a national identity. However, sometimes such actions create controversy because they threaten the values of minority groups.

Nation-building activities help instill common world views, values, and expectations. Using a concept discussed more in Chapter 3, governments can help create a national **political culture.** The political culture defines the public's expectations toward the political process and its role within the process. The more the political culture is shared, the easier it is to live in peaceful coexistence and engage in activities for mutual gain, such as commerce.

Security and Order

Government activities partially reflect Hobbes' belief that only strong governments can make society safe for their inhabitants. Providing security and law and order is among the most essential tasks that governments perform. Externally, security means protecting against attacks from other political systems. Armies, navies, and air forces typically perform this function. Internally, security means protecting against theft, aggression, and violence from members of one's own society. In most societies providing this protection is the function of the police.

Providing security and order is a critical role of modern governments. While governments worldwide have privatized many of the services they once performed—for example, those involving post offices, railroads, and telecommunications, few, if any, governments have privatized their police or defense forces. This shows how security is one of the most essential roles of government. The international terrorist attacks in New York City and Washington, D.C. on September 11, 2001, and subsequent attacks in London, Madrid and other cities underscore the importance of security.

Protecting Rights

John Locke considered property rights to be particularly critical to the development of prosperous communities. Without effective protection of property rights, people will not invest their goods or energies in productive processes. Also, unless property rights exist and contracts can be negotiated and enforced, people will not trust their neighbors enough to engage in trade and commerce. Anything beyond a subsistence economy requires effective property rights and contracts. Therefore, Locke believed that the primary role of government is to establish and protect such rights. Similarly, contemporary authors argue that social order is a prerequisite for development and democratization.[5]

Effective property rights allocate ownership and provide security against trespass and violations. Such rights must also make the buying and selling of property relatively inexpensive and painless. Finally, people must have faith that their property rights can be defended. Thus, many analysts argue that one of the most restrictive limitations on development in the Third World is the government's inability (or unwillingness) to guarantee such rights. Peasant families who have lived for generations on a plot of land cannot claim ownership, which erodes their incentive and opportunity to invest in the future.

Although Locke was most concerned with economic property rights, governments also protect many other social and political rights. Among them are freedoms of speech and association and protection against various forms of discrimination and harassment. Indeed, the protection of these rights and liberties is one of the prime goals of government—with other factors such as nation-building, security and property rights providing a means toward this goal. Governments also play a key role in protecting the rights of religious, racial and other social groups. Human development stresses the expansion of these rights and liberties, and governments play a key role in this process.

Promoting Economic Efficiency and Growth

Economists have long debated the government's potential role in promoting economic development. Neoclassical economics shows that markets are efficient when property rights are defined and protected, when competition is rigorous, and when information is freely available. When these conditions do not hold, markets may fail and the performance of the economy may suffer.[6] At least in some circumstances, governments can lessen the results of market failure.

Governments may be especially important in providing **public goods,** such as clean air, a national defense, or disease prevention. Public goods have two things in common. One is that if one person enjoys them, they cannot be withheld from anyone else. The second is that one person's enjoyment or consumption of the goods does not detract from anyone else's. Consider clean air. For most practical purposes, it is impossible to provide one person with clean air without also giving it to his or her neighbors. Moreover, my enjoyment of clean air does not mean that my neighbors have any less of it. Analysts therefore argue that people in a market economy will not pay enough for public goods. They claim that only government can provide such public goods. Otherwise, people will not voluntarily pay for public goods because they can benefit from the goods that others provide, or they will not act until they are assured others will also contribute.

Governments can also benefit society by controlling the **externalities** that occur when an activity produces costs that are not borne by the producer or the user. For instance, many forms of environmental pollution occur when those who produce or consume goods do not pay all of the environmental costs. Polluting factories, waste dumps, prisons, and major highways can impose large costs on those who live near them. NIMBY ("not in my backyard") groups are an example of citizens complaining about these costs. Governments can help protect people from such unfair externalities or ensure that burdens are fairly shared.

Governments also can promote fair competition in economic markets. For example, governments can assure that all businesses follow minimum standards of worker protection and product liability. In other cases, the government may control potentially monopolistic parts of the economy to ensure that suppliers do not take advantage of their market power. This happened in the nineteenth century with railroad monopolies, and now in the twenty-first century with technology monopolies, such as Microsoft, or telecommunications companies. In these cases the government acts as the policeman to ensure that the economically powerful do not exploit their power. Sometimes, the government itself may become the monopolist. There are some markets in which very large start-up costs or prohibitive costs of coordination mean that there should be only one producer. The government may then set itself up as that monopolist, or it may decide to tightly control a private monopolist.

Telecommunications have commonly been a government monopoly, as have mail services and strategic defense industries.

Social Justice

Governments can also play a role in dividing the fruits of economic growth in equitable ways. Many people argue that governments are needed to promote social justice by redistributing wealth and other resources among citizens. In many countries the distribution of income or property is highly uneven. Moreover, in many societies income and wealth inequalities worsen over time. Brazil, for example, has one of the most severe income inequalities in the world, an inequality that grew in every decade from the 1930s to the 1990s.

Under such circumstances, social justice may require a "new deal," especially if inequalities deprive many individuals of education, adequate health care, or other basic needs. Government can intervene to redistribute resources from the better-off to the poor. Some theorists argue that such transfers should attempt to equalize the conditions of all citizens. Others prefer governments to redistribute enough to equalize opportunities, and then let individuals be responsible for their own fortunes.

Many private individuals, organizations, and foundations attempt to help the poor, but they generally lack the capacity to effect large-scale redistribution. Governments do, at least under some circumstances. Many tax and welfare policies effectively redistribute income, although the degree of redistribution is often hotly disputed. Yet most individuals agree that governments should provide their citizens with the opportunities to reach certain minimum standards of living and a social safety net.

Protecting the Weak

We commonly rely on the government to protect individuals and groups that are not able to speak for themselves. Groups such as the poor or the homeless or future generations cannot effectively protect their own interests. Governments, however, can protect the interests of the unborn and prevent them from getting saddled with economic debts or environmental degradation. In recent decades, governments have become much more involved in protecting groups that are politically weak or disenfranchised, such as children, the old, and the infirm or disabled, as well as nonhumans—from whales and birds to trees and other parts of our natural environment.

WHEN DOES GOVERNMENT BECOME THE PROBLEM?

There are many reasons that governments may become involved in human affairs, but such intervention is not always welcomed. When and how government intervention is necessary and desirable are among the most disputed issues in modern politics. During the twentieth century, the role of governments expanded enormously in most nations. At the same time, criticisms of many government policies have persisted and sometimes intensified. Such skepticism is directed at virtually all government activities, especially the economic role of government.

Destruction of Community

Whereas some see governments as a way to build community, others argue that governments destroy natural communities. Government, they hold, implies power and inequality among human beings. And power corrupts. In Lord Acton's famous words, "Power corrupts, and absolute power corrupts absolutely."

While those who have power are corrupted, those without it are degraded and alienated. According to Rousseau, only human beings unfettered by government can form bonds that allow them to develop their full human potential. By imposing an order based on coercion, hierarchy, and the threat of force, governments destroy natural communities. The stronger government becomes, the more it creates inequalities of power that have negative consequences. Such arguments stimulated Western criticism of communism as limiting the potential and freedom of its citizens.

Others argue that strong governments create a "client society," in which people learn to be subservient to authorities and to rely on governments to meet their needs. In such societies, governments patronize and pacify their citizens, as seen in many developing nations today.

Violations of Basic Rights

Just as governments can help establish many essential rights, they can also use their powers to violate these rights in the most serious manner. The twentieth century witnessed enormous progress in the extension of political, economic, and social rights in societies worldwide. At the same time, however, some governments violated basic **human rights** on an unprecedented scale. The millions of lives lost to political persecution is the most serious example of this. Such horrors happened not only in Nazi extermination camps and during Stalin's Great Terror in the Soviet Union, but also on a huge scale in China, Cambodia, and Rwanda, and on a smaller scale in Iraq, Argentina, the Sudan, and Afghanistan.

These extreme abuses of government power illustrate a dilemma that troubled James Madison and other Founders of the American Revolution: the tension between creating a government strong enough to govern effectively but not so strong that it could destroy the rights of its citizens. They understood the irony that to protect individuals from each other, societies can create a government that has even more power to coerce the individual.

Economic Inefficiency

Governments can help economies flourish, but they also can distort and restrict a state's economic potential. President Robert Mugabe, for instance, has destroyed the economy of a once developing Zimbabwe, and similar examples exist in many struggling economies. Economic problems might arise even if government officials do not actively abuse their power. Government regulation of the economy may distort the terms of trade and lower people's incentives to produce. Further inefficiencies may arise when governments actually own or manage important economic enterprises. This is particularly likely if the government holds a monopoly on an important good, since monopolies generally cause goods to be undersupplied and overpriced. Moreover, government industries may be especially prone to inefficiency and complacency because management and workers often have better job protection than those in the private sector. Therefore, they may worry less about the economic performance of the firm. Such experiences stimulate calls to restrict the economic role of governments in both developing and advanced industrial economies.

Government for Private Gain

Society also may suffer if government officials make decisions to benefit themselves personally, or select policies to get themselves reelected regardless of whether those policies would be the best for the society. These actions are like a game in which one person's gain is another person's loss. A politician or political group may use the government to unfairly reap benefits at the public's expense—what is called "rent seeking." *Rents* are benefits created through government intervention in the economy—for example, tax revenue or profits created because the government has restricted competition. Rent seeking refers to efforts by individuals, groups, firms, or organizations to reap such benefits. The idea is really quite simple. For instance, a local mayor plans an economic development project that will benefit his friends who own land in the area or who will supply contracts for the project. Rent seeking can impose large net costs on society because policies are chosen for the private benefits that they produce rather than for their social efficiency and because groups may expend large amounts of resources to control the spoils of government. Rent seeking may turn into outright corruption when influence is traded for money or other advantage (see Box 1.2).

Political exploitation is a particularly serious problem in poor societies. Holding political office is often an effective way to enrich oneself when other political actors are too weak to constrain the abuse of government officials. Besides, many developing societies do not have strong norms against using government for private gain. On the contrary, people often expect those in government to use their power to benefit themselves, their families, and their neighbors. Even in many advanced democratic societies public officeholders are expected to appoint their supporters to ambassadorships and other public posts, constrained in part by civil service rules designed to reward merit over patronage. The temptations of officeholding are great. Despite formal rules, press scrutiny, and citizen concerns, few governments anywhere finish their terms of office untainted by some corruption scandal.

Vested Interests and Inertia

Government-created private gains are difficult to change or abolish once they have been established. Some people enjoy the benefits of government jobs, contracts, or other favors that they otherwise might not have had. The larger the government and

BOX 1.2

The Case of Mobutu Sese Seko

What happens if politicians use their power in their own self-interest or to benefit individuals or groups that support them? President Mobutu Sese Seko (1930–1997) of Zaire offers a tragic example of the costs that rent-seeking politicians can impose on their societies. After seizing power in a 1965 coup, Mobutu ruled the large African state of Congo (which he renamed Zaire) for more than thirty years. During his long rule, President Mobutu used government funds, including aid from Western states such as the United States, to amass a huge personal fortune, which he invested abroad. In addition to large sums of money, he is reported to have owned about thirty luxury residences abroad, including a number of palatial estates on the French Riviera. Meanwhile, living standards in Zaire, a poor country despite significant natural resources, plummeted, and the country was racked with epidemic disease and civil war. Mobutu died of natural causes shortly after his ouster.

the more attractive the benefits it provides, the more likely it is that such vested interests will resist change (unless change means even larger benefits). Therefore, any government will foster a group of people with a vested interest in maintaining or enlarging the government itself. Such groups may become a powerful force in favor of the status quo.

Vested interests make it difficult to change government policies or make them more efficient. Once established, agencies and policies can live on far beyond their usefulness. For example, when the Spanish Armada threatened to invade England in 1588, the government posted a military observation post at Land's End in southwest England. This observation post remained in place for four centuries! In the United States, the Rural Electrification Administration was created in 1935 to bring electricity to rural America; it persisted for almost sixty years until it was finally merged into the Rural Utilities Service in 1994.

Vested interests are particularly likely in political systems that contain a lot of safeguards against rapid political change. While the checks and balances in political systems as the United States are designed to safeguard individual rights, they may also protect the privileges of vested interests. Yet, even political systems that contain far fewer such checks may exhibit an excess of political inertia. Britain is an excellent example. Until recently, the House of Lords represented the social groups that dominated British society before the Industrial Revolution more than 200 years ago (noblemen, bishops, and judges). Only in the last few years has Britain begun reforming the House of Lords to eliminate features that reflect Britain's feudal and preindustrial past.

This debate and struggle over the proper role of government are an ongoing part of politics. In the past twenty-five years or so, there has been a clear trend away from extensive government regulation of many economic sectors. Since the 1970s especially, many societies have moved to privatize many economic sectors and to deregulate others. Government regulation has become less extensive in some areas, but it has grown in others—for example, through enacting laws to protect the environment or the rights of children. The overall size of governments in advanced industrial countries has not changed very much. In the former communist countries and in some developing countries, however, the government's size has shrunk quite dramatically. Yet, countries vary widely in the size of their governments, and they are likely to continue to do so.

POLITICAL SYSTEMS AND STATES

We began by discussing governments, but governments are only one part of a larger political system. Since the term **political system** is a main organizing concept of this book, it deserves a full explanation. A system necessarily has two properties: (1) it has a set of interdependent parts, and (2) it has boundaries between its environment.

Political systems are a particular type of social system that is involved in the making of authoritative public decisions. Central elements of a political system are the institutions of government—such as parliaments, bureaucracies, and courts—that formulate and implement the collective goals of a society or of groups within it.

Political systems also include important parts of the society in which governments operate. For example, political organizations, such as political parties or interest groups, are part of the political system. Such organizations do not have coercive authority, except insofar as they control the government. Likewise, the mass media only indirectly affect elections, legislation, and law enforcement. A whole host of institutions—beginning with the family and including communities, churches, schools, corporations, foundations, and think tanks—influence political attitudes and public policy. The term *political system* refers to the whole collection of related, interacting institutions and agencies.

The political systems that we compare in this book are all independent states. They represent some of the important countries in the contemporary world. At the same time, they reflect the diversity of political systems that exist today. A **state** is a particular type of political system. It has **sovereignty**—an independent legal authority over a population in a particular territory, based on the recognized right to self-determination. Sovereignty rests with those who have the ultimate right to make political decisions.

External sovereignty means the right to make binding agreements (treaties) with other states. For instance, France's external sovereignty means that it can enter into treaties with other states. The city of Bordeaux, however, does not have this right (nor do other subnational units of government in France). Internal sovereignty means the right to determine matters having to do with one's own citizens. For example, the French government has internal sovereignty so that it can impose taxes on French citizens.

Yet, states mold and are molded by a domestic environment and an international environment. The system receives inputs from these environments and shapes them through its outputs. The boundaries of political systems are defined in terms of persons, territory, and property. Most people have citizenship rights in only one country. Similarly, territory is divided between states. A given piece of land is supposed to belong to only one country. Of course, disputes over citizenship, territory, and property are by no means uncommon and are among the most frequent causes of international conflict.

Every state faces some constraints on its external and internal sovereignty. For example, with the increasing integration of France into the **European Union (EU),** the French government has given up parts of its sovereignty to the EU, and this loss of sovereignty is a major topic of political debate. In the United States, we confuse things a bit by calling the fifty constituent units "states," even though they enjoy much less sovereignty than France. The states of the United States share the power and authority of the "state" with the federal government in Washington, D.C.

We often think of the world as a patchwork of states with sizable and contiguous territories and a common identity shared by their citizens. A nation is a group of people, often living in a common territory, who have such a common identity. We call the cases in which national identification and sovereign political authority largely coincide **nation-states**. We have come to think of nation-states as the natural way to organize political systems, and often as an ideal. The national right to self-determination—the idea that every nation has a right to form its own state if it wants to do so—was enshrined in the Treaty of Versailles signed at the end of World War I.

Nation-states are often a desirable way to organize a political system. However, the national right to self-determination—is a relatively modern invention. Until the end of the Middle Ages, Europe consisted of many very small political systems and a few very large ones, whose territorial possessions were not always very stable or contiguous. Nor did states always consist of people with the same national identity. Gradually, a set of European nation-states evolved, and the 1648 Treaty of Westphalia established that principle for the political organization of Europe. The nation-state thus emerged as the dominant political system during the eighteenth and nineteenth centuries in Europe.

Since then, Europe has transformed itself into distinct nation-states. This did not happen accidentally—indeed, the governments of the emerging nation-states had a lot to do with it. They sought to instill a common national identity among the peoples they controlled. They did so, often heavy-handedly, by promoting a common language, a common educational system, and often a common religion. While this process of *nation-building* was often harsh, it produced a Europe in which the inhabitants of most states have a strong sense of community.

Many societies in the developing world today face similar challenges. Especially in Africa, the former colonial powers (particularly Britain and France) left the newly independent states with very weak national identities. In many parts of Africa, large-scale national communities simply did not exist at the time of colonization. Even where they did exist, they were rarely reflected in the boundaries that the colonial powers drew between their possessions. After independence, many new states have therefore faced huge nation-building tasks.

There are additional challenges to contemporary nation-states. After World War II, power in Western states began to shift downward from the state to local governments, and upward to supranational organizations, such as the EU. Most of the industrialized countries of Western Europe have gradually created a common market economy. Originally consisting of six countries—France, Germany, Italy, Belgium, the Netherlands, and Luxembourg—the EU has expanded to twenty-seven members with the addition of two members in 2006.

The **United Nations (UN),** formed at the end of World War II in 1945, has also acquired new responsibilities since the collapse of the Soviet Union in the 1990s. As of early 2006, UN forces were peacekeepers in fifteen countries. These operations—involving more than 100,000 peacekeepers—separate combatants in domestic and international conflicts, settle disputes, and form effective governing institutions. The UN has increased authority over world security, constraining, supporting, and sometimes replacing the unilateral actions of individual states. While the sovereignty of states may be diminishing, they are still the most important political systems. That, of course, is the main reason that they are the subject of our study.

THE DIVERSITY OF STATES

Just about the entire surface of the world today is covered by independent states. There were 192 UN "member-states" in 2006.[7] A few countries are not members of the UN (Taiwan, Switzerland, and the Vatican), and some independence movements would create even more states. When the United States declared its independence in 1776, most independent states were European (see Figure 1.1). Much of the rest of the world existed as colonies to one of the European empires. In the nineteenth and early twentieth centuries, the number of states increased, principally in Latin America, where the Spanish and Portuguese empires broke up into twenty independent states. In Europe, newly independent countries emerged in the Balkans, Scandinavia, and the Low Countries.

Between the two world wars, national proliferation extended to North Africa and the Middle East; and Europe continued to fragment as the Russian and Austro-Hungarian empires broke up. Since World War II, the development of new states has taken off. By 2006, 125 new countries have joined the sixty-eight states that existed in 1945. The largest group of new states is in Sub-Saharan Africa. More than twenty new countries formed in the 1990s—mostly the successor states of the Soviet Union, Yugoslavia, and Czechoslovakia.

All these countries—new as well as old—share certain characteristics. They have legal authority over their territories and people; most have armies, air forces, and in some cases navies; they collect taxes and spend money; they regulate their economies, maintain public order, and pursue their general welfare. Countries send and receive ambassadors; most belong to several international organizations. They also vary, often profoundly, in physical size, histories, institutions, cultures, religions, economies, and social structures—factors that shape their politics.

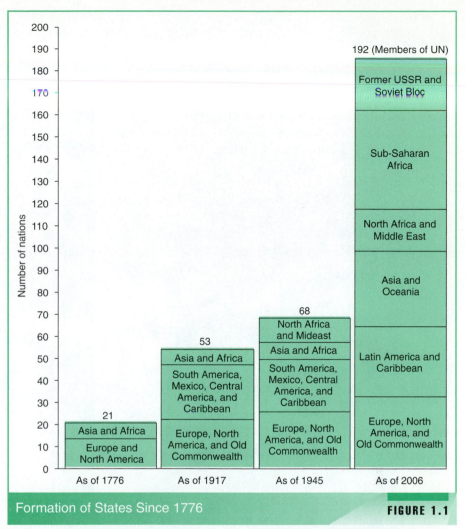

Formation of States Since 1776

FIGURE 1.1

Source: For contemporary members, Information Office, United Nations, Data to 1945 from Charles Taylor and Michael Hudson, *World Handbook of Political and Social Indicators* (New Haven, CT: Yale University Press, 1972), 26 ff.

Big and Small States

Nations come in all sizes. The smallest legally independent political entity in both geographic extent and population is Vatican City, the headquarters of the Catholic Church, with less than half a square kilometer of turf and less than a thousand residents.

The contrasts between geographic size and population size can be graphically seen in the following two maps. Map 1.1 is the familiar global map in which countries are displayed according to their size. Russia, with its landmass extending over eleven

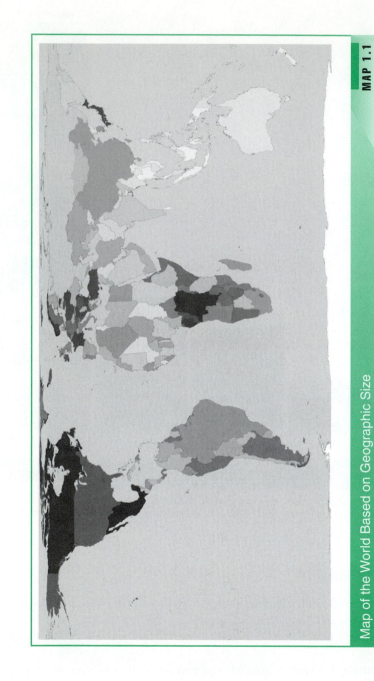

Map of the World Based on Geographic Size

Source: Copyright © *The Real World Atlas*, Thames & Hudson, Ltd., London, 2008.

MAP 1.1

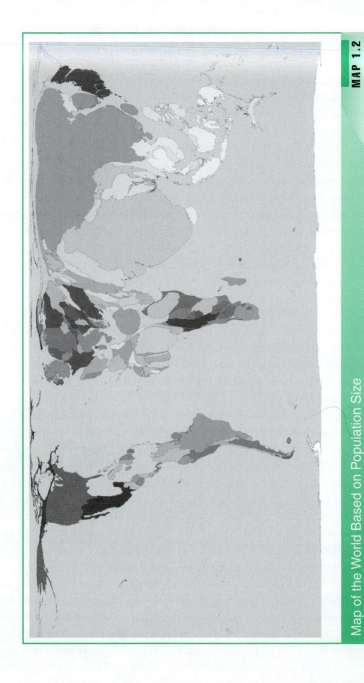

Map of the World Based on Population Size

MAP 1.2

contiguous time zones, is the world's largest state with more than 17 million square kilometers. The United States falls about midpoint in this range, with just more than 9 million square kilometers. Many of the established democracies in Europe are relatively small (Britain has 242,000 square kilometers and Germany 349,000).

Map 1.2 is more provocative because it displays nations by their population size. Instantly we see China and India balloon in size because of their large populations. China alone accounts for almost a quarter of the world's population (with 1.3 billion people) and India is not far behind (with 1.1 billion). The European democracies we compare—Britain, France, and Germany—look smaller in these comparisons because their populations range from about 60 million to 80 million. Even more dramatically, Australia shrinks from a continent in the first map to a small dot in the population map because of its small population size (20 million). The United States in this global perspective seems relatively small in population terms (298 million), even though it has roughly the same area as China and is geographically larger than India. And even though Russia has almost twice as much land as any other country, it has a modest population size (142 million) that is barely half as large as the United States and Russia is shrinking.

The political implications of these striking contrasts in population size and geographic area are not always obvious. Big countries are not always the most important and do not always prevail over the small ones: Cuba has challenged the United States for almost forty years; Israel stands off the Arab world; and tiny Vatican City has great power and influence. Nor do area and population size determine a country's political system. Both little Luxembourg and large India are democracies. Authoritarian regimes are found in small, medium, and large countries. These enormous contrasts in size show only that the states now making up the world differ greatly in their physical and human resources.

A state's geographic location can also have important strategic implications. In the sixteenth through nineteenth centuries, European states typically required a large land army to protect themselves from the threats of their neighbors. These nations had difficulties developing free political institutions, since they needed a strong government to extract resources on a large scale and keep the population under control. Britain was protected by the English Channel and could defend itself through its navy, a smaller army, lower taxation, and less centralization of power—which aided political liberalization. Most peoples of Asia, Africa, and Latin America were colonized by the more powerful Western nations. Those that had the richest natural resources and the most benign climates tended to attract the largest numbers of settlers.

Whether they are old or new, large or small, most of the world's states face a number of common challenges. The first is building community. Most states do not have a homogeneous population, and instilling a sense of shared identity can be a serious challenge. Second, the ability to foster economic and social development is a challenge that is shared even by the wealthiest states. Finally, most states face significant challenges in advancing democracy and civil liberties. These challenges should be familiar from our discussion of the purposes and dangers of governments. In the remainder of this chapter, we discuss these challenges successively.

BUILDING COMMUNITY

One of the most important challenges facing political systems worldwide is to build a common identity and a sense of community among the citizens. The absence of a common identity can have severe political consequences. Conflicts over national, ethnic, or religious identities are among the most explosive causes of political turmoil, as we have witnessed in Northern Ireland, the former Yugoslavia, Rwanda, and elsewhere. But while building community is a pervasive challenge, some countries are in a much better situation than others. Japan, for example, has an ethnically homogeneous population, a common language, and a long national political history. A large majority of the Japanese share in the religions of Buddhism and Shintoism, and the country is separated by miles of ocean from its most important neighbors. Nigeria, in contrast, is an accidental and artificial creation of British colonial rule and has no common precolonial history. The population is sharply divided between Muslims and Christians; the Christians are divided equally into Catholics and Protestants. There are some 250 different ethnic groups, speaking a variety of local languages, in addition to English. Obviously, the challenges of building community are much greater in Nigeria than they are in Japan. Although few countries face problems as complicated as those of the Nigerians, the community-building challenge is one of the most serious issues facing many states today.

States and Nations

The word *nation* is sometimes used to mean almost the same as the word *state*, as in the name the United Nations. Strictly speaking, however, we wish to use the term **nation** to refer to a group of people with a common identity. When we speak of a "nation," we thus refer to the self-identification of a people. That common identity may be built upon a common language, history, race, or culture, or simply upon the fact that this group has occupied the same territory. Nations may or may not have their own state or independent government. In some cases—such as Japan, France, or Sweden—there is a close correspondence between the memberships of the state and the nation. Most people who identify themselves as Japanese do in fact live in the state of Japan, and most people who live in Japan identify themselves as Japanese.

In many instances, the correspondence between the nation and the state is not so neat. Nor is it obvious that it should be. In some cases, states are *multinational*—consisting of a multitude of different nations. The Soviet Union, Yugoslavia, and Czechoslovakia were multinational states that broke apart. In other cases, some nations are much larger than the corresponding states, such as Germany for most of its history, or China. Some nations have split into two or more states for political reasons, such as Korea today and Germany between 1949 and 1990. Some groups with claims to be nations have no state at all, such as the Kurds, the Basques, and the Tamils. When states and nations do not coincide, it can cause explosive political conflict, as discussed later. At the same time, the presence of several nations within the same state can also be a source of diversity and cultural enrichment.

Nationality and Ethnicity

There is a fine line between nations and *ethnic groups,* which may have common physical traits, languages, cultures, or history. Like nationality, **ethnicity** need not have any objective basis in genetics, culture, or history. The German sociologist Max Weber defined ethnic groups as "those human groups that entertain a subjective belief in their common descent because of similarities of physical type or of customs or both, or because of memories of colonization and migration. . . . [I]t does not matter whether or not an objective blood relationship exists."[8] Similarly, groups that are physically quite similar, but differ by language, religion, customs, marriage patterns, and historical memories (for example, the Serbs, Croats, and Muslim Bosnians) may believe they are descended from different ancestors and hence are physically different as well. Over centuries, originally homogeneous populations may intermix with other populations, even though the culture may continue. This is true, for example, of the Jewish population of Israel, which has come together after more than two millennia of global dispersion.

Ethnic differences can be a source of political conflict.[9] Since the end of the Cold War, many states of the former Soviet bloc have come apart at their ethnic and religious seams. In the former Yugoslavia, secession by a number of provinces triggered several wars. The most brutal of these was in Bosnia-Herzegovina, where a Muslim regime faced rebellion and murderous "ethnic cleansing" by the large Serbian minority. Intervention by the UN, the North Atlantic Treaty Organization (NATO) and the United States contained Serbian aggression and led to an uneasy settlement, but considerable tension remains. Similar tensions and violent aggression occurred in Kosovo as well.

In many developing countries, boundaries established by former colonial powers cut across ethnic lines. In 1947 the British withdrew from India and divided the subcontinent into a northern Muslim area—Pakistan—and a southern Hindu area—India. The most immediate consequence was a terrible civil conflict and "ethno-religious" cleansing. There still are almost 100 million Muslims in India. Similarly, thirty years ago the Ibo "tribe" of Nigeria fought an unsuccessful separatist war with the rest of Nigeria, resulting in the deaths of millions of people. The Tutsi and Hutu peoples of the small African state of Rwanda engaged in a civil war of extermination in the 1990s, with hundreds of thousands of people slaughtered, and millions fleeing the country in fear of their lives.

The migration of labor, forced or voluntary, across state boundaries is another source of ethnic differentiation. The American descendants of Africans forcefully enslaved between the seventeenth and the nineteenth centuries are witnesses of the largest coercive labor migration in world history. In contrast, voluntary migration takes the form of Indians, Bangladeshi, Egyptians, and Palestinians seeking better lives in the oil sheikhdoms around the Persian Gulf; Mexican and Caribbean migrant workers moving to the United States; and Turkish and North African migrants relocating to Europe. Some migration is politically motivated, triggered by civil war and repression. Two scholars refer to the contemporary world as living through an "Age of Migration,"[10] comparable in scale to that of the late nineteenth and early twentieth centuries.

| Examples of Ethnicity: Its Bases and Their Salience* | | | | TABLE 1.1 | |

	Physical Differences	Language	Norms Against Intermarriage	Religion	Negative Historical Memories
Brazil: Blacks	XX	O	XX	X	X
Britain: South Asians	X	O	X	XX	X
China: Tibetans	X	XX	XX	XX	XX
France: Algerians	X	X	XX	XX	XX
Germany: Turks	X	XX	XX	XX	O
India: Muslims	O	X	XX	XX	XX
Iran: Kurds	X	XX	XX	XX	XX
Japan: Buraku-min	O	O	XX	O	XX
Mexico: Mayan	X	X	XX	X	XX
Nigeria: Ibo	O	X	XX	XX	XX
Russia: Chechens	X	XX	XX	XX	XX
United States:					
African-Americans	XX	X	XX	O	XX
Hispanics	X	X	X	O	X

*Salience is estimated at the following levels: O = none or almost none; X = some; XX = much importance in affecting differences.

Table 1.1 provides examples of politically significant "ethnicity," broadly defined, in our selected twelve countries. Five sets of traits are included, beginning with physical differences, then language, norms against intermarriage, religion, and negative historical memories. The table illustrates the importance of each distinction to ethnic identity. The most important bases of distinction lie in intermarriage, religion, and historical memories. Language differences are of great importance in four cases and of some importance in six; and finally, and perhaps surprisingly, physical differences are of great importance in only two cases. Recent migration has made such previously homogeneous states as France, Japan, and Germany more multiethnic. Other countries, such as the United States and Canada, have long been multiethnic and have become even more so. Indeed, globalization and migration seem destined to increase the diversity of many societies worldwide.

Language

Language can be a source of social division that may overlap with ethnicity. There are approximately 5,000 different languages in use in the world today, and a much smaller number of language families. Most of these languages are spoken by relatively small tribal groups in North and South America, Asia, Africa, or Oceania. Only 200 languages have a million or more speakers, and only eight may be classified as world languages.

English is the most truly international language. There are approximately 380 million people who speak English at home, and 1.8 billion who live in countries where it is one of the official languages. Other international languages include Spanish (more than 300 million home speakers), Arabic (200 million), Russian (165 million), Portuguese (165 million), French (100 million), and German (100 million). The language with the largest number of speakers, though in several varieties, is Chinese (1.2 billion). The major languages with the greatest international spread are those of the former colonial powers—Great Britain, France, Spain, and Portugal.[11]

Linguistic divisions can create particularly thorny political problems. Political systems can choose to ignore racial, ethnic, or religious differences among their citizens, but they cannot avoid committing themselves to one or several languages. Linguistic conflicts typically show up in controversies over educational policies, or over language use in the government. Occasionally, language regulation is more intrusive, as in Quebec, where English-only street signs are prohibited and large corporations are required to conduct their business in French.

Religious Differences and Fundamentalism

States also vary in their religious characteristics. In some—such as Israel, the Irish Republic, and Pakistan—religion is a basis of national identity for a majority of the population. Iran is a theocratic regime, in which religious authorities govern and religious law is part of the country's legal code. In other societies, such as Poland under communism, religion can be a rallying point for political movements. In many Latin American countries, the clergy have embraced a liberation theology that fosters advocacy of the poor and criticism of government brutality.

Table 1.2 indicates that Christianity is the largest and most widely spread religion, which is divided into three major groups—Roman Catholics, Protestants (of many denominations), and Orthodox (e.g., Greek and Russian). The Catholics are dominant in Europe and Latin America; there is a more equal distribution of Catholics and Protestants elsewhere. While the traditional Protestant denominations have declined in North America in the last decades, three forms of Protestanism—Fundamentalist, Pentecostal, and Evangelical—have increased.

The Muslims are the second largest religious group and the most rapidly growing religion. Muslims are primarily concentrated in Asia and Africa, as well as substantial numbers in Europe and North America, and are becoming revitalized in the Asian successor states of the Soviet Union. Muslims have been particularly successful in missionary activities in Sub-Saharan Africa.

Religion can be a source of intense antagonism, since beliefs may take the form of deep personal convictions that are difficult to compromise. Religious groups often battle over such issues as the rules of marriage and divorce, childrearing, sexual morality, abortion, euthanasia, the emancipation of women, and the regulation of religious observances. Religious communities often take a special interest in educational

TABLE 1.2

Adherents of All Religions by Six Continents (mid-2004, in millions)

Religion	Africa	Asia	Europe	Latin America	North America	Oceania	Total	Percentage
Christians	401.7	341.3	553.6	510.1	273.9	26.1	2,106.2	33.0
Muslims	350.4	892.4	33.2	1.7	5.1	.4	1,283.4	20.1
Nonreligious and Atheists	6.4	724.2	130.6	18.6	33.1	4.2	917.7	14.4
Hindus	2.6	844.5	1.4	.8	1.4	.4	851.2	13.3
Buddhists	.1	369.3	1.6	.7	3.0	.4	375.4	5.9
Jews	.2	5.3	1.9	1.2	6.1	.1	14.9	.2
Other	107.7	693.5	3.2	17.6	6.3	1.0	828.8	13.1
Total	869.1	3,870.5	725.5	550.7	328.9	32.6	6,377.6	100%

Source: Adherents as defined in *Encyclopedia Britannic 2006*.

policies in order to transmit their ideas of nature and humankind, right and wrong. On such issues, religious groups may clash with one another as well as with more secular groups. Although religious groups can coexist peacefully, and are often the source of exemplary acts of compassion and reconciliation, they may also commit acts of violence, cruelty, and terrorism.[12]

Even societies in which most people supposedly belong to the same community of faith may be split by conflicts between "fundamentalists" and those who are more moderate in their beliefs. **Religious fundamentalism** has recently emerged in some form in all major faiths in reaction to social modernization. Fundamentalists have frequently been technologically adaptive, even while militantly rejecting some elements of modernity (see Box 1.3).

Judaism, Christianity, and Islam are all "religions of the book," although not exactly the same book. The Jews believe only in the Old Testament; the Christians add on the New Testament; and the Muslims add the Koran to these two. While each religion disagrees over the interpretation of these texts, Jewish, Christian, and Muslim, fundamentalists all believe in the truth of their respective sacred books and attack some of their own clergy for lukewarm defense of these sacred texts. There are also Hindu and Buddhist fundamentalists. The rise of fundamentalism has affected the entire world.

The extremist wings of fundamentalist movements employ violence in many forms: from threats and property destruction to assassination and destructive suicide, as young people turn themselves into bombs. The terrorism of these acts lies in their enormity. They stagger the imagination and are intended to weaken the will. From this point of view, the September 11, 2001, attacks on the World Trade Center and the Pentagon were acts of mega-terrorism, involving not only suicide pilot-hijackers but also aircraft filled with volatile fuel and innocent passengers

BOX 1.3

The Origins of "Fundamentalism"

Fundamentalism got its name in the decades before World War I when some Protestant clergymen in the United States banded together to defend the "fundamentals" of religious belief against the secularizing influences of a modernizing society. This was a reaction to new biblical scholarship at the time that questioned the divine inspiration and authorship of the Bible, and to the expansion of science and Darwinist theories of evolution. These church leaders were also distressed by the apparent erosion of morality and tradition in the United States. In 1920, a journalist and Baptist layman named Curtis Lee Laws appropriated the term "fundamentalist" as a designation for those who were ready "to do battle royal for the Fundamentals." The fundamentalists affirmed the inerrancy (the absolute truth) of the Bible and formed enclaves to protect themselves from error and sin. Religious fundamentalism has recently emerged in some form in all major faiths in reaction to social modernization.

converted into immense projectiles. These attacks were followed by terrorist assaults in Bali, Madrid, London, Riyadh, and other cities. Dealing with international terrorism by religious fundamentalists is now a challenge that faces many nations worldwide.

FOSTERING ECONOMIC DEVELOPMENT

Two major forces are transforming political systems and nations, and the lives of their citizens; they provide major sources of comparison across the nations in this book. The first is the process of economic development, and the second is political democratization.

A political system cannot generally satisfy its citizens unless it can foster social and economic development. Thus, as significant as nation-building may be, the level of economic and social development and the rate of economic growth are exceptionally important. Economic development implies that citizens can enjoy new resources and opportunities. Many people are primarily concerned that government can improve their living conditions through economic growth, providing jobs and raising income standards. However, development can also create social strains and damage nature. For better or worse, the social changes that result from economic development transform the politics of developing countries. The success of governments—both democratic and autocratic—is often measured in these terms.

For many affluent advanced industrial societies, contemporary living standards provide for basic social needs (and much more) for most of the public. Indeed, the current political challenges in these nations often focus on problems resulting from the economic successes of the past, such as protecting environmental quality or managing the consequences of growth. New challenges to social welfare policies are emerging from the medical and social security costs of aging populations. For most of the world, however, substantial basic economic needs still exist, and governments focus on improving the socioeconomic conditions of the nation.

Over the past two decades, globalization, democratization, and marketization have begun to transform living conditions in many nations. The United Nations Development Program (UNDP) combines measures of economic well-being, life expectancy, and educational achievement into what it calls the Human Development Index (HDI).[13] The HDI shows dramatic improvements in life conditions in many regions of the world over the past three decades (Figure 1.2). East Asia and South Asia have made substantial improvements since 1975. For instance, in 1975 South Korea and Taiwan had a standard of living close to many poor African nations, and they are now affluent societies. Even more striking is the change in the two largest nations in the world. China improved from a HDI of .52 in 1975 (the same as Botswana or Swaziland) to .75 in 2003 (similar to the Philippines or Ecuador); India improved from an HDI of .41 to .60. These statistics represent improved living conditions for billions of people. At the same time, other regions of the world are not sharing in these advances. Living conditions have changed only marginally in Sub-Saharan Africa over

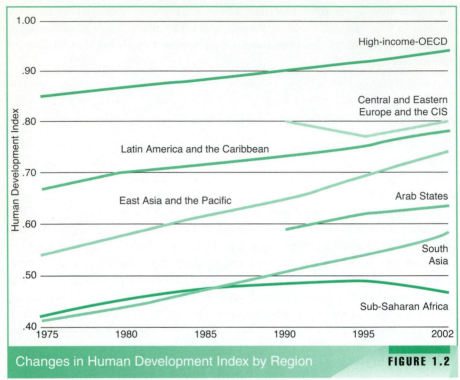

Changes in Human Development Index by Region   **FIGURE 1.2**

Source: United Nations Development Program, *Human Development Report 2004* (New York: United Nations, 2004), 134.

this period—the poorest of the poor nations have not improved. In addition, many of the postcommunist nations of Central and Eastern Europe have suffered economically following the transition from communism to capitalism and democracy. The HDI for Russia, for instance, has stagnated since 1990.

The process of economic development typically follows a similar course. One element is a transformation of the structure of the labor force. The five advanced industrial countries in our comparisons all have agricultural employment as less than 10 percent of the labor force. The three poorest countries—China, India, and Nigeria—have more than two-thirds of their labor forces employed in agriculture. The middle-income countries—Mexico and Brazil—have about a third to a fifth of their labor forces in agriculture. In addition, economic development is typically linked to urbanization, as peasants leave their farms and move to the cities. In nations undergoing rapid economic development, such as China, urban migration creates new opportunities for the workers but also new economic and social policy challenges for the governments.

The UNDP's Human Development Index provides a means to compare the differences in current life conditions across the twelve comparison nations in this chapter (Table 1.3). Perhaps the most striking feature of this table is the wide gap in

TABLE 1.3

Human Development Indicators

Nation	Life Expectancy	Percent Enrolled in School	GNP/capita (ppp)	2003 HDI	1975 HDI	2003 World Rank
United States	77.4	93	37,562	.944	.867	10
Japan	82.0	84	27,967	.943	.857	11
United Kingdom	78.4	—	27,147	.939	.845	15
France	79.5	92	27,677	.938	.853	16
Germany	78.7	89	27,756	.930	—	20
Mexico	75.1	75	9,168	.814	.689	53
Russia	65.3	90	9,230	.795	—	62
Brazil	70.5	91	7,790	.792	.645	63
China	71.6	69	5,003	.755	.525	85
Iran	70.4	69	6,995	.736	.566	99
India	63.3	60	2,892	.602	.412	127
Nigeria	43.4	64	1,050	.453	.318	158

Source: United Nations Development Program, *World Development Report 2005* (New York: United Nations, 2005) (www.undp.org).

living standards that still exist across nations worldwide. For instance, the **gross national product (GPN)** per capita, which is a measure of national economic development, is nearly thirty times higher in the Western advanced industrial democracies than in Nigeria.[14] Similarly, there are notable gaps in life expectancy and educational opportunities between the affluent Northern societies and the developing nations in Africa and Asia. In highly industrialized countries, education is virtually universal and practically everyone over age 15 can read and write. In India and Nigeria, less than two-thirds of the adult population has this minimal level of education. Moreover, the countries with the fewest literate citizens also have the fewest radios and television sets—even though these devices do not require literacy. Economic development is also associated with better nutrition and medical care. In the economically advanced countries, fewer children die in infancy, and the average citizen has a life expectancy at birth of over seventy-five years. Improvements in living conditions have substantially increased life expectancy in many low-income nations, such as Mexico and China. However, the average life expectancy of an Indian is sixty-three years; and the Nigerian little more than forty years. Material productivity, education, exposure to communications media, and longer and healthier lives are closely interconnected.

In order to become more productive, a country needs the resources to develop a skilled and healthy labor force and to build the infrastructure that material welfare requires. Preindustrial nations face most urgently the issues of economic development: how to improve the immediate welfare of their citizens yet also build and invest for the future. Typically, these are newer nations that also face the challenges of building community and effective political institutions. Political leaders and celebrities, such as Bono and Angelina Jolie, have mobilized public awareness that these differences in living conditions are a global concern—for those living in the developing world, the affluent nations and their citizens, and international organizations such as the United Nations and the World Bank.

Problems of Economic Development

The HDI or GNP per capita measure the overall wealth, income, and opportunity in a nation, but these factors are not evenly distributed within nations. The unequal distribution of resources and opportunities is among the most serious causes of political conflict. A large GNP may conceal significant differences in the distribution of resources and opportunities. A high rate of national growth may benefit only particular regions or social groups, leaving large parts of the population unrewarded or even less well off than before. The "inner cities" of the United States, the older parts of such Indian cities as Delhi and Calcutta, the peripheral ramshackle settlements around the cities of Latin America, many rural areas in China, and the arid northeast of Brazil all suffer from poverty and hopelessness. At the same time, other parts of the countries experience growth and improved welfare. Moreover, there is some evidence that rapid economic development tends to increase such inequalities.

A country's politics may be sharply affected by internal divisions of income, wealth, and other resources. Table 1.4 displays income distributions for our twelve comparison countries. Generally speaking, economic development improves the

Income Distribution for Selected Nations			TABLE 1.4
Country	Year	Wealthiest 10%	Poorest 40%	Wealthy/Poor Gap
Germany	2000	22.1	22.2	−0.1
Russia	2002	23.8	20.9	2.9
Japan	1993	21.7	24.8	3.1
France	1995	25.1	19.8	5.3
India	1999	28.5	21.2	7.3
Britain	1999	28.5	17.5	11.0
United States	2000	29.9	16.2	13.7
Iran	1998	33.7	19.5	14.2
China	2001	33.1	13.7	19.4
Nigeria	1996	35.4	12.6	22.8
Mexico	2000	43.1	10.3	32.8
Brazil	2001	46.9	8.3	38.6

Source: World Bank, *World Development Indicators 2005*, table 2-7 (www.worldbank.org); distribution of income or consumption.

equality of income, at least past a certain stage of economic growth. Wealthy nations like Japan, Germany, and France have relatively more egalitarian income distributions than middle- or low-income countries. Still, the wealthiest 10 percent in Japan receive about the same total income as the poorest 40 percent receive. This is a large gap in life conditions between rich and poor, but the gap is even wider in less affluent nations. In Mexico, a middle-income country, the ratio is closer to 10 to 1; and in Brazil it is more than 20 to 1. The table also suggests that a nation's political characteristics make a difference. India has consciously worked to narrow inequality, which places it higher in the table, while inequality in the United States is as great as several poor nations, such as China.

Although industrialization and high productivity may eventually encourage a more equal distribution of income, the first stages of industrialization may actually increase **income inequality.** As economies modernize they create a dual economy—a rural sector and an urban industrial and commercial sector, both with inequalities of their own. These inequalities increase as education and communication spread more rapidly in the modern sector, which may contribute to the political instability of developing countries. Moreover, there is no guarantee that inequality will diminish in later stages of development. In Brazil, for instance, income inequality has increased for decades, even as the economy has developed. In the United States, income inequality increased substantially from the 1970s to the mid-1990s because of changes in economic structure, the increase in single-parent families, and a lowering of income taxes. In Russia and other postcommunist societies, the development of new capitalist markets was accompanied by new income inequalities. Inequality is an issue that many nations face.

Several studies have proposed various policy solutions to mitigate the hardships economic inequality causes in developing societies.[15] Taiwan and South Korea are models showing how early land reforms equalized opportunity at the outset of the developmental process. Investment in primary and secondary education, in agricultural inputs and rural infrastructure (principally roads and water), and in labor-intensive industries produced remarkable results for several decades. A comparative advantage in cheap and skilled labor enabled Taiwan and South Korea to compete effectively in international markets. Thus, some growth policies mitigate inequalities, but it can be very difficult to put them into practice, especially where substantial inequalities already exist.

Another correlate of development is population growth. The book *The Population Explosion* drew attention to the social burden that may follow from the population growth that typically accompanies economic development.[16] As health care improves, living standards increase, and life expectancies lengthen, population sizes grow. This is a positive development because it represents improved living conditions for these people, but rapid population growth also can pose policy challenges for many developing nations.

Table 1.5 puts this issue in sharp relief. The table divides the world population into three strata: low-income economies, middle-income economies, and high-income economies. In 1990 the low-income countries had a population total of almost 2 billion,

Population by Economic Development Level in 1990 and Projected to 2015 (in millions)				TABLE 1.5
	In 1990		**Projected to 2015**	
Economic Development Level	**Number**	**Percentage**	**Number**	**Percentage**
Low-income economies	1,777	33.9	2,794	39.4
Middle-income economies	2,588	49.3	3,299	46.5
High-income economies	887	16.8	1,007	14.1
Total	5,252	100	7,100	100

Source: World Bank, *World Development Report Indicators 2005*, table 2-1 (www.worldbank.org) population dynamics.

or about a third of the total world population. In contrast, the high-income nations had about a sixth of the world's population.

Some projections estimate that world population in 2015 will increase to 7 billion and that the poorer countries will see a more rapid rate of growth. In 2005, Hania Zlotnik of the UN population division estimated that "out of every 100 persons added to the [world's] population in the coming decade, 97 will live in developing countries."[17] Rapid economic growth in the developing world can create significant burdens for these nations.

These prospects have produced a development literature that mixes both light and heat. Economist Amartya Sen warns of a "danger that in the confrontation between apocalyptic pessimism on one hand, and a dismissive smugness, on the other, a genuine understanding of the nature of the population problem may be lost."[18] He points out that the first impact of "modernization" on population is to increase it rapidly, as new sanitation measures and modern pharmaceuticals reduce the death rate. As an economy develops, however, changing conditions tend to reduce fertility. With improved education (particularly of women), health, and welfare, the advantages of lower fertility become clear, and population growth declines.

Fertility decreased in Europe and North America as they underwent industrialization. Today, in many European nations the native populations are decreasing because fertility rates are below levels necessary to sustain a constant population size. This pattern appears to be occurring in the developing world. Thus annual population growth in the world has declined from 2.2 percent to 1.7 percent in the last two decades. The rate of population growth in India, for example, rose to 2.2 percent in the 1970s and has since declined. Latin America peaked at a higher rate and then came down sharply. The major problem area is Sub-Saharan Africa, with an average growth rate of more than 2.7 percent each year during the 1990s.[19] The fertility rate in Africa has recently dropped dramatically because of the tragically, rising death rate from the AIDS epidemic.

While population growth rates appear to be slowing, governments are addressing this issue in different ways. China adopted a coercive policy of limiting families to a single child, which in urban areas produced dramatic results at great costs. India followed a collaborative approach involving governmental intervention and market and education to affect family choices.[20] Kerala in southern India is a dramatic example of what can be accomplished by the collaborative approach, where expanding education (particularly among women) and otherwise improving living conditions has reduced fertility more than in China.

Economic growth can have other social costs. For instance, advanced industrial societies are dealing with the environmental costs of their industrial development. Despoiled forests, depleted soils and fisheries, polluted air and water, nuclear waste, endangered species, and a threatened ozone layer now burden their legislative dockets. With increasing industrialization and urbanization in the developing world, many of these environmental problems could worsen. Thus, economic development can impose serious environmental costs as well as benefits. At the same time, some environmental problems are even more acute in less developed countries, where rapid increases in population and urbanization create shortages of clean air, clean water, and adequate sanitation.[21] Thus, economic development generally improves living conditions of the public, but in the process it produces new policy problems that governments must address.

FOSTERING DEMOCRACY, HUMAN RIGHTS, AND CIVIL LIBERTIES

The second major force transforming contemporary political systems is the process of democratization, which includes the enhancement of human rights and the expansion of freedom. Democracy is the form of government to which most contemporary countries, more or less sincerely and successfully, aspire. A **democracy,** briefly defined, is a political system in which citizens enjoy a number of basic civil and political rights, and in which their most important political leaders are elected in free and fair elections and are accountable under a rule of law. Democracy literally means "government by the people."

In small political systems, such as local communities, it may be possible for "the people" to share directly in debating, deciding, and implementing public policy. In large political systems, such as contemporary states, democracy must be achieved largely through indirect participation in policymaking. Elections, competitive political parties, free mass media, and representative assemblies make some degree of democracy, some degree of "government by the people," possible. This indirect, or representative, democracy is not complete or ideal. But the more citizens are involved and the more influential their choices, the more democratic the system.

The most important general distinction in classifying political systems is between democratic systems and authoritarian systems. *Authoritarian* states lack one or several of the defining features of democracy. In democracies, competitive elections give citizens the chance to shape the policymaking process through their selection of key policymakers. In authoritarian systems the policymakers are chosen by military councils, hereditary families, dominant political parties, and the like. Citizens are either ignored or pressed into symbolic assent to the government's choices.

Authoritarian states can take several forms. (See Chapter 6.) In **oligarchies,** literally "rule by the few," important political rights are withheld from the majority of the population. South Africa until the abolition of apartheid in the early 1990s is a good example. Other authoritarian states, such as Egypt, are controlled by an individual dictator and his party or military supporters. **Totalitarian systems**—such as Nazi Germany, or the Soviet Union under Stalin, or North Korea today—are systems in which the government constricts the rights and privacy of its citizens in a particularly severe and intrusive manner.

As societies become more complex, richer, and more technologically advanced, the probability of citizen involvement and democratization increases. In the first half of the twentieth century most Western states were transformed from authoritarian regimes or oligarchies to democracies. After World War II, a second democratic wave—which lasted from 1943 until the early 1960s—saw both newly independent states (such as India and Nigeria) and defeated authoritarian powers (such as Germany and Japan) set up the formal institutions of democracy.[22]

Another round of democratic transitions began in 1974, involving Southern Europe, East Asia, Latin America, and a number of African states. The most dramatic changes came in Central and Eastern Europe, where in a few short years the Soviet empire collapsed, the nations of Eastern Europe rapidly converted to democracy, and many of these nations have now joined the European Union. The people power revolution in the Philippines, the end of the apartheid regime in South Africa, and the public protests for democratization in Indonesia were equally dramatic. Samuel P. Huntington speaks of the latest move toward democracy as a "Third Wave" of worldwide **democratization.**[23]

As a result of these three democratization waves, democracy has become a common goal of the global community (see Figure 1.3). As late as 1978, only a third of the world's independent countries had competitive party and electoral systems. Communist and other single-party governments and other authoritarian regimes dominated the landscape. By 2004, almost two-thirds of states had a system of electoral democracy, and human rights and liberties were similarly spreading to more of the world's population.[24] This democratization trend is continuing in the new millennium, with prospects for further progress in many nations.

This democratization process results from a combination of factors. Economic development transforms societies in ways that typically encourage democratization by creating autonomous political groups that demand political influence, by expanding the political skills of the citizenry, and by creating economic complexity that encourages systems of self-governance. Social modernization transforms the political values and political culture of the public, which increases demands for a more participatory system (see Chapter 3). New democracies are also much more likely to endure when founded in economically developed societies.[25]

Democracy is not an all-or-nothing proposition, however. No democracy is perfect, and we can speak of shades or gradations of democracy. Democracy typically

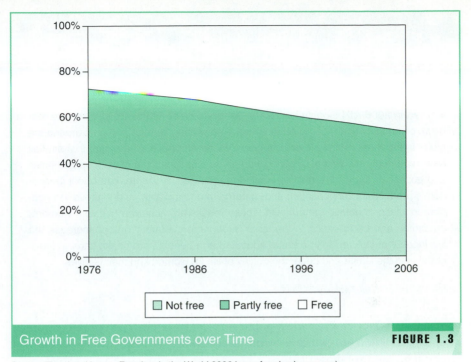

Growth in Free Governments over Time   **FIGURE 1.3**

Source: Freedom House, *Freedom in the World 2006* (www.freedomhouse.org).

does not come about overnight. It often takes time to establish democratic institutions and to have citizens recognize them and comply with the rules of the democratic process.

It can be especially difficult to consolidate democracy in less economically developed societies. Not all of the newly democratizing countries are succeeding beyond the first few years. In some, democratic processes fail to produce stable institutions and effective public policies and give way to some form of authoritarianism. In Nigeria, a democratic-leaning regime installed in 1979 was overthrown by a military coup in 1983, and a partial movement toward redemocratization was again aborted by the military in 1993 before being reestablished in 1999. Nigeria is by no means unique. Transition can move in either direction, toward or away from democracy. The recent wave of democratization is supported by the more favorable environments of more modernized societies and because there are now more democracies in the world to support new democracies. However, democracy is difficult to sustain when severe economic or political problems face a nation, or where the public remains uncertain about democracy.

Even when states democratize, there is no guarantee that they will grant human rights and civil liberties to all their people. In some countries, majority rule turns into a "tyranny of the majority" against ethnic or religious minorities. Therefore, democracies have to balance between respecting the will of the majority and protecting the

Women and Political Development

BOX 1.4

If a poor nation could do one thing to stimulate its development, what should it do? Opening the fiftieth session of the United Nations Commission on the Status of Women in 2006, UN Deputy-Secretary General Louise Fréchette said the international community finally comprehends that empowering women and girls around the globe is the most effective tool for a country's development. She stated that studies have repeatedly shown that by giving women equal education and work opportunities and access to a society's decision-making processes, a country can boost its economic productivity, reduce infant and maternal mortality rates, and improve the general population's nutrition and health. These results are achieved because women's education and participation in the labor force increase family output, increase the likelihood that children will be better educated and benefit from health care, improve nutrition in the family, and better the quality of life for women and their families.

Source: UN News Center, February 27, 2006.

rights of the minority. Even when political rulers sincerely try to promote human rights and civil liberties (which is by no means always the case), they do not always agree on the nature of those rights.

A good example of the spread of rights and liberties—and cultural differences in the definition of rights—involves gender issues. Governments in Western industrial societies favor gender policies that guarantee equality for women in society, the workplace, and politics. The United Nations and other international organizations have become advocates of women's rights. But gender norms often vary across cultural zones. The UN's statistics indicate that many developing nations hesitate to grant equal rights to women, restricting their education and involvement in the economy and politics.[26] Restrictions on women's rights are even starker in many Arab states. Ironically, other research indicates that improving the status of women is one of the most productive ways to develop a nation politically and economically (see Box 1.4). In short, expanding human rights is an ongoing process in the world today, and there is much room for further progress.

LOOKING FORWARD

The last several decades have been a period of tremendous social, economic, and political change in the world. Economic development, improved living standards, the spread of human rights, and democratization improved the life chances and life conditions of billions of individuals. In most of the world, the average child born today can look forward to a longer, better, and freer life than his or her parents—especially if she is a girl.

At the same time, continuing social, economic, and political problems remain. Progress in one area can create new opportunities, but also new problems in another. Economic development, for example, can sometimes stimulate ethnic strife and destabilize political institutions. Economic development can also disrupt social life. And the process of development has been uneven across and within nations. Many basic human needs still remain in too short supply.[27]

Even in the affluent democracies, as one set of policy issues is addressed, new issues come to the fore. Western democracies struggle to address issues of environmental quality, changing lifestyles, and the challenges of globalization and multiculturalism. A more affluent and information-driven citizenry can also limit the effectiveness of political parties, interest groups, parliaments, and political executives. Success in meeting these old and new challenges can improve the living conditions for the world's populations, decrease international conflict, and come closer to meeting the ideals of humankind.

Governments and politics have played a large role in promoting the successes and failures of the past. Just as we can point to governments whose actions improved life for their citizens, there are other governments that took regressive actions. Governments and their activities are central to our political futures. Our goal in this book is to examine the ways in which citizens, policymakers, and governments address the policy challenges that face them today.

REVIEW QUESTIONS

- What is politics?
- What are the contrasting images of the "state of nature" of humankind?
- What are the potential positive and negative outcomes of government activity?
- What are the main challenges that countries face in building a political community?
- What are the causes and consequences of economic development?
- What are the causes and consequences of democratization?

KEY TERMS

democracy	human rights	public goods
democratization	income inequality	religious fundamentalism
ethnicity	nation	sovereignty
European Union (EU)	nation-states	state
externalities	oligarchies	state of nature
governments	political culture	totalitarian systems
gross national product (GNP)	political system	United Nations (UN)

SUGGESTED READINGS

Chenery, Hollis et al. *Redistribution With Growth.* New York: Oxford University Press, 1981.

Cornelius, Wayne et al., eds. *Controlling Immigration: A Global Perspective.* Stanford, CA: Stanford University Press, 1995.

Dalton, Russell, and Doh Chull Shin, eds. *Citizens, Democracy, and Markets Around the Pacific Rim.* Oxford: Oxford University Press, 2006.

Diamond, Larry, ed. *Developing Democracy: Towards Consolidation.* Baltimore: Johns Hopkins University Press, 1999.

Ehrlich, Paul, and Anne Ehrlich. *The Population Explosion.* New York: Simon Schuster, 1990.

Horowitz, Donald. *Ethnic Groups in Conflict.* Berkeley: University of California Press, 1985.

Huntington, Samuel. *The Third Wave: Democratization in the Late Twentieth Century.* Norman: University of Oklahoma Press, 1991.

————. *The Clash of Civilizations and the Remaking of World Order.* New York: Simon & Schuster, 1996.

Lijphart, Arend. *Patterns of Democracy.* New Haven, CT: Yale University Press, 1999.

Linz, Juan, and Alfred Stepan, eds. *Problems of Democratic Transitions and Consolidation.* Baltimore: Johns Hopkins University Press, 1996.

Marty, Martin, and Scott Appleby. *Fundamentalism Observed.* Chicago: University of Chicago Press, 1991.

Putnam, Robert. *Making Democracy Work: Civic Traditions in Modern Italy.* Princeton, NJ: Princeton University Press, 1993.

Przeworski, Adam et al. *Democracy and Development: Political Institutions and Well-being in the World 1950–1990.* New York: Cambridge University Press, 2000.

Sachs, Jeffrey. *The End of Poverty: Economic Possibilities for Our Time.* New York: Penguin, 2005.

United Nations. *World Development Report.* New York: Oxford University Press, annual editions.

Weiner, Myron. *The Global Migration Crisis: Challenge to States and to Human Rights.* New York: HarperCollins, 1995.

Zakaria, Fareed. *The Future of Freedom: Illiberal Democracy at Home and Abroad.* New York: Norton, 2003.

ENDNOTES

1. Thomas Hobbes, *Leviathan,* ed. C. B. Macpherson (New York: Penguin, 1968), 186.

2. J. J. Rousseau, *Second Discourse on Inequality, The First and Second Discourses* (New York: St. Martin's Press, 1964), pp. 109–10.

3. Two other philosophical groups are especially outspoken critics of government: libertarians and anarchists. Adherents of **libertarianism** are individualists who see society as composed of individual human beings with fundamental rights that must be protected. The main problem with government, libertarians argue, is that the more tasks it takes on, the more prone it is to violate such basic rights. Adherents of **anarchism** claim that governments produce undesirable effects; they see societies not as collections of individuals but as communities of people who in their natural condition are equal. Governments and power corrupt such communities and lead to oppression and alienation.

4. Martin Greenberg and Mark Tier, *Visions of Liberty* (New York: Baen Publishers, 2004).

5. See, for example, Fareed Zakaria, *The Future of Freedom: Illiberal Democracy at Home and Abroad* (New York: Norton, 2003).

6. See, for example, Douglas North, *Institutions, Institutional Change, and Economic Performance* (Cambridge: Cambridge University Press, 1990); Mancur Olson, "The New Institutional Economics: The Collective Choice Approach to Economic Development," in C. Clague, ed., *Institutions and*

Economic Development. (Baltimore: Johns Hopkins University Press, 1997); S. Knack and P. Keefer, "Institutions and Economic Performance," *Economics and Politics* 7 (1995), 207–29.

7. The Vatican and Switzerland are not members of the UN but maintain permanent observer missions at the UN headquarters. Taiwan was expelled from the UN in 1971 to accommodate mainland China (the People's Republic).

8. Max Weber, *Economy and Society,* ed. Guenther Roth and Claus Wittich (Berkeley: University of California Press, 1978), 389.

9. Even before the end of the Cold War, ethnic autonomy movements in parts of old countries—such as the United Kingdom (the Scots and Welsh) and Canada (the Quebecois)—sought to break free or achieve greater autonomy.

10. Stephen Castles and Mark J. Miller, *The Age of Migration: International Population Movements in the Modern World* (New York: Guilford, 1994).

11. Erik V. Gunnemark, *Countries, Peoples, and Their Languages: The Geolinguistic Handbook* (Gothenburg: Lanstryckeriet, 1991).

12. A book dealing with this theme is R. Scott Appleby, *The Ambivalence of the Sacred* (Lanham, MD: Rowman & Littlefield, 2000).

13. United Nations Development Program, *Human Development Report 2005* (New York: United Nations). See also (www.undp.org.) for additional data and interactive presentations.

14. The per capita *gross national product (GNP)* is the total economic output per person. Rather than the traditional measures computed according to the exchange rates of the national currencies, the *purchasing power parity (PPP)* index takes into account differences in price levels from one country to another. Most analyses assume that the GNP/ppp statistics are more comparable measures of living conditions. The income gap increases, however, if one uses the traditional exchange rate measure of GNP.

15. For example, see Hollis Chenery et al., *Redistribution With Growth* (New York: Oxford University Press, 1981).

16. Paul Ehrlich and Anne Ehrlich, *The Population Explosion* (New York: Simon & Schuster, 1990).

17. Hania Zlotnik, "Statement to the Thirty-Eighth Session of the Commission on Population and Development," April 4, 2005 (www.un.org/esa/population/cpd/Statement_HZ_open.pdf).

18. Amartya Sen, "Population: Delusion and Reality," *New York Review of Books,* 22 Sept., 1994, pp. 62ff.

19. World Bank, *World Development Report, 1998–1999* (New York: Oxford University Press, 1999).

20. Sen, "Population: Delusion and Reality."

21. Regina Axelrod, David Downie, and Norman Vig, eds., *The Global Environment: Institutions, Law, and Policy* (Washington, DC: CQ Press, 2004)**;** Yale Center for Environmental Law and Policy and Center for International Earth Science Information Network, *2005 Environmental Sustainability Index: Benchmarking National Environmental Stewardship* (New Haven, CT: Yale University, 2005) (http://www.yale.edu/esi/).

22. While many countries became formally democratic in these years, most of them quickly lapsed into authoritarianism. Many of these would-be democracies failed in their first decade; another "reverse wave" in the 1960s and early 1970s swept away some older democracies (Chile, Greece, and Uruguay, for example) as well.

23. Samuel Huntington, *The Third Wave* (Norman: University of Oklahoma Press, 1991).

24. Freedom House, *Freedom in the World 2004* (Washington, DC: Freedom House, 2005) (www .freedomhouse.org).

25. Seymour Martin Lipset, "Some Social Requisites of Democracy," *American Political Science Review* 53 (September 1959), 69–105; Larry Diamond, "Economic Development and Democracy Reconsidered," in G. Marks and L. Diamond, eds., *Reexamining Democracy* (Newbury Park, CA: Sage, 1992); Tatu Vanhanen, *Prospects of Democracy* (New York: Routledge, 1997); Adam Przeworski et al., *Democracy and Development: Political Institutions and Well-being in the World 1950–1990* (New York: Cambridge University Press, 2000).

26. See United Nations Development Program, *Human Development Report 2005* (New York: United Nations) (http://hdr.undp.org/reports/global/2005/), tables 25-30, and associated discussion.

27. Many of these issues are addressed by the United Nations' Millennium Development Goals. Visit the UN website (http://www.un.org/millenniumgoals/) or see United Nations, *Millennium Development Goals Report 2005* (New York: United Nations) (http://unstats.un.org/unsd/mi/pdf/MDGBook.pdf).

COMPARING POLITICAL SYSTEMS

WHY WE COMPARE

The great French interpreter of American democracy, Alexis de Tocqueville, while traveling in America in the 1830s, wrote to a friend explaining how his own ideas about French institutions and culture entered into his writing of *Democracy in America*. Tocqueville wrote: "Although I very rarely spoke of France in my book, I did not write one page of it without having her, so to speak, before my eyes."[1]

On a more general note about the comparative method, he offered this comment: "Without comparisons to make, the mind does not know how to proceed."[2] Tocqueville was telling us that comparison is fundamental to all human thought. We add that it is the methodological core of the humanistic and scientific methods. It is the only way we can fully understand our own political system. Comparing our experience with that of other countries deepens our understanding of our own institutions. Examining politics in other societies permits us to see a wider range of political alternatives. It illuminates the virtues and shortcomings of our own political life. By taking us beyond our familiar arrangements and assumptions, comparative analysis helps expand our awareness of the possibilities of politics.

Comparison is also at the methodological core of the scientific study of politics. Comparative analysis helps us develop explanations and test theories of the ways in which political processes work and in which political change occurs. The goals of the comparative methods used by political scientists are similar to those used in more exact sciences. But political scientists cannot normally design experiments, a major path to knowledge in many of the natural sciences. We cannot control and manipulate political arrangements and observe the consequences. We are especially limited when dealing with large-scale events that drastically affect many people. For example, researchers cannot and would not want to start a social revolution to see its effects.

We can, however, use the comparative method to describe and explain the different combinations of political events and institutions found in different societies. More than two thousand years ago, Aristotle in his *Politics* contrasted the economies

BOX 2.1

Aristotle's Library

There is historical evidence that Aristotle had accumulated a library of more than 150 studies of the political systems of the Mediterranean world of 400–300 B.C. Many of these had probably been researched and written by his disciples.

While only the Athenian constitution survives of this library of Aristotelian polities, it is evident from the references to such studies that do survive that Aristotle was concerned with sampling the variety of political systems then in existence, including the "barbarian" (Third World?) countries, such as Libya, Etruria, and Rome: "[T]he references in ancient authorities give us the names of some 70 or more of the states described in the compilation of 'polities.' They range from Sinope, on the Black Sea, to Cyrene in North Africa; they extend from Marseilles in the Western Mediterranean to Crete, Rhodes, and Cyprus in the East. Aristotle thus included colonial constitutions as well as those of metropolitan states. His descriptions embraced states on the Aegean, Ionian, and Tyrrhenian Seas, and the three continents of Europe, Asia, and Africa."

Source: Ernest Barker, ed., *The Politics of Aristotle* (London: Oxford University Press, 1977), 386.

and social structures of Greek city-states in an effort to determine how the social and economic environments affected political institutions and policies (see Box 2.1). More contemporary political scientists also try to explain differences between the processes and performance of political systems. They compare two-party democracies with multiparty democracies, parliamentary with presidential regimes, democracies in poor countries with those in rich countries, elections in new party systems with those in established democracies. These and many other comparisons have greatly enriched our understanding of politics.

HOW WE COMPARE

We study politics in several different ways: we describe it; we seek to explain it; sometimes we try to predict it. These are all parts of the scientific process. Each of them may use the comparative method.

The first stage in the study of politics is description. If we cannot describe a political process or event, we cannot really hope to understand or explain it. Much less can we predict what might happen next or in similar situations. In order to describe politics, we need a set of concepts that are clearly defined and well understood. We speak of this as a conceptual framework. The easier this set of concepts is to understand, and the more generally it can be applied, the more helpful it is to the study of politics. Conceptual frameworks are not generally right or wrong, but they may be more or less useful to the task at hand.

POLITICAL SYSTEMS: ENVIRONMENT AND INTERDEPENDENCE

Comparative Politics Today suggests that we compare political systems with a structural-functional systems framework. To do so, we need to discuss three general concepts that we use throughout this book: (1) system, (2) structure, and (3) function. **System,** as we defined it in Chapter 1, suggests an object having interdependent parts, acting within a setting or an **environment.** The **political system** is a set of institutions and agencies concerned with formulating and implementing the collective goals of a society or of groups within it. **Governments** are the **policymaking** parts of political systems. The decisions of governments are normally backed up by legitimate coercion, and obedience may be compelled. (We discuss legitimacy at greater length in Chapter 3.)

Figure 2.1 tells us that a political system exists in both an international environment and a domestic environment. It is molded by these environments and it tries to mold them. The system receives **inputs** from these environments. Its policymakers attempt to shape them through its outputs. In the figure, which is quite schematic and simple, we use the United States as the central actor. We include other countries

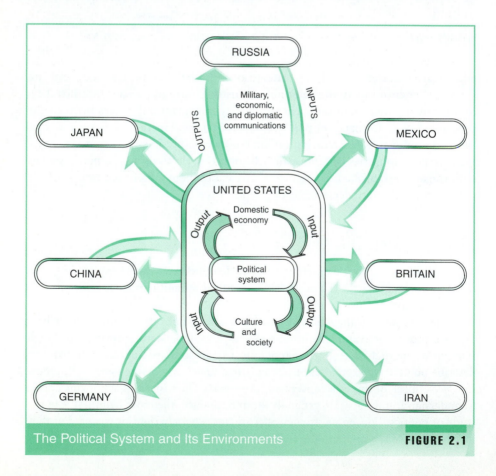

The Political System and Its Environments   **FIGURE 2.1**

as our environmental examples—Russia, China, Britain, Germany, Japan, Mexico, and Iran.

Exchanges among countries may vary in many ways. For example, they may be "dense" or "sparse"; U.S.–Canadian relations exemplify the dense end of the continuum, while U.S.–Nepalese relations would be at the sparse end.

Relationships among political systems may be of many different kinds. The United States has substantial trade relations with some countries and relatively little trade with others. Some countries have an excess of imports over exports, whereas others have an excess of exports over imports. Military exchanges and support with such countries as the NATO nations, Japan, South Korea, Israel, and Saudi Arabia have been of significant importance to the United States.

The interdependence of countries—the volume and value of imports and exports, transfers of capital, international communication, the extent of foreign travel and immigration—has increased enormously in the last decades. This increase is often called **globalization.** We might represent this process as a thickening of the input and output arrows between the United States and other countries in Figure 2.1. Fluctuations in this flow of international transactions and traffic attributable to depression, inflation, protective tariffs, international terrorism, war, and the like may wreak havoc with the economies of the countries affected.

The interaction of a political system with its domestic environment—the economic and social systems and the political culture of its citizens—is also depicted in Figure 2.1. We can illustrate this interaction in the U.S. case by the rise of the "high-tech information-based economy."

The composition of the U.S. labor force, and consequently its citizenry, has changed dramatically in the last century. Agriculture has declined to under 2 percent of the gainfully employed. Employment in heavy extractive and manufacturing industries has decreased substantially. Newer, high-technology occupations, the professions, and the service occupations have increased sharply as proportions of the labor force. The last half-century has also witnessed significant improvements in the educational level of the U.S. population. Many more young people complete high school and go on to college. Moreover, people move more easily from one region to another. These and other changes in the U.S. social structure have altered the challenges facing the U.S. system and the resources available to meet these challenges.

These changes in the economy and the citizenry are associated with changes in American **political culture.** (Political culture—the attitudes, beliefs, and values of the people in a country—is discussed at more length in Chapter 3.) People want different things from politics. For example, an educated and culturally sophisticated society is more concerned with quality of life, the beauty and healthfulness of the environment, and similar issues.

At the same time, the globalization of the economy leads to demands from firms and workers in some industries for protection of their jobs. Natural disasters, such as the hurricane that devastated New Orleans in 2005, spur calls for the national government to lead reconstruction. Local issues are seen as the responsibility of the entire country. People live longer. An aging population demands that governments do more to help with medical benefits. In input-output terms, socioeconomic changes transform the political demands of the electorate and the kinds of policies that it supports.

Thus a new pattern of society results in different policy outputs, different kinds and levels of taxation, changes in regulatory patterns, and changes in welfare expenditures. The advantage of the system-environment approach is that it directs our attention to the **interdependence** of what happens between and within countries. It provides us with a vocabulary to describe, compare, and explain these interacting events.

If we are to make sound judgments in politics, we need to be able to place political systems in their domestic and international environments. We need to recognize how these environments both set limits on and provide opportunities for political choices. This approach keeps us from reaching quick and biased political judgments. If a country is poor in natural resources and lacks the capabilities necessary to exploit what it has, we cannot fault it for having a low industrial output or poor educational and social services. Each country chapter in the second half of this book begins by discussing the current policy challenges facing the country and its social and economic environment.

POLITICAL SYSTEMS: STRUCTURES AND FUNCTIONS

Governments do many things—from establishing and operating school systems, to maintaining public order, to fighting wars. In order to carry on these disparate activities, governments have specialized agencies, or **structures**, such as parliaments, bureaucracies, administrative agencies, and courts. These structures perform **functions**, which in turn enable the government to formulate, implement, and enforce its policies. The policies reflect the goals; the agencies provide the means to achieve them.

Figure 2.2 locates six types of political structures—political parties, interest groups, legislatures, executives, bureaucracies, and courts—within the political system. These are formal organizations engaged in political activities. They exist in most contemporary political systems. This list is not exhaustive. Some structures, such as ruling military councils or governing royal families, are found in only a few countries. Some, such as Iran's Council of Guardians, are unique to their political system.

We might think that if we understand how such structures work in one political system, we can apply this insight to any other system. Unfortunately, that is not always the case. The sixfold classification will not carry us very far in comparing political systems with each other. The problem is that similar structures may have very different functions across political systems. For example, Britain and China have all six types of political structures. However, these institutions are organized differently in the two countries. More importantly, they function in dramatically different ways. They do different things in the political processes of their countries.

The political executive in Britain consists of the prime minister, the ministers assigned to the Cabinet, and the larger ministry, which consists of all the heads of

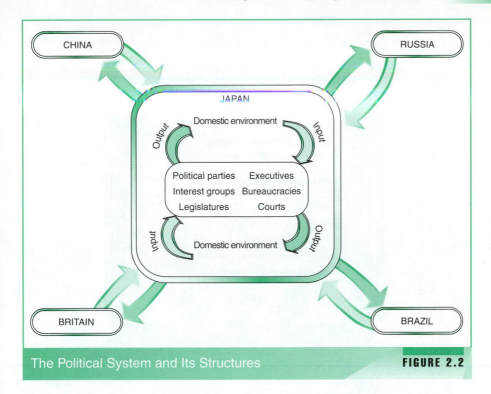

CHINA

RUSSIA

JAPAN

Output

Domestic environment

Input

Political parties   Executives

Interest groups   Bureaucracies

Legislatures   Courts

Input

Domestic environment

Output

BRITAIN

BRAZIL

The Political System and Its Structures

FIGURE 2.2

departments and agencies. All these officials are usually selected from Parliament. There is a similar structure in China, called the State Council, headed by a premier and consisting of the various ministers and ministerial commissions. But while the British prime minister and Cabinet have substantial policymaking power, the State Council in China is closely supervised by the general secretary of the Communist Party, the Politburo, and the Central Committee of the party.

Both Britain and China have legislative bodies—the House of Commons in Britain and the National People's Congress in China. Their members make speeches to each other and vote on prospective public policies. But while the House of Commons is a key institution in the policymaking process, the Chinese Congress meets for only brief periods, ratifying decisions made mainly by the Communist Party authorities. Usually the Chinese delegates do not even consider alternative policies.

There are even larger differences between political parties in the two countries. Britain has a competitive party system. The majority in the House of Commons and the Cabinet are constantly confronted by an opposition party or parties, competing for public support. They look forward to the next election when they may unseat the incumbent majority, as happened in 1997, when the Labour Party replaced the Conservatives in government. In China the Communist Party controls the whole political process. There are no other political parties. The principal decisions are taken in the Politburo and to some extent in the Central Committee of the

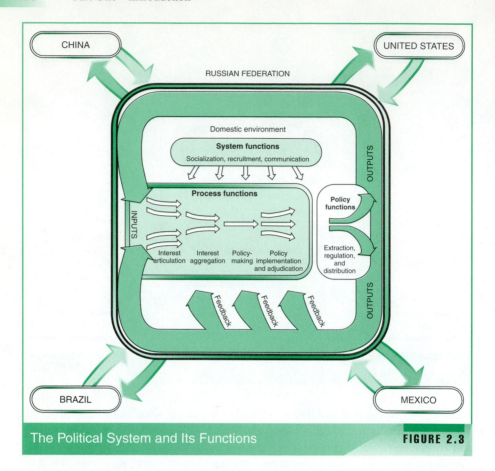

The Political System and Its Functions

FIGURE 2.3

Communist Party. The governmental agencies implement the policies, which are initiated or approved by the top Communist Party leaders.

Thus, an institution-by-institution comparison of British and Chinese politics that did not spell out their interdependence and the functions that they perform would not bring us far toward understanding the important differences in the politics of these two countries. Each country study in this book includes a figure that shows how some of the major structures select and control each other. Another figure illustrates how they fit into the policymaking process.

Figure 2.3 shows the functions of the political process that we can use to compare all political systems. The center of Figure 2.3 under the heading **"process functions"** lists the distinctive activities necessary for policy to be made and implemented in any kind of political system.

- **Interest articulation** involves individuals and groups expressing their needs and demands.
- **Interest aggregation** combines different demands into policy proposals backed by significant political resources.

- **Policymaking** decides which policy proposals are to become authoritative rules.
- **Policy implementation** carries out and enforces public policies; **policy adjudication** settles disputes about their application.

(We discuss each concept in greater detail in Chapters 4, 5, and 6.) We call these process functions because they play a direct and necessary role in the process of making policy.

Before policy can be decided, some individuals and groups in the government or the society must decide what they want and hope to get from politics. The political process begins as these interests are expressed or articulated. The many arrows on the left of the figure show these initial expressions.

To be effective, however, these demands must be combined (aggregated) into policy alternatives—such as higher or lower taxes or more or fewer social security benefits—for which substantial political support can be mobilized. Thus the arrows on the left are consolidated as the process moves from interest articulation to interest aggregation.

Governments then consider alternative policies. Whoever controls the government backs one of them and authoritative policymaking takes place. The policy must be enforced and implemented, and if it is challenged, there must be some process of adjudication. Each policy may affect several different aspects of a society, as reflected in the three arrows for the implementation phase.

These process functions are performed by such political structures as parties, legislatures, political executives, bureaucracies, and courts. The **structural-functional approach** stresses two points. One is that in *different countries, the same structure may perform different functions.* A second is that while a particular institution, such as a legislature, may have a special relationship to a particular function, such as policymaking, *institutions often do not have a monopoly on any one function.* Presidents and governors may share in the policymaking function (veto powers), as do the higher courts (judicial review of statutes for their constitutionality).

The three functions listed at the top of the figure—socialization, recruitment, and communication—are not directly involved in making and implementing public policy but are of fundamental importance to the political system. We refer to these three functions as **system functions.** They determine whether or not the system will be maintained or changed. For example, will policymaking continue to be dominated by a military council or be replaced by competitive parties and a legislature? Will a sense of national community persist, or will it be eroded by new experiences?

The arrows leading from these three functions to all parts of the political process suggest their crucial role in underpinning and permeating the political process.

- **Political socialization** involves families, schools, communications media, churches, and all the various political structures that develop, reinforce, and transform the political culture, the attitudes of political significance in the society. (See Chapter 3.)

- **Political recruitment** refers to the selection of people for political activity and government offices. In a democracy, competitive elections play a major role in political recruitment. In authoritarian systems, recruitment may be dominated by a single party, as in China, or unelected religious leaders, as in Iran.
- **Political communication** refers to the flow of information through the society and through the various structures that make up the political system. Gaining control over information is a key goal of most authoritarian rulers, as shown in the elaborate efforts of Chinese leaders to control content on the Internet.

Understanding the performance of the system functions is essential to understanding how political systems respond to the great contemporary challenges of building community, fostering economic development, and securing democracy that we discussed in Chapter 1.

On the right side of Figure 2.3 we see the consequences of the policy process. The **outputs** are the implementations of the political process. These are the substantive impacts on the society, the economy, and the culture. They include various forms of **extraction** of resources in the form of taxes and the like, **regulation** of behavior, and **distribution** of benefits and services to various groups in the population. The **outcomes** of all these political activities reflect the way the policies interact with the domestic and international environments. Sometimes these outcomes are the desired results of public policies. But sometimes the complexities of policy and society result in unintended consequences. Among these may be new demands for legislation or for administrative action, or increases or decreases in the amount of support given to the political system and incumbent officeholders. We shall return to the policy level, after providing an example of a structural-functional comparison.

The functional concepts shown in Figure 2.3 describe the activities carried on in any society regardless of how its political system is organized or what kinds of policies it produces. Using these functional categories, we can determine how institutions in different countries combine in making and implementing different kinds of public policy. Each country study in this book discusses the ways the different political functions are performed.

AN ILLUSTRATIVE COMPARISON: REGIME CHANGE IN RUSSIA

Figures 2.4 and 2.5[3] offer a simplified graphic comparison of structures and functions in Russia before and after the breakdown of communist rule in the Soviet Union. They illustrate the use of the comparative method to assess the way a political regime changed significantly in a short period of time. The point here is to illustrate how we can use the tools of political analysis, rather than provide the details of the Russian case (which are discussed in depth in Chapter 12).

The figures depict the changes in the functioning of the major structures of the political system brought about by the collapse of communism. These include two revolutionary changes. One is the end of the single-party political system dominated

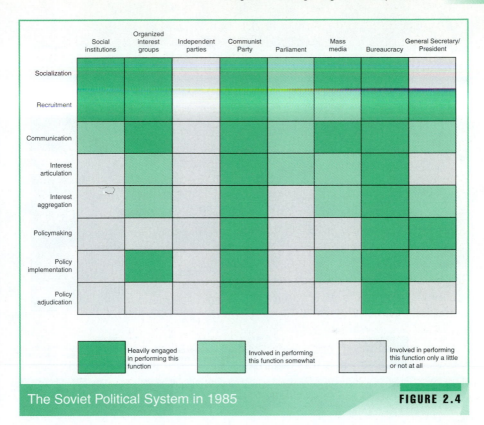

The Soviet Political System in 1985   **FIGURE 2.4**

by the Communist Party of the Soviet Union, which held together the vast, multinational Soviet state. The other is the dissolution of the Soviet Union itself into its fifteen member republics. As a result of these two remarkable events, Russia, the republic that was the core republic of the old union, became an independent noncommunist state.

In June 1991, Boris Yeltsin, a bitter rival to the Soviet president, Mikhail Gorbachev, was elected president of Russia. Six months later, the Soviet Union collapsed and Gorbachev gave up his office. In December 1993, Russian voters were called on to ratify a new constitution, which provided for a powerful executive presidency and at the same time elected a new parliament dominated by a diverse range of political parties.

In the new Russia, democratic tendencies competed with pressures for authoritarian rule. Overall, the new system was a mixture of pluralism with vestiges of the old, bureaucratically run, state socialist order. New political parties were represented in Parliament and tried to develop national political bases of support for the next elections. A reborn Communist Party—called the Communist Party of the Russian Federation—regularly denounced Yeltsin and called for the restoration of a strong state and more social protection. Parliament had become a meaningful site for policy debate and decisionmaking. The mass media were no longer tightly controlled by the Communist Party. New organized interest groups, such as business associations and

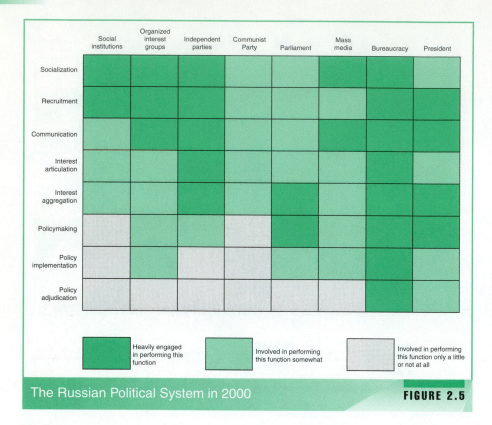

	Social institutions	Organized interest groups	Independent parties	Communist Party	Parliament	Mass media	Bureaucracy	President
Socialization								
Recruitment								
Communication								
Interest articulation								
Interest aggregation								
Policymaking								
Policy implementation								
Policy adjudication								

Heavily engaged in performing this function

Involved in performing this function somewhat

Involved in performing this function only a little or not at all

The Russian Political System in 2000   **FIGURE 2.5**

labor unions, were actively involved in policymaking. The bureaucracy remained a powerful central player in the political process, however, with substantial continued control over the economy.

These and subsequent changes are reflected in the differences between the two figures. In 1985 (the year that the reform leader Mikhail Gorbachev came to power), the Soviet Union was a communist regime. Its Communist Party ruled the country. The top leader of the country was the general secretary of the Communist Party. Although the country had the formal trappings of democracy, power actually flowed downward from the decisionmakers at the top to government and society.

Figure 2.4 therefore shows how the basic functions of the political system were performed in 1985. The Communist Party was the dominant political institution of the country, overseeing schools and media, the arts and public organizations, the economy and the courts. For this reason, all the cells of the chart in the column marked "Communist Party" are shaded dark, as are the cells under the column marked "Bureaucracy." Although social institutions—such as the family, workplace, arts, and hobby groups—exercised some influence over such system-level functions as socialization, recruitment, and communication, it was the Communist Party and state bureaucracy that dominated process-level functions. Under their tutelage, the mass media in 1985 were a key agent of communist political socialization and communication. Parliament was a compliant instrument for ratifying decisions made by the party and bureaucracy. No other parties could exist beside the Communist Party. The only organized interest groups were those authorized by the party. The party's general secretary was the most powerful official in the country, since there was no state presidency.

By 2000 the political system had undergone fundamental changes, as shown in Figure 2.5. Many more structures played a role in the political process, as is immediately evident by the larger number of cells that are heavily shaded. In particular, Parliament, independent political parties, and regional governments all acquired important new powers in policymaking. The freedom enjoyed by ordinary citizens to articulate their interests and to organize to advance them had expanded enormously. The Communist Party, no longer an official or monopolistic party, had declined substantially in power and was playing by the rules of the parliamentary game. The lighter shading for the Communist Party in Figure 2.5 shows its diminished influence. The state bureaucracy remained an important element in the political system, although adapting itself to the new trend of movement toward a market economy by adopting quasi-commercial forms.

The presidency, now occupied by Vladimir Putin, has been a dominating policymaking institution in the new Russia, as shown in Figure 2.5. The Parliament, although fairly representative of the diversity of opinion in the country, was frustrated in its policymaking and oversight roles by the inertia of the vast state bureaucracy, by its inability to compel compliance with its laws, by its weak links with the electorate, and by the president's power to make policy by decree. Nevertheless, it played a much greater role than before in aggregating interests and making policy, as shown when comparing Figures 2.4 and 2.5.

A further updating of Figure 2.5 would show the eclipse of independent parties and Parliament by President Putin after 2000. This movement in a more authoritarian direction, although not back to communism, would be shown by fewer dark shaded columns in the middle of the figure. These further developments are discussed in detail in Chapter 12.

The brief comparisons presented here illustrate the use of the structural-functional approach. This approach enables us to examine how the same functions are performed in different countries, or in the same country at two different points in time. Similarly, we may examine changes in the functions performed by the same structures over time or across different political systems. In a country undergoing as rapid and dramatic a transition as Russia in the 1990s, this framework helps us to analyze changes in the distribution of power among the major institutions making up the political system.

Neither the analysis of structures nor that of functions is complete without the other. A structural analysis tells us the number of political parties, or the organization of the legislature. It describes how the executive branch, the courts, the bureaucracy, the mass media, interest groups, and other structures of a political system are set up and by what rules or standards they operate. A functional analysis tells us how these institutions and organizations interact to produce and implement policies. This kind of analysis is especially essential when we are comparing very different kinds of political systems.

The country chapters of this book do not present formal structural-functional sketches like Figures 2.4 and 2.5. But at the core of each chapter is a set of discussions of these functions and the structures that perform them. We can see these in the section headings of the country studies and in the analytic guide at the beginning of this book. These tools make it possible to compare the workings of the very different political systems in this book.

THE POLICY LEVEL: PERFORMANCE, OUTCOME, AND EVALUATION

The important question is what these differences in structure and function do for the interests, needs, and aspirations of people. We call this the **policy level** of the political system.

Looking again at Figure 2.3, we see reflections of the relationships between the international environment, the domestic society, and the political system. At the left of Figure 2.3 are arrows signifying inputs of demands and supports from the society and the international system. Inputs also come from the independent initiatives of political leaders and bureaucrats. The structures performing the political process functions convert these inputs into the policies of the government. These policies extract resources, distribute benefits, and regulate behavior. They are designed to achieve broad goals, such as welfare, justice, and freedom—or control and domination—as well as special benefits for groups and individuals. At the right are arrows signifying outputs and outcomes, the end products of the political process, the things a government does for and to its people.

We call the outputs of a political system—its extractions, distributions, regulations, and symbolic acts—its policy performance. We have to distinguish among these efforts, the things a government does, and the actual outcome of these efforts. Governments may spend equal amounts on education and health, or defense, but with different consequences. Government efficiency or corruption plays a role in the effectiveness of politics. But so do the underlying cultural, economic, and technological levels.

Americans spend more per capita on education than any other people in the world. But their children perform less well in some subjects, such as mathematics, than do children in some other countries that spend substantially less. The United States spent enormous sums and many lives on the war in Vietnam in the 1960s and 1970s, as did the Soviet Union on its war in Afghanistan in the 1980s. Yet, both countries were held at bay by small countries resolved to resist at all costs. Because of these costly failures, they were weakened internally. The outcome of public policy is never wholly in the hands of the people and their leaders. Conditions in the internal environment, conditions and events in the larger external world, and simple chance may frustrate the most thoughtfully crafted programs and plans. Each country study in this book concludes with a discussion of the country's performance, describing both policies and their outcomes.

Finally, we must step even further back to consider the whole situation of political system, process, and policy, and the environment in order to evaluate what political systems are doing. Evaluation is complex because people value different things and put different emphasis on what they value. We will refer to the different things people may value as political "goods." In Chapter 7, we discuss goods associated with the system level, such as the stability or adaptability of political institutions. We also discuss goods associated with the process level, such as citizen participation in politics. Finally, we consider goods associated with the policy level, such as welfare, security, and liberty. To evaluate what a political system is doing, we assess performance and outcomes in each of these areas. We must also be aware of how outcomes affect individuals and subgroups in the society, of specific changes that may often be overlooked in presenting averages.

A particularly important problem of evaluation concerns building for the future as well as living today. The people of poor countries wish to survive and alleviate the suffering of today but also to improve their children's lot for tomorrow. The people of all countries, but especially rich ones, must deal with the costs to their children of polluted and depleted natural resources as the result of the thoughtless environmental policies of the past.

HOW WE EXPLAIN

Once we are able to describe politics with the help of the conceptual framework that we choose, the next task is to explain it. What we mean by explaining political phenomena is seeking to identify relationships among them. For example, we might be interested in the relationship between democracy and international peace (see Box 2.2). Are democratic states more peaceful than others? If so, are they peaceful because they are democratic, are they democratic because they are peaceful, or are they perhaps both peaceful and democratic because they are more prosperous than other states?

These questions show that we often want explanations to go beyond associating one thing with another. Ideally, we want to put many political relationships in causal terms, so that we can say that one political feature is the cause of another, and the latter is the effect of the former.

Theories are statements about causal relationships between general classes of events—for example, about what causes democracy, war, or welfare policies. Scientific theories are always tentative; they are always subject to modification or falsification as our knowledge improves. And theories need to be testable. A good theory is one that holds up after continued trials and experiments. Yet, it can be further confirmed or modified as we test the theory again and again. A well-tested theory allows us to explain confidently what happens in specific cases or groups of cases: these two countries have a peaceful relationship because they are democracies (see Box 2.2).

BOX 2.2

Statistical Methods

A popular contemporary research program known as *democratic peace research* illustrates the pros and cons of statistical and case study research. It has been of primary interest to international relations scholars, who took the diplomatic history of the Cold War period and asked whether democratic countries are more peaceful in their foreign policy than authoritarian and nondemocratic ones. Many scholars in the democratic peace research group took the statistical route. They counted each year of interaction between two states as one case. With roughly half a century of diplomatic history involving a state system of 100 countries or more, they had a very large number of cases, even after eliminating the many irrelevant cases of countries that never, or rarely, had any relations with one another. Political scientists Andrew Bennett and Alexander George drew these conclusions after surveying the statistical research:

> Statistical methods achieved important advances on the issue of whether a nonspurious inter-democratic peace exists. A fairly strong though not unanimous consensus emerged that: (1) democracies are not less war-prone in general; (2) they have very rarely if ever fought one another; (3) this pattern of an interdemocratic peace applies to both war and conflicts short of war; (4) states in transition to democracy are more war prone than established democracies; and (5) these correlations were not spuriously brought about by the most obvious alternative explanations.

> Yet, although much was learned from the statistical studies, they were not as successful at answering "why" questions. Case studies make clinical depth possible, revealing causal interconnections in individual cases. Careful repetition of these causal tracings from case to case strengthens confidence in these relationships. Thus Bennett and George concluded that the best research strategy uses statistical and case study methods together, with each method having its own strengths.

Source: Andrew Bennett and Alexander George, "An Alliance of Statistical and Case Study Methods: Research on the Interdemocratic Peace," APSA-CP: *Newsletter of the APSA Organized Section in Comparative Politics* 9 (1998) no. 1: 6.

Researchers in political science distinguish between studies based on large numbers (large "n") and small numbers (small "n"). In large "n" studies, it is often possible and helpful to use statistical analysis. Such studies are usually referred to as *statistical studies;* small "n" studies are usually called *case studies.* Large "n" studies have a sufficient number and variety of cases to enable the researcher to examine the relation among the variables. Variables are the features on which our cases differ—for example, "form of government: democracy or dictatorship." Statistical analysis enables us to consider possible alternative causes at the same time, accepting some and rejecting others. Small "n" studies permit investigators to go deeply into a case, identify the particularities of it, get the clinical details, and examine each link in the causal process. Most researchers recognize that these methods are complementary (see Box 2.2).

Large "n" statistical studies allow us to be more certain and precise in our explanations. On the other hand, we need the depth that case studies provide. They encourage us to formulate insightful hypotheses for statistical testing in the first place. They allow us to trace the nature of the cause-and-effect relations (sometimes called "causal mechanisms") better than large "n" studies. In this manner, political scientists may come to know not only whether democracies are more peaceful than dictatorships, but more precisely why democratic leaders behave in the way that they do.

We can also generate and test hypotheses about the causes and consequences of political change by comparing countries at different historical periods. Tocqueville's study of the French Revolution contributed to a general theory of revolution by comparing pre- and postrevolutionary France.[4] Theda Skocpol based her theories of the causes of revolution on a comparison of the "old regimes" of France, Russia, and China with their revolutionary and postrevolutionary regimes.[5]

An example may suggest how you might go about theorizing in comparative politics, going beyond "just mastering the facts." It is well known that rich countries are more likely to be democracies than are poor countries; democracy and economic development are strongly associated. But there are many possible reasons for this association. Some have suggested that this relationship comes about because democracy encourages education and economic development. Others have argued that as countries develop economically, their new middle classes or better organized working class are more likely to demand democratization. Yet others have seen that both democracy and economic development are commonly found in some regions of the world, such as Western Europe, while both tend to be scarce in the Middle East and Africa. This fact suggests that certain cultures may encourage or discourage both of them.

We want to understand the causal nature of this association, for reasons of both science and policy. Fostering economic development and securing democracy are two of the significant political challenges that we discussed in Chapter 1. It is vitally important that we understand how they relate to each other.

A work of Adam Przeworski and his associates examined the full experience of democracies, nondemocracies, and transitions between them in all parts of the world between 1950 and 1990.[6] Their statistical analysis led them to conclude that the explanation for the association did not lie in regional effects or superior economic growth in democracy. Moreover, countries at any level of development seemed able to introduce democracy, although economically developed countries are somewhat more likely to do so. They argue that key to the relationship lies rather in the consistently greater fragility of democracies in societies at lower levels of economic development. Democracy can easily be introduced in poor societies with less educated populations. But in these social conditions it is often replaced by some kind of dictatorship. In rich countries, on the other hand, democracy tends to survive once it has been introduced. These democratic failures in poor countries produce a strong association between development and democracy. We still need to understand just why democracy is more precarious in less developed societies. But we are making progress in understanding the causal element in the relationship. We are better able to explain the relationship between development and democracy, as well as the failures of democratization in specific countries.

Comparative analysis is a powerful and versatile tool. It enhances our ability to describe and understand political processes and political change in any country by offering concepts and reference points from a broader perspective. The comparative approach also stimulates us to form general theories of political relationships. It encourages and enables us to test our political theories by confronting them with the experience of many institutions and settings.

REVIEW QUESTIONS

- How do the main elements in the environment of a political system affect the way it performs?
- Why can't we compare political systems by just describing the different structures we find in them?
- What are the functions performed in all political systems as policies are made?
- What is the difference between outputs and outcomes of policy?
- How do we use theories to explain political events?

KEY TERMS

distribution
environment
extraction
functions
globalization
governments
inputs
interdependence
interest aggregation
interest articulation

outcomes
outputs
policy adjudication
policy implementation
policy level
policymaking
political culture
political communication
political recruitment

political socialization
political system
process functions
regulation
structural-functional approach
structures
system
system functions

SUGGESTED READINGS

Collier, David. "The Comparative Method," in Ada W. Finifter, ed., *Political Science: The State of the Discipline II.* Washington; DC: American Political Science Association, 1993.

Dogan, Mattei, and Dominique Pelassy. *How to Compare Nations: Strategies in Comparative Politics.* Chatham, NJ: Chatham House, 1990.

Goodin, Robert E., and Hans-Dieter Klingemann. Chapters 2 and 3, and Part 4 of *A New Handbook of Political Science*. New York: Oxford University Press, 1996.

King, Gary, Robert O. Keohane, and Sidney Verba. *Scientific Inference in Qualitative Research*. New York: Cambridge University Press, 1993.

Lichbach, Mark, and Alan Zuckerman. *Comparing Nations: Rationality, Culture, and Structure*. New York: Cambridge University Press, 1997.

Przeworski, Adam, and Henry Teune. *The Logic of Comparative Social Inquiry*. New York: Wiley, 1970.

ENDNOTES

1. Alexis de Tocqueville to Louis de Kergolay, 18 October 1847, in *Alexis de Tocqueville: Selected Letters on Politics and Society*, ed. Roger Boesche (Berkeley: University of California Press, 1985), 191.
2. Alexis de Tocqueville to Ernest de Chabrol, 7 October 1831, *ibid*, 59.
3. Figures 2.4 and 2.5 and the text of this section were contributed by Thomas Remington.
4. Alexis de Tocqueville, *The Old Regime and the French Revolution,* trans. Stuart Gilbert (New York: Doubleday, 1955).
5. Theda Skocpol, *States and Social Revolutions* (New York: Cambridge University Press, 1979).
6. Adam Przeworski, et al., *Democracy and Development* (Cambridge: Cambridge University Press, 2000).

POLITICAL CULTURE AND POLITICAL SOCIALIZATION

Do you remember the first time you traveled to a foreign country? You probably were surprised by how many of the normal things in your life were different there. The food was different, people wore different clothes, houses were constructed and furnished differently, and the pattern of social relations differed (for instance, whether they talked to strangers or stood in queues). You were observing how social norms shape what people eat, how they dress, how they live, and maybe even on which side of the road they drive.

Similarly, each nation has its own political norms that influence how people think about and react to politics. Americans' strong feelings of patriotism, the Japanese deference to political elites, and the French proclivity for protest all illustrate how cultural norms shape politics. The way political institutions function at least partially reflects the public's attitudes, norms, and expectations. Thus, the English use their constitutional arrangements to sustain their liberty, while the same institutions were once used as a means of repression in South Africa and Northern Ireland. When a new regime forms, a supportive public can help develop the new system, while the absence of public support may weaken the new system. To understand the political tendencies in a nation, we must begin with public attitudes toward politics and their role within the political system—what we call a nation's political culture.

Chapter 1 stated that one main goal of any government, and a special challenge for a new government, is to create and maintain a political community. In part, this involves developing common structures and systems (such as a single economy), common political institutions, and common political processes. At the level of the public, this involves developing common world views, values, and expectations among the public that together comprise the nation's political culture. So studying political culture partially explains how a political community is created and sustained.

In this chapter we map the important parts of political culture. We then discuss political socialization: how individuals form their political attitudes and thus, collectively, how citizens form their political culture. We conclude by describing the major trends in political culture in world politics today.

MAPPING THE THREE LEVELS OF POLITICAL CULTURE

A nation's **political culture** includes its citizens' orientations at three levels: the political system, the political and policymaking process, and policy outputs and outcomes (Table 3.1). The *system* level involves how people view the values and organizations that comprise the political system. Do citizens identify with the nation and accept the general system of government? The *process* level includes expectations of how politics should function, and individuals' relationship to the political process. The *policy* level deals with the public's policy expectations for the government. What should be the policy goals of government and how are they to be achieved?

The System Level

Orientations toward the political system are important because they tap basic commitments to the polity and the nation. It is difficult for any political system to endure if it lacks the support of its citizens.

Feelings of national pride are considered an affective, emotional tie to a political system. National pride seems strongest in nations with a long history that has emphasized feelings of patriotism—the United States is a prime example (see Figure 3.1). Such a common sense of identity and national history often binds a people together in times of political strain. The figure indicates that high levels of pride exist in nations with very different political and economic systems, such as the United States and Poland. In contrast, national pride is low in Japan and Germany, two nations that have avoided nationalist sentiments in reaction to the World War II regimes and their excesses. In other cases, ethnicity, language, or history divide the public, which may strain national identities and ultimately lead to conflict and division.

The Aspects of Political Culture	**TABLE 3.1**

Aspects of Political Culture	Examples
System	Pride in nation National identity Legitimacy of government
Process	Role of citizens Perceptions of political rights
Policy	Role of government Government policy priorities

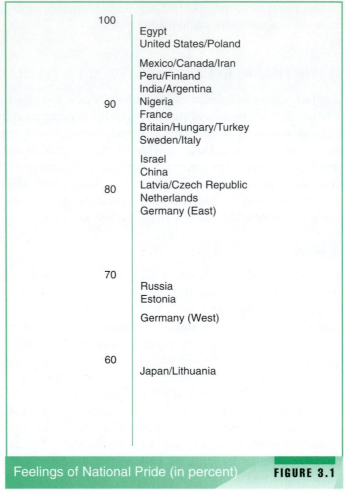

100	Egypt
	United States/Poland
	Mexico/Canada/Iran
	Peru/Finland
	India/Argentina
90	Nigeria
	France
	Britain/Hungary/Turkey
	Sweden/Italy
	Israel
	China
80	Latvia/Czech Republic
	Netherlands
	Germany (East)
70	
	Russia
	Estonia
	Germany (West)
60	
	Japan/Lithuania

Feelings of National Pride (in percent)   **FIGURE 3.1**

Source: Selected nations from the 2000–2002 *World Values Survey* and the 1999 *European Values Survey*. Figure entries are the percent "proud" and "very proud"; missing data are excluded from the calculation of percentages.

Feelings of popular **legitimacy** are another foundation for a successful political system. When people believe that they ought to obey the laws, legitimacy is high. If they see no reason to obey or if they comply only from fear, legitimacy is low. Because it is much easier for government to function when citizens believe in the legitimacy of the system, virtually all governments, even the most brutal and coercive, try to encourage people to believe that they should obey the laws. A political system and a government with high legitimacy are typically more effective in carrying out policies and are more likely to overcome hardships and reversals.

Citizens may grant legitimacy to a government for different reasons. In a traditional society, legitimacy may depend on the ruler's inheriting the throne or on the ruler's commitment to religious customs. In a modern democracy, the legitimacy of the authorities depends on their selection by voters in competitive elections and on the government following constitutional procedures. In other political cultures, the leaders may base their claim to legitimacy on their special wisdom or ideology, which they claim will transform people's lives for the better, even though the government does not respond to specific public demands or follow prescribed procedures.[1] Theocratic regimes, such as Iran, base their legitimacy on adherence to religious principles. Thus, legitimacy also presumes an agreement on the broad form of government that defines the political system and thus the standards of legitimacy: monarchical rule, a tribal system, a communist order, or a democratic system.

Whether legitimacy is based on tradition, ideology, elections, or religion, feelings of legitimacy reflect a basic understanding between citizens and political authorities. Citizens obey the laws and in return the government meets the obligations set by the terms of its legitimacy. As long as the government meets its obligations, the public is supposed to be supportive and act appropriately. If legitimacy is violated—the line of succession is broken, the constitution is subverted, or the ruling ideology is ignored—the government may expect resistance and perhaps rebellion.

In systems with low legitimacy, people often resort to violence or extra-governmental actions to solve political disagreements. Legitimacy is lacking where the public disputes the boundaries of the political system (as in Northern Ireland or Kashmir), rejects the current arrangements for recruiting leaders and making policies (as when Indonesians took to the streets in 1998 demanding a new democratic regime), or loses confidence that the leaders are fulfilling their part of the political bargain (as when the Thai opposition forced the prime minister from office in 2006).

The Soviet Union disintegrated in the early 1990s because all three legitimacy problems appeared. After the communist ideology failed as a legitimizing force, there was no basis for a national political community in the absence of common language or ethnicity. Similarly, the loss of confidence in the Communist Party as a political organization led many people to call for institutional reform. Finally, shortages of food and consumer goods caused people to lose faith in the government's short-term economic and political policies. Soviet President Mikhail Gorbachev failed in his efforts to deal with all three problems at the same time.

The Process Level

The second level of the political culture involves what the public expects of the political process. Whether you are English or Nigerian, what do you think about the institutions of your political system and what is expected of you as a citizen?

Broadly speaking, three different patterns describe the citizen's role in the political process:[2]

- **Participants** are, or have the potential to be, involved in the political process. They are informed about politics and make demands on the polity, granting their support to political leaders based on performance.

- **Subjects** passively obey government officials and the law, but they do not vote or actively involve themselves in politics.
- **Parochials** are hardly aware of government and politics. They may be illiterates, rural people living in remote areas, or simply people who ignore politics and its impact on their lives.

As shown in Figure 3.2, in a hypothetical modern industrial democracy a majority are participants, a third are simply subjects, and a small group are parochials. This distribution provides enough political activists to ensure competition among political parties and sizable voter turnout, as well as critical audiences for debate on public issues by parties, candidates, and pressure groups. At the same time, not all citizens feel the need to be active in or concerned about in the political system.

The second column in Figure 3.2 shows the pattern we expect in an industrialized authoritarian society, such as the former communist nations of Eastern Europe. A small minority of citizens are involved in a one-party system, which penetrates and oversees the society, as well as decides government policies. Most other citizens are mobilized as subjects by political institutions: political parties, the bureaucracy, and government-controlled mass media. People are encouraged and even forced to cast a symbolic vote of support in elections and to pay taxes, obey regulations, and follow the dictates of government. Because of the effectiveness of modern social organization and the efforts of the authoritarian power structure, few people are unaware of the government and its influence on their lives. If such a society suddenly

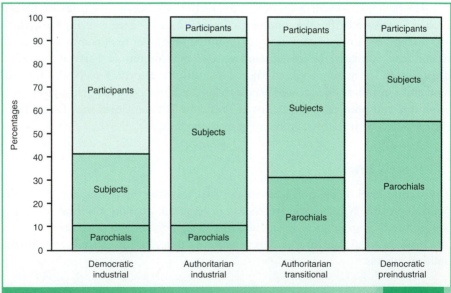

Models of Political Culture: Orientations Toward Involvement in the Political Process

FIGURE 3.2

attempts to democratize its politics, many people must learn to become democrats and participants.

The third column shows an authoritarian society that is partly traditional and partly modern, such as in Iran or China. In spite of an authoritarian political system, some participants—students and intellectuals, for example—oppose the system and try to change it by persuasion or acts of protest. Favored groups, like business people and landowners, discuss public issues and engage in lobbying. Most people in such systems are passive subjects, aware of government and complying with the law but not otherwise involved in public affairs. The parochials—poor and illiterate urban dwellers, peasants, or farm laborers—have limited contact with the political system.

The fourth column shows the democratic preindustrial system, perhaps India or Nigeria, which has a predominantly rural, illiterate population. In such a country, the few political participants are chiefly educated professionals, business people, and landowners. A much larger number of employees, workers, and farmers are directly affected by government taxation and other official policies. The largest group of people are illiterate peasants, whose knowledge of and involvement with national politics are minimal. Such a society faces significant challenge to create a more aware public that can participate meaningfully and shape government policies through democratic means.

Attitudes toward the citizen's role are also shaped by the political form of the regime. In the early 1900s, many different political systems existed worldwide. Fascism was on the rise in Europe, communism was establishing itself in the Soviet Union, colonial administrations governed large parts of the world, and monarchical or authoritarian governments ruled other nations. All of these systems encouraged a restrictive role for the citizens. Western Europe and North America were the democracies in this sea of conflicting currents.

Today, many of these nondemocratic forms of governance are no longer widely accepted. Communism still has strongholds in China and Cuba, but it has lost its image as a progressive force for global change. Some nations still accept autocratic or religiously based systems of government. However, the global wave of democratization since the early 1990s has raised democratic principles to a position of prominence (see Figure 1.3 in Chapter 1). Democratic norms emphasize the importance of a participatory system, majority rule and minority rights, and the values of political tolerance. Most of the people in the world today seem to favor democratic principles even if they differ in how those principles should be applied.[3]

The distribution of these citizen types and political norms is affected by the process of social and economic **modernization** that we introduced in Chapter 1. Industrialization, urbanization, and improved living standards transform the social base of a nation. Exposure to modernity through work, education, and the media shapes an individual's personal experiences and sends messages about norms in other societies. It encourages citizen participation, a sense of individual equality, the desire for improved living standards and increased life expectancy, and government legitimacy based on policy performance. It also frequently disrupts familiar ways of life, traditional bases of legitimacy, and political arrangements that depend on citizens

Becoming Modern

Alex Inkeles and David Smith report how one Nigerian worker replied to a question about how his new job in a factory made him feel. "Sometimes like 9 feet tall with arms a yard wide. Here in the factory I alone with my machine can twist any way I want a piece of steel that all the men in my home village together could not begin to bend at all." Such experiences—and the parallel changes in educational levels and access to information—can create a more modern political culture.

Source: Alex Inkeles and David Smith, *Becoming Modern* (Cambridge, Harvard University Press, 1974), 158.

remaining parochials or subjects. In addition, the secularizing influences of science can alter economic and social systems, which then reshapes the political culture. This modernization trend has powerful effects as it penetrates societies (or parts of societies). Alex Inkeles and David Smith's classic study of modernization emphasized how factory experience can create an awareness of the possibilities of organization, change, and control over nature that empowers the individual (see Box 3.1).

This modernization process is spread unevenly across the globe. The advanced industrial societies have the largest proportion of citizens who are participants and cognitively engaged in politics. The recent economic growth in East Asia is similarly transforming the political culture and political behavior in these nations.[4] In contrast, modernization has proceeded more slowly and uncertainly in Africa and Arab nations. Some political leaders in these nations even reject the principles of modernization as incongruent with their national values. However, there is persuasive evidence that where social and economic modernization occurs, it transforms the political culture to emphasize self-expression, participatory values, and autonomy.[5]

The Policy Level

What is the appropriate role of government? If you ask political theorists, you get a wide range of answers—from the minimal state to the all-encompassing polity (see Chapter 1). And if you travel to other nations, you quickly realize that there is wide variation in how people answer this question.

The policy activities of a country are influenced by public images of what constitutes the good society and the government's role in achieving these goals. Should government manage the economy, or should private property rights and market forces guide economic activity? Should the state intervene in addressing social and moral issues, or should it follow a minimalist strategy? The ongoing debates over "big government" versus "small government" in democratic states, and between socialist and market-based economies reflect these different images of the scope of government.

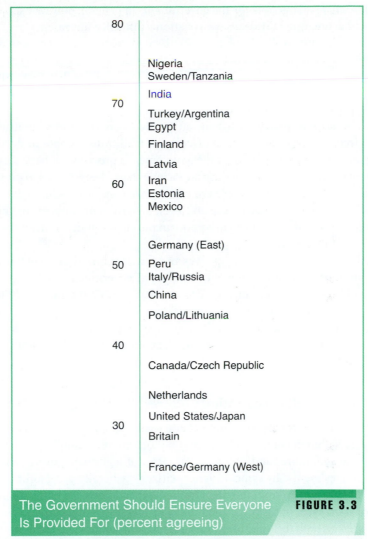

80	
	Nigeria
	Sweden/Tanzania
70	India
	Turkey/Argentina
	Egypt
	Finland
	Latvia
60	Iran
	Estonia
	Mexico
	Germany (East)
50	Peru
	Italy/Russia
	China
	Poland/Lithuania
40	
	Canada/Czech Republic
	Netherlands
	United States/Japan
30	Britain
	France/Germany (West)

The Government Should Ensure Everyone Is Provided For (percent agreeing)   **FIGURE 3.3**

Source: Selected nations from the 2000–2002 *World Values Survey* and 1999 *European Values Survey*; missing data are excluded from the calculation of percentages.

We can illustrate differences in policy expectations with an opinion survey question that asks whether the government is responsible to provide for everyone (see Figure 3.3). The range in opinions is considerable, about three-quarters of respondents in Nigeria and Sweden believe this is a government responsibility compared with only a quarter of the French or West Germans. In general, people in developing nations and in the formerly communist nations of Eastern Europe are more supportive of a large government role—reflecting both their social condition and their past political ideologies. In some Western nations, such as Sweden and Finland, traditions include a large role for the government. In general, however, support for government action generally decreases as national affluence increases.[6]

Policy expectations also involve specific issue demands.[7] Indeed, each country study in this book begins with a discussion of the policy challenges facing the nation and the public's issue concerns. This sets the agenda of politics that responsive governments should address.

Some policy goals, such as economic well-being, are valued by nearly everyone. Concern about other policy goals may vary widely across nations because of the nation's circumstances and because of cultural traditions. People in developing countries are more likely to focus on the government's provision of basic services to ensure public welfare. Advanced industrial societies have the resources to provide for basic needs. In these nations, people are often more concerned with quality-of-life goals, such as preservation of nature and even government support for the arts.[8] One basic measure of a government's performance is its ability to meet the policy expectations of its citizens.

Another set of expectations involves the functioning of government. Some cultures put more weight on the policy outputs of government, such as providing welfare and security. Other cultures also emphasize how the process functions, which involves values such as the rule of law and procedural justice. Among Germans, for example, the rule of law is given great importance; in many developing nations political relations are personally based, and there is less willingness to rely on legalistic frameworks.

Consensual or Conflictual Political Cultures

Although political culture is a common characteristic of a nation, values and beliefs can also vary within it. Political cultures may be consensual or conflictual on issues of public policy and, more fundamentally, on views of legitimate governmental and political arrangements. In some societies, citizens generally agree on the norms of political decisionmaking and their policy expectations. In other societies— because of differences in histories, conditions, or identities—the citizens are sharply divided, often on both the legitimacy of the regime and solutions to major problems.[9]

When a country is deeply divided in its political values and these differences persist over time, distinctive **political subcultures** may develop. The citizens in these subcultures may have sharply different points of view on some critical political matters, such as the boundaries of the nation, the nature of the regime, or the correct ideology. They may affiliate with different political parties and interest groups, read different newspapers, and even have separate social clubs and sporting groups. Thus, they are exposed to different information about politics. For instance, such subcultural differences characterize the publics in India, Nigeria, and Russia today.

In some instances, historical or social factors generate different cultural trajectories. For instance, *ethnic, religious*, or *linguistic* identities in many parts of the world shape citizen values.[10] Moreover, as such groups increase their political skills and self-confidence, they may express their identities and demand equal treatment.

In fact, the processes of globalization might actually heighten these cultural contrasts.[11] The migration of peoples into new areas—made possible by easier transportation and encouraged by wars, political conflicts, and the desire for economic betterment—can seem to threaten the way of life of the host society. The exposure to values from other cultures also may intensify one's own self-image, which may increase cultural tensions. Although such exposure may eventually lead to greater tolerance, that outcome is not guaranteed.

WHY CULTURE MATTERS

Political culture does not explain everything about politics. Even people with similar values and skills might behave differently from each other when they face different situations. Nor is political culture unchangeable. However, cultural norms typically change slowly and reflect stable values. Thus, political culture is important first because it encapsulates the history, traditions, and values of a society. To understand how most people in a nation think and act politically, we can begin by understanding their political culture. Political culture can create the common political community that is one goal of government.

In addition, the distribution of cultural patterns is typically related to the type of political process that citizens expect and support. This is the principle of *congruence theory*. For instance, support for a democratic system is typically higher in societies that have a more participatory political culture. Authoritarian states are more likely to endure when the public is characterized by subjects and parochials—where individuals lack the skills or motivations to participate and the state discourages their participation. These cultural norms represent the "rules of the game" for the political system, and the system works better when citizens accept these rules. Where political structures and political cultures are mutually reinforcing, a more stable political system is likely to emerge.

We can illustrate the logic of congruence theory in terms of the relationship between political culture and the democratic development of a nation (Figure 3.4). The horizontal axis of the figure displays the public's adherence to self-expressive values, reflecting the participatory norms we discussed earlier. The vertical axis represents the democratic development of the nation based on a variety of expert evaluations. You can see that as participatory values increase, so too does the democratic development of the nation. The nations in this book that are included in these analyses show a clear differentiation between the established Western democracies, relatively new democracies (such as Russia and other East European nations), and nondemocracies (such as China and several Middle East nations). Structure and culture do overlap in these nations.[12]

Do democracies create a participatory democratic public or does such a political culture lead to a democratic political system? It works both ways. For example, immediately after World War II, Germans were less supportive of democracy, but political institutions and political experiences transformed their culture over the next

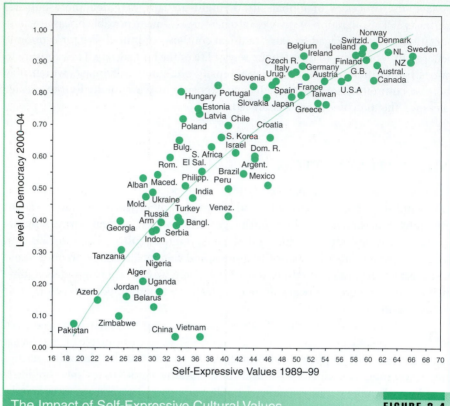

The Impact of Self-Expressive Cultural Values on the Level of Democracy

FIGURE 3.4

Source: The self-expressive values measure is from the *Word Values Survey*; higher scores represent more citizen emphasis on self-expression. The level of democracy measure is a composite of the ranking of democracy by the Freedom House and other national rankings. Higher scores indicates a higher level of democratic development. For additional discussion of these measures see Ronald Inglehart and Christian Welzel, *Modernization, Cultural Change and Democracy: The Human Development Sequence* (New York: Cambridge University Press, 2005).

generation.[13] At the same time, democracy endured in Britain during the strains of the Great Depression and World War II, at least in part because the British public supported the democratic process. The important conclusion is that there is normally a relationship between political culture and political structures.

Beyond shaping the structure of the political system, a nation's political culture also influences the style of politics and the content of policymaking. We have stressed how the policy elements of a political culture can influence the content of policy. In addition, research suggests that cultural factors, such as social trust and engagement, influence the efficiency and effectiveness of government.[14]

Finally, while the political culture may help build a national community, it may also provide a basis of division. For instance, where political subcultures coincide with ethnic, linguistic, or religious differences—as in Northern Ireland, Bosnia, and Lebanon—the divisions can be enduring and threatening. The fragmentation of the Soviet empire, the breakup of Yugoslavia, and the impulses toward autonomy and secession among ethnically distinct regions (such as in Scotland or separatist movements in Africa) all reflect the lasting power of language, culture, and historical memory to create and sustain the sense of ethnic and national identity among parts of contemporary states. In broader international terms, Samuel Huntington has divided the world into different civilizations defined by their religious and cultural traditions.[15] He then predicted that these cultural differences will be a major source of international conflict in this century. While culture may have the power to divide, it is counterbalanced by its potential to build a common political community.

POLITICAL SOCIALIZATION

Political cultures are sustained or changed as people acquire their attitudes and values. **Political socialization** refers to the way in which political values are formed and the political culture is transmitted from one generation to the next. Most children acquire their basic political values and behavior patterns by adolescence.[16] Some of these attitudes will evolve and change throughout their lives, while other attitudes may remain part of their political self throughout life.

At any specific time, a person's political beliefs are a combination of various feelings and attitudes. At the deepest level, there are general identifications, such as nationalism, ethnic or class self-images, religious and ideological commitments, and a fundamental sense of rights and duties in the society. At the middle level, people develop attitudes toward politics and governmental institutions. Finally, there are more immediate views of current events, policies, issues, and personalities. All these attitudes can change, but those in the first level usually were acquired earliest, have been most frequently reinforced, and tend to be the most durable.

Three points about political socialization deserve mention. First, the socialization process can occur in different ways. Direct socialization involves an actor explicitly communicating information, values, or feelings toward politics. Examples of direct socialization include civics courses in the schools, public education programs of the government, and the political information campaigns of interest groups. Communist political systems also heavily use direct indoctrination programs (see Box 3.2). Indirect political socialization occurs when political views are inadvertently molded by our experiences. For example, children normally learn important political values by observing the behavior of their parents, teachers, and friends. Or, people may learn by observing the political and social context that surrounds them, watching what governments do and how other citizens react.

Second, socialization is a lifelong process. Early family influences can create an individual's initial values, but subsequent life experiences—becoming involved in new social groups, moving from one part of the country to another, shifting up or

Socializing Values

BOX 3.2

Communist East Germany had a special ceremony for eighth graders to mark their passage to adulthood. The heart of the ceremony was the endorsement of the following four pledges:

- As young citizens of our German Democratic Republic, are you prepared to work and fight loyally for the great and honorable goals of socialism, and to honor the revolutionary inheritance of the people?
- As sons and daughters of the worker-and-peasant state, are you prepared to pursue higher education, to cultivate your mind, to become a master of your trade, to learn permanently, and to use your knowledge to pursue our great humanist ideals?
- As honorable members of the socialist community, are you ready to cooperate as comrades, to respect and support each other, and to always merge the pursuit of your personal happiness with the happiness of all the people?
- As true patriots, are you ready to deepen the friendship with the Soviet Union, to strengthen our brotherhood with socialist countries, to struggle in the spirit of proletarian internationalism, to protect peace and to defend socialism against every imperialist aggression?

down the social ladder, becoming a parent, finding or losing a job—may change one's political perspectives. More dramatic experiences—such as relocating to a new country or suffering through an economic depression or a war—can alter even basic political attitudes. Such events seem to have their greatest impact on young people, but people at any age are affected to some degree.

Third, patterns of socialization can unify or divide. Governments design public education systems, for instance, to create a single national political culture. Some events, such as international conflict or the death of a popular public figure, can affect nearly the entire nation similarly. In contrast, subcultures in a society can have their own distinctive patterns of socialization. Social groups that provide their members with their own newspapers, their own neighborhood groups, and perhaps their own schools can create distinctive subcultural attitudes. Divisive patterns of socialization can lead to a political gap among members of a nation.

AGENTS OF POLITICAL SOCIALIZATION

Individuals in all societies are affected by **agents of political socialization:** individuals, organizations, and institutions that influence political attitudes. Some, like civics courses in schools, are direct and deliberate sources of political learning. Others, like playgroups and work groups, affect political socialization indirectly.

The Family

The direct and indirect influences of the family—the first socialization source that an individual encounters—are normally powerful and lasting. The family has distinctive influences on attitudes toward authority. Participation in family decisionmaking can increase a child's sense of political competence, providing skills for political interaction and encouraging active participation in the political system as an adult. Similarly, unquestioning obedience to parental decisions may lead a child toward a role as a political subject. The family also shapes future political attitudes by defining a social position for the child: establishing ethnic, linguistic, class, and religious ties; affirming cultural values; and influencing job aspirations.

The nature of the family is changing in many societies. Family sizes are generally decreasing, which changes the pattern of family life. In addition, there has been a marked rise of single-parent families, especially in the advanced industrial democracies. The impact of these structural changes on family socialization patterns is still unclear.

In addition, gender roles are changing in many industrial nations, although they persist in many less-developed nations.[17] The rise of the women's movement and self-help groups has encouraged women to become politically active and change social cues about how women should relate to politics. The lessening of gender differences in self-images, in parental roles, and in relations to the economy and the political system is significantly affecting patterns of political recruitment, political participation, and public policy. A more open family, equality of parenting, and the early exposure of children to childcare and preschool group experiences have modified the impact of the family in the socialization process. Especially in the developing world, the changing role of women may have profound influences in modernizing the society.[18]

Schools

Schools educate children about politics and their role in the process, provide them with information on political institutions and relationships. Schools can also help shape attitudes about the political system, the rules of the political game, the appropriate role of the citizen, and expectations about the government. Schools typically reinforce attachments to the political system and reinforce common symbols, such as the flag and pledge of allegiance, that encourage emotional attachments to the system. When a new nation comes into being, or a revolutionary regime comes to power in an old nation, it usually turns immediately to the schools as a means to supplant "outdated" values and symbols with new ones more congruent with the new ideology.

In some nations, educational systems do not provide unifying political socialization but send starkly different messages to different groups. For instance, some Muslim nations segregate girls and boys within the school system. Even if educational experiences are intended to be equal, segregation creates different experiences and expectations. Moreover, the content of education often differs between boys and girls. Perhaps the worst example occurred under the Taliban in Afghanistan, where for several years young girls were prohibited from attending school. Such treatment of young girls severely limits their life changes, and ensures they will have restricted roles in society and the economy—which was the intent of the Taliban system. The new Afghanistan government reversed this policy, and now young girls are being included in the education system, and their future life prospects are improving as a result.

Education also affects the political skills and resources of the public. Educated people are more aware of the impact of government on their lives and pay more attention to politics.[19] The better educated have mental skills that improve their ability to manage the world of politics. They also have more information about political processes and participate in a wider range of political activities.

Religious Institutions

The religions of the world are carriers of cultural and moral values, which often have political implications. The great religious leaders have seen themselves as teachers, and their followers have usually attempted to shape the socialization of children through schooling, preaching, and religious services. In most nations, there are formal ties between the dominant religion and the government. In these instances, religious values and public policy often overlap. Catholic nations, for instance, are less likely to have liberal abortion policies, just as Islamic governments enforce strict moral codes.

Religious institutions of many kinds offer valuable moral and ethical guidance that individuals often need to make choices in complex societies. Religious affiliations are often important sources of partisan preferences and can guide people in making other political choices. Thus, even though church attendance is decreasing in many nations, the political relevance of religion continues.

Where churches teach values that may be at odds with the controlling political system, the struggle over socialization can be intense. These tensions can take a wide variety of forms: the clash between secular and religious roles in the French educational system, the efforts of American fundamentalists to introduce prayer in the schools, or the conflict between Islamic fundamentalists and secular governments in Algeria and Egypt. In such cases, religious groups may oppose the policies of the state, or even the state itself.

The emergence of religious fundamentalism in recent decades has influenced the society and politics of countries as diverse as the United States, India, Israel, Lebanon, Iran, Pakistan, Algeria, and Nigeria. Such **fundamentalism** is often a defensive reaction against the spread of scientific views of nature and human behavior, and the libertarian values and attitudes that accompany these views.[20] The influence of fundamentalism has been most visible in the Middle East and in Muslim countries, but it is important in Christian countries as well. Both Protestant and Catholic versions of fundamentalism exist in the United States, Europe, and Latin America. Versions of fundamentalism also exist, combined with ethnic and nationalist tendencies, in the Confucian, Buddhist, and Hindu countries of Asia. Broadly speaking, fundamentalism seeks to raise conservative social, moral, and religious issues to the top of the contemporary policy agenda.

Peer Groups

Peer groups also shape political attitudes. They include childhood playgroups, friendship cliques, school college fraternities, small work groups, and other groups in which members share relatively equal status and close ties. They can be as varied as a group of Russian mothers who meet regularly at the park, to a street gang in Brazil, to a group of Wall Street executives who are members of a health club.

A peer group socializes its members by motivating or pressuring them to conform to the attitudes or behavior accepted by the group. Individuals often adopt the views of their peers because they like or respect them or because they want to be like them. Similarly, an individual may become interested in politics or attend a political demonstration because close friends do so. One example of peer networks is the international youth culture symbolized by rock music, T-shirts, and blue jeans (and more liberal political values). Some observers claim that it played a major role in the failure of communist officials to mold Soviet and Eastern European youth to the "socialist personality" that was the Marxist-Leninist ideal. Likewise, the "skinheads" groups that have sprouted up among lower class youth in many Western countries have adopted political views that are based on peer interactions.

Social Class

Most societies have significant social divisions based on class or occupation. Individuals live in different social worlds defined by their class position. For instance, industrialization in Britain created a working class that was concentrated in particular neighborhoods. This working class developed its own forms of speech, dress, recreation, and entertainment, as well as its own social organizations (such as social clubs, trade unions, and political parties). Similarly, the life experience of the rural peasantry in many less developed nations is radically different from urban dwellers. Often, these social divisions are politically relevant: identifying yourself as a member of the working class or the peasantry leads to distinct political views about what issues are important and which political groups best represent your interest.

Interest Groups

Interest groups, economic groups, and similar organizations also shape political attitudes. In most industrial countries, the rise of trade unions transformed the political culture and politics, created new political parties, and ushered in new social benefit programs. Today, unions are active participants in the political process and try to persuade their members on political matters. Other professional associations—such as groups of peasants and farmers, manufacturers, wholesalers and retailers, medical societies, and lawyers—also regularly influence political attitudes in modern and modernizing societies. These groups ensure the loyalty of their members by defending their economic and professional interests. They can also provide valuable political cues to nonmembers, who might identify with a group's interests or political ideology. For instance, when a group that you like (or dislike) publicly supports a policy, it gives you information on the likely content of the policy.

The groups that define a civil society are also potential agents of socialization. These groups might include ethnic organizations, fraternal associations, civic associations (such as parent-teacher associations), and policy groups (such as taxpayers' associations, women's groups, and environmental groups). Such groups provide valuable political cues to their members and try to reinforce distinct social and political orientations. They also provide settings to learn about how making political choices in small groups can be extended to politics. For instance, Vietnam has an active network of social groups that socialize individuals into the norms of the communist regime; while civil society groups in the United States are treated as democracy-building organizations.[21] In addition, these groups—using the media and other sources—send out large quantities of information on political, social, and economic issues to the public and elites.

Political Parties

Political parties normally play an important role in political socialization. In democratic systems, political parties attempt to mold issue preferences, arouse the apathetic, and find new issues to mobilize support. Party representatives provide the public with a steady flow of information on the political issues of the day. Party organizations regularly contact voters by mail or phone, and in many nations party activists visit voters at home. In addition, every few years there is an election in which parties present their accomplishments and discuss the nation's political future. Elections can serve as national civics lessons, and the political parties are the teachers.

In competitive democratic party systems, partisan socialization can be also a divisive force. In their efforts to gain support, party leaders may appeal to class, language, religion, and ethnic divisions and make citizens more aware of these differences. The Labour and Conservative parties in Britain, for example, use traditional symbols of class to attract supporters. Similarly, the Congress Party in India tries to develop a national program and appeal, but other parties emphasize the ethnic and religious divisions. Leaders of preindustrial nations often oppose competitive parties because they fear such divisiveness. Although this is sometimes a sincere concern, it is also self-serving to government leaders, and is increasingly difficult to justify against contemporary demands for multiparty systems.

Authoritarian governments often use a single party to inculcate common attitudes of national unity, support for the government, and ideological agreement. The combination of a single party and controlled mass media is potent: the media present a single point of view, and the party activities reinforce that perspective by directly involving the citizen. In a closed environment, single-party governments can be potent agents of socialization.

Mass Media

The mass media—newspapers, radio, television, magazines—are important in socializing attitudes and values in nations around the globe. The mass media are typically the prime source of information on the politics of the day. There is virtually no place so remote that people lack the means to be informed about events elsewhere: in affluent nations the public is wired to the Internet, satellite dishes sprout from houses in Iran, inexpensive transistor radios are omnipresent even in Third World villages far removed from urban centers.

There is one thing most people in the world share in common: we sit before our televisions to learn about the world.[22] Television can have a powerful cognitive and emotional impact on large public audiences by enlisting the senses of both sight and sound. Watching events on television—such as the broadcasts of government affairs or the war in Iraq—gives a reality to the news. Seeing the world directly can shape political attitudes. Today, the Internet provides another powerful source of news for those with access to it.

Access to information thus becomes an important political commodity in the contemporary world. Western democracies put a premium on freedom of the media, even if they frequently complain about what the media reports. In many European nations, the government still manages television and radio stations because it views the media as a public service. Autocratic governments typically seek to control the media and what they can report, as well as the public's access to information (see Box 3.3). Similarly, the communist regimes of Eastern Europe had tried to limit access to news reports from the West because they feared it would undermine their regimes, and the movements for democracy in the region were partially created by the image of the way of life in the West. In the contemporary world of Internet and

---

BOX 3.3

The Great Firewall of China

The People's Republic of China currently has the largest number of Internet users of any nation in the world, except the United States, and this fact has government officials worried. Chinese "netizens" find themselves surfing in the shadow of the world's most sophisticated censorship machine. There is now an estimated 30,000-strong Internet police force, which—with the aid of Western-provided technology—is dedicated to monitoring websites and e-mails. On a technical level, the five gateways that connect China to the global Internet filter traffic coming into and going out of the country. Keyword blocking technology—much of it provided by U.S. companies such as Microsoft and Google—prevents access to offending sites. Even the country's 110,000 Internet cafes are now highly regulated and state-licensed, and all are equipped with standard surveillance systems.

Source: Richard Taylor, "The Great Firewall of China," *BBC News*, January 6, 2006.

satellite broadcasting, it is becoming increasingly difficult for governments to control the spread of information.

Direct Contact with the Government

In modern societies, the wide scope of governmental activities brings citizens into frequent contact with various bureaucratic agencies. One survey of Americans found that about a third had had contact with a government official (federal, state, or local) in the preceding year.[23] Citizens contacted a wide range of government offices, from federal officials, to state and local governments, to school boards and the police. In addition, the government touches our lives in a myriad of other ways, from running the public schools to providing retirement checks to providing social services. The degree of government intervention in daily life, and hence the necessity for contacts with government, varies greatly across nations as a function of their political system and the role of government in the society.

These personal experiences are powerful agents of socialization, strengthening or undercutting the images presented by other agents. Does the government send retirement checks on time? Do city officials respond to citizen complaints? Are the schools teaching children? Do unemployment offices help people find jobs? Are the highways well maintained? These are very direct sources of information on how well the government functions. No matter how positive the view of the political system that people have learned as children, citizens who face a different reality in everyday life are likely to change their early-learned views. Indeed, the contradictions between ideology and reality proved to be one of the weaknesses of the communist systems in Eastern Europe.

In summary, the sources of political socialization often determine the content of what is learned about politics. If people learn about new events from their friends at church, they may hear different information than people who rely on their workplace or the television for information. The role of these different socialization agents and the content of their political messages also vary systematically across nations. In addition, the ability of a nation to recreate its political culture in succeeding generations is an important factor in perpetuating the political system. Finally, cultures change when new elements are added to the process of political learning. Thus, socialization provides the feedback mechanism that enables a political culture to endure or change.

TRENDS SHAPING CONTEMPORARY POLITICAL CULTURES

A political culture exists uniquely in its own time and place. Citizens' attitudes and beliefs are shaped by personal experiences and by the agents of political socialization. Yet, in any historical period there may be trends that change the culture in many nations. The major social trends of our time reflect both general societal developments and specific historic events.

For the past two decades, a major new development is the trend toward democracy in Eastern Europe, East Asia, and other parts of the developing world. This **democratization** trend reflects long-term responses to modernity as well as immediate reactions to current events. Modernization gradually eroded the legitimacy of nondemocratic ideologies, while the development of citizens' skills and political resources made their claim to equal participation in policymaking (at least indirectly) more plausible. Thus, many studies of political culture in Eastern Europe and the former Soviet Union uncovered surprising support for democratic norms and processes among the citizenry as the new democratic system formed.[24]

Ironically, as democracy has begun taking root in Eastern Europe, citizens in many Western democracies are increasingly skeptical about politicians and political institutions. In 1964, three-quarters of Americans said they trusted the government; today only a third of the public say as much—and the malaise is spreading to Western Europe and Japan.[25] At the same time, public support for democratic norms and values has strengthened over time in most Western democracies. Thus, these publics are critical of politicians and political parties when they fall short of these democratic ideals. Although this cynicism is a strain on democratic politicians, it presses democracy to continue to improve and adapt, which is ultimately democracy's greatest strength.

Another recent major trend affecting political cultures is a shift toward **marketization**—that is, an increased public acceptance of free markets and private profit incentives, rather than a government-managed economy. One example of this movement appeared in the United States and many Western European nations beginning in the 1980s, where economies had experienced serious problems of inefficiency and economic stagnation. Margaret Thatcher in Britain and Ronald Reagan in the United States rode to power on waves of public support for reducing the scale of government. Public opinion surveys show that people in these nations felt that government had grown too large (see again Figure 3.3).

Just as Western Europeans began to question the government's role in the economy, the political changes in Eastern Europe and the Soviet Union transformed the discussion. The command economies of Eastern Europe were almost exclusively controlled by state corporations and government agencies. The government set both wages and prices and directed the economy. The collapse of these systems raised new questions about public support for marketization. Public opinion surveys generally find that Eastern Europeans support a capitalist market system and the public policies that would support such an economic system.[26]

Globalization is another trend affecting political cultures of many nations. Increasing international trade and international interactions tend to diffuse the values of the overall international system. Thus, as developing nations become more engaged in the global economy and global international system, the development of certain norms—such as human rights, gender equality, and democratic values—increases.[27] People in developing nations also learn about the broader opportunities existing in other nations, which can spur cultural change as well as economic change. Thus, although globalization has been a deeply divisive political issue for the past decade in many nations, the Pew Global Values Survey found broad support for globalization among citizens worldwide—especially in developing nations where it is seen as improving living standards and life chances.[28]

Clearly, political culture is not a static phenomenon, so our understanding of political culture must be dynamic. It must encompass how the agents of political socialization communicate and interpret historic events and traditional values. It must juxtapose these factors with the exposure of citizens and leaders to new experiences and new ideas. But it is important to understand the political culture of a nation, because these cultural factors influence how citizens act, how the political process functions, and what policy goals the government pursues.

REVIEW QUESTIONS

- What are the three key elements of a political culture?
- Why does political culture matter?
- Why is the process of political socialization important?
- What are the main agents of political socialization?
- What are the major trends in cultural change in the contemporary world?

KEY TERMS

agents of political
   socialization
democratization
fundamentalism
legitimacy

marketization
modernization
parochials
participants
political culture

political socialization
political subcultures
subjects

SUGGESTED READINGS

Almond, Gabriel A., and Sidney Verba. *The Civic Culture.* Princeton, NJ: Princeton University Press, 1963.

———, eds. *The Civic Culture Revisited.* Boston: Little Brown, 1980.

Barnes, Samuel, and Janos Simon, eds. *The Postcommunist Citizen.* Budapest: Erasmus Foundation, 1998.

Bratton, Michael, Robert Mattes, and E. Gyimah-Boadi. *Public Opinion, Democracy, and Market Reform in Africa.* Cambridge: Cambridge University Press, 2004.

Cleary, Matthew, and Susan C. Stokes. *Democracy and the Culture of Skepticism: Political Trust in Argentina and Mexico.* New York: Russell Sage, 2006.

Dalton, Russell. *Democratic Challenges, Democratic Choices: The Erosion of Political Support in Advanced Industrial Democracies.* Oxford: Oxford University Press, 2004.

Harrison, Lawrence, and Samuel P. Huntington, eds. *Culture Matters: How Values Shape Human Progress.* New York: Basic Books, 2000.

Horowitz, Donald. *Ethnic Groups in Conflict.* Berkeley: University of California Press, 1985.

Huntington, Samuel. *The Clash of Civilizations and the Remaking of World Order.* New York: Simon & Schuster, 1996.

Inglehart, Ronald, and Pippa Norris. *Sacred and Secular: Religion and Politics Worldwide.* Cambridge: Cambridge University Press, 2004.

Inglehart, Ronald, and Christian Welzel. *Modernization, Cultural Change, and Democracy: The Human Development Sequence.* New York: Cambridge University Press, 2005.

Inkeles, Alex, and David H. Smith. *Becoming Modern.* Cambridge: Harvard University Press, 1974.

Jennings, M. Kent. "Political Socialization," in Russell Dalton and Hans-Dieter Klingemann, eds. *Oxford Handbook of Political Behavior.* Oxford: Oxford University Press, 2007.

Jennings, M. Kent, and Richard Niemi. *Generations and Politics: A Panel Study of Young Adults and Their Parents.* Princeton, NJ: Princeton University Press, 1981.

Klingemann, Hans Dieter, Dieter Fuchs, and Jan Zielonka, eds. *Democracy and Political Culture in Eastern Europe.* London: Routledge, 2006.

Norris, Pippa, ed. *Critical Citizens: Global Support for Democratic Government.* Oxford: Oxford University Press, 1999.

Norris, Pippa, and Ronald Inglehart. *Rising Tide: Gender Equality and Cultural Change Around the World.* New York: Cambridge University Press, 2003.

Pharr, Susan, and Robert Putnam. *Disaffected Democracies: What's Troubling the Trilateral Democracies?* Princeton, NJ: Princeton University Press, 2000.

Putnam, Robert. *The Beliefs of Politicians.* New Haven, CT: Yale University Press, 1973.

———. *Making Democracy Work: Civic Traditions in Modern Italy.* Princeton, NJ: Princeton University Press, 1993.

Pye, Lucian W., and Sidney Verba, eds. *Political Culture and Political Development.* Princeton, NJ: Princeton University Press, 1965.

Rochon, Thomas. *Culture Moves: Ideas, Activism, and Changing Values.* Princeton, NJ: Princeton University Press, 1998.

Rose, Richard, Christian Haerpfer, and William Mishler. *Testing the Churchill Hypothesis: Democracy and Its Alternatives in Post-communist Societies.* Cambridge, UK: Polity/Baltimore: Johns Hopkins University Press, 2000.

ENDNOTES

1. This concept of legitimacy and its bases in different societies draws on the work of Max Weber. See, for example, Max Weber, *Basic Concepts in Sociology*, trans. H. P. Secher (New York: Citadel Press, 1964), chs. 5–7.

2. These terms were developed in Gabriel A. Almond and Sidney Verba, *The Civic Culture: Political Attitudes and Democracy in Five Nations* (Princeton, NJ: Princeton University Press, 1963).

3. Ronald Inglehart and Christian Welzel, *Modernization, Cultural Change, and Democracy: The Human Development Sequence* (New York: Cambridge University Press, 2005); Pippa Norris, ed., *Critical Citizens: Global Support for Democratic Government* (Oxford: Oxford University Press, 1999).

4. Russell Dalton and Doh Chull Shin, eds., *Citizens, Democracy, and Markets Around the Pacific Rim* (Oxford: Oxford University Press, 2006).

5. Inglehart and Welzel, *Modernization, Cultural Change, and Democracy.*

6. Ronald Inglehart, *Modernization and Postmodernization* (Princeton, NJ: Princeton University Press, 1997), chs. 6–7.

7. Ole Borre and Elinor Scarbrough, eds., *The Scope of Government* (Oxford: Oxford University Press, 1995).

8. Ronald Inglehart, *Culture Shift in Advanced Industrial Societies* (Princeton, NJ: Princeton University Press, 1990).

9. Even within established Western democracies, there are internal differences in the appropriate role of government, the role of the citizen, and the perceived goals of government. See Max Kaase and Ken Newton, *Beliefs in Government* (Oxford: Oxford University Press, 1995).

10. W. Kymlicka and N. Wayne, eds., *Citizenship in Divided Societies* (Oxford: Oxford University Press, 2000); Donald Horowitz, *Ethnic Groups in Conflict* (Berkeley: University of California Press, 1985).

11. Amy Chua, *World on Fire: How Exporting Free Market Democracy Breeds Ethnic Hatred and Global Instability* (New York: Doubleday, 2003).

12. See also Inglehart and Welzel, *Modernization, Cultural Change, and Democracy.*

13. Kendall Baker, Russell Dalton, and Kai Hildebrandt, *Germany Transformed* (Cambridge: Harvard University Press, 1981).

14. Robert Putnam, *Making Democracy Work: Civic Traditions in Modern Italy* (Princeton, NJ: Princeton University Press, 1993); Robert Putnam, *Bowling Alone* (New York: Simon & Schuster, 2000).

15. Samuel P. Huntington, *The Clash of Civilizations and the Remaking of World Order* (New York: Simon & Schuster, 1996); see also Fareed Zakaria, *The Future of Freedom* (New York: Norton, 2003).

16. See Almond and Verba, *Civic Culture,* ch. 12; M. Kent Jennings, Klaus R. Allerbeck, and Leopold Rosenmayr, "Generations and Families," in Samuel H. Barnes, Max Kaase, et al., *Political Action* (Beverly Hills, CA: Sage, 1979), chs. 15–16.

17. Pippa Norris and Ronald Inglehart, *Rising Tide: Gender Equality and Cultural Change Around the World* (New York: Cambridge University Press, 2003).

18. Martha Nussbaum and Jonathan Glover, eds., *Women, Culture, and Development* (New York: Oxford University Press, 1995).

19. For example, see Sidney Verba, Norman H. Nie, and Jae-on Kim, *Participation and Political Equality* (New York: Cambridge University Press, 1978); Barnes, Kaase, et al., *Political Action,* ch. 4.

20. See Martin Marty and Scott Appleby, *Fundamentalism Observed* (Chicago: University of Chicago Press, 1991).

21. Robert Putnam, ed., *Democracies in Flux* (Oxford: Oxford University Press, 2002).

22. The Pew Global Attitudes Project found that over two-thirds of the public in most nations cited television as their main source of political information. Only in poor African nations did this statistic fall below 50 percent, and in these nations the radio provided an alternative. Pew Global Attitudes Project, *What the World Thinks in 2002* (Washington, DC: Pew Global Attitudes Project, 2002) (http://pewglobal.org/).

23. Sidney Verba et al., *The American Participation Study 1990* (Ann Arbor: Interuniversity Consortium for Political and Social Research, University of Michigan).

24. Arthur Miller, William Reisinger, and Vicki Hesli, eds., *Public Opinion and Regime Change* (Boulder, CO: Westview Press, 1993); William Mishler and Richard Rose, "Trajectories of Fear and Hope: Support for Democracy in Post-communist Europe," *Comparative Political Studies* 28 (1995): 553–81. Compare to Robert Rohrschneider, "Institutional Learning Versus Value Diffusion," *Journal of Politics* 58 (1996): 442–66.

25. Norris, *Critical Citizens;* Russell Dalton, *Democratic Challenges, Democratic Choices.*

26. See William Zimmerman, *The Russian People and Foreign Policy: Russian Elite and Mass Perspectives* (Princeton: Princeton University Press, 2002), ch. 2; Raymond Duch, "Tolerating Economic Reform," *American Political Science Review* 87 (1993): 590–608. Russian support for marketization noticeably lags behind that of most Eastern Europeans.

27. Wayne Sandholtz and Mark Gray, "International Integration and National Corruption," *International Organization* 57 (Autumn 2003): 761–800; Mark Gray, Miki Kittilson, and Wayne Sandholtz, "Women and Globalization: A Study of 180 Countries, 1975–2000," *International Organization* 60 (Spring 2006): 293–333.

28. Pew Global Attitudes Project, *Views of a Changing World, June 2003* (Washington, DC: Pew Global Attitudes Project, 2003): 71–81 (http://pewglobal.org/reports/display.php?ReportID=185).

INTEREST ARTICULATION

Every political system has some way for people and social groups to express their needs and demands to the government. This process, known as **interest articulation,** can take many forms. For example, a person might contact a city council member or in a more traditional system she might meet with the village head or tribal chieftain. Or, a group of people might work together on a common concern. In large, established political systems, formal interest groups are a primary means of promoting political interests.

As societies have become internally more complex and the scope of government activity has widened, the quantity and variety of methods to articulate public interests have grown proportionately. People work together to address local and national needs, ranging from providing clean water in a village to passing national clean water standards. Social movements involve the public in issues as diverse as protecting the rights of indigenous people in the Amazon to debating nuclear power. Formal, institutionalized interest groups develop to represent labor, farmers, businesses, and other social interests. Interest groups, in large numbers, work in capitals like London, Washington, D.C., and Tokyo. Some of these headquarter buildings are as imposing as those housing major governmental agencies. Today, Internet chatrooms or blogging provides another forum for expression. In countries with powerful local governments, interest groups are active at the provincial or local level as well.

This chapter considers the multiple ways that people can express their interests in contemporary political systems. First we discuss the means of interest articulation that are available to individual citizens. Then we describe how formal interest groups and associations provide another means of interest articulation. For example, in most countries that allow them, labor unions, manufacturers' associations, farm groups, and associations of doctors, lawyers, engineers, and teachers represent these interests. In the end, most political systems rely on many different forms of interest articulation to determine what the public and social groups want from their government.

CITIZEN ACTION

One aspect of interest articulation involves what you might do as an individual citizen. Suppose an unjust or unfair law was being passed by the government, what could you do to express your dissatisfaction and try to stop the legislation? Or suppose you see a need that the government is not addressing, what could you do to encourage government action? These are the questions that often face us as citizens—what choices do we have for making our interests and needs known to policymakers?

Individual citizens can use various methods to make requests and demands for policies (Table 4.1).[1] Each of these forms of citizen action has different characteristics, as described in the table. The most common form of citizen participation is voting in an election. When elections are free and meaningful, they enable people to express their interests and to make a collective choice about the government's past progress and the future policies for the nation. Although elections select political elites, they often are a blunt policy tool because they involve many different issues, and between elections officeholders may stray from the voters' preferences.

People can also work with others in their community to address common needs, as when parents work to better the local schools or residents express their worries about how the community is developing. These activities are typically very policy focused and exert direct pressure on decisionmakers. Such group activity exists in both democratic and authoritarian systems, although nondemocracies may limit the methods of expression to ones that do not openly confront authorities.

Some interest articulation involves direct contact with government, such as writing a letter to an elected official or to a government bureaucracy (see Box 4.1, page 84).

Forms of Citizen Interest Articulation   **TABLE 4.1**

Form	Scope of Interests	Degree of Pressure on Elites
Voting, participation in elections	Broad, collective decision on government leaders and their programs	Modest pressure, but not policy focused
Informal group	Collective action focused on a common interest	High pressure
Direct contact on personal matter	Normally deals with specific, personal problem	Low pressure
Direct contact on policy issue	Action on a government policy	Modest pressure
Protest activity	Highly expressive support for specific interests	High pressure
Political consumerism	Focused on specific issues, activities	High pressure

Some direct contact involves personal issues, such as when a veteran writes to his legislator for help in getting benefits approved, or when a homeowner asks the local party precinct leader to get her driveway snowplowed regularly. These forms of personal contact are universal across political systems, including the authoritarian ones. Other direct contact involves broader political issues facing the government, such as campaigns to support or block new legislation. Direct contact on policy issues occurs primarily in democratic systems, where citizen input is broadly encouraged. However, even in autocratic nations the public often finds ways to petition the government on policy matters.[2]

The expression of interests also may involve **protests** or other forms of contentious action. The spontaneous gathering of outraged ghetto dwellers, the public protests that overthrew the communist governments of Eastern Europe, and the environmental protests of Greenpeace are all examples of how protest articulates policy interests. Protests and other direct actions tend to be high-pressure activities that can both mobilize the public and directly pressure elites; these activities can also be very focused in their policy content.

Recent participation studies found that political consumerism—buying or boycotting a product for political reasons—is another active form of participation, at least in Western democracies.[3] Such participation allows individuals to protest the activities of a firm that pollutes or has unfair labor practices. Several boycotts of American and Western products have been organized in Arab nations to protest Western policies toward the region. Such efforts are very focused. If they become politically visible, they can have broader policy effects as well.

In summary, people can take many routes to express their interests, and each of these routes has particular characteristics associated with it.

HOW CITIZENS PARTICIPATE

The amount of citizen political participation varies widely according to the type of activity and the type of political system. Table 4.2 shows examples of the types of citizen participation in several of the nations examined in this book.

The most frequent forms of political participation revolve around elections: turning out to vote, trying to convince others how to vote, or working with political parties. Because elections are the most common form of public involvement in the political process, they are important forms of interest articulation. During elections, citizens speak their minds on current issues by engaging in conversations, attending meetings, contributing to campaigns, and even expressing their opinions to pollsters. Ultimately, individuals decide their preferences in their ballot choices. At the same time, however, elections perform many other functions: aggregating political interests, recruiting political elites, and even socializing political values and preferences through the campaign process (see Chapter 2).

Among the democracies, the United States stands out for its rather low levels of national voting participation: both West Europeans (with their long democratic

TABLE 4.2

Citizen Participation Across Nations (percentage)

Type of Participation	United States	Britain	France	Germany	Japan	Russia	Mexico	Brazil	China	Iran	Nigeria
Voter turnout in most recent national elections	54%	61%	60%	78%	68%	56%	69%	78%	—	60%	49%
Discussed politics with others	74	46	65	84	64	75	58	58	70	69	74
Participated in political party activity	18	3	2	3	4	1	5	—	10	—	—
Participated in citizen interest group	36	7	6	7	9	2	11	—	3	—	—
Signed a petition	81	81	68	52	63	12	19	47	—	—	7
Participated in lawful protest demonstration	21	13	39	28	13	24	4	25	—	—	17

Sources: Election turnout data is percent of registered public for most recent national legislative election from the International Institute for Elections and Democracy, downloaded from www.idea.org; 2000–2002 *World Values Survey* and the 1999 *European Values Survey* for other participation statistics. Some of the participation questions were not asked in each survey, and these missing items are noted by a dash in the table.

experience) and Russians (who are new to democratic elections) vote more frequently than Americans. However, as the table shows, Americans' low level of election turnout does not simply reflect apathy. Americans are much more likely than the British to try to discuss politics with others, and Americans are much more likely to work for a party or candidate than either the British or Germans.

Public efforts to express political interests and influence public policy extend beyond elections. Grassroots politics—people working together to address a common problem—is a very direct method for articulating political interests and attempting to influence policy. Alexis de Tocqueville considered such grassroots community action as the foundation of democracy in America. Today, such activities are often identified with middle-class participation in affluent societies—such as parent-teacher association groups, community associations, and public interest groups—but group activity occurs in almost any nation.[4] Indian villagers working together to build a communal latrine or to develop rural electricity, and indigenous people protecting their land rights are other examples of community action.

Table 4.2 indicates that group action is frequent in the advanced industrial democracies. Nearly a third of Americans are members of a citizen interest group, and significant numbers are active in Europe as well.[5] Such activity is high in Mexico, perhaps because this survey overlaps with the politicization of Vicente Fox's election in 2000. However, surveys from the developing world suggest that these activities are regularly used, albeit less frequently than in more developed nations.

Perhaps the most expressive and visible form of citizen action involves participation in protests, demonstrations, or other direct actions (see Box 4.2). For instance, many environmentalists believe that direct actions—hanging an environmental banner from a polluting smokestack, staging a mass demonstration outside of parliament, or boycotting polluters—effectively generate media attention and public interest in their cause. Political protests arise for quite different reasons. On the one hand, protest and direct action is often used by individuals and groups that feel they lack access to legitimate political channels. The mass demonstrations in Eastern Europe in the late 1980s and the public rallies and marches of black South Africans against apartheid illustrate protests as the last resort of the disadvantaged. On the other hand, peaceful protests are also increasingly used by the young and better-educated citizens in Western democracies. To many democratic citizens, protest is the continuation of "normal" politics by other means.

A majority in most nations have signed a petition, a form of political action that has become so common that it no longer can be described as unconventional (see again Table 4.2). Roughly a fifth of Americans and Germans have at some time participated in a legal demonstration. Many different sectors of society now use protests and direct action.[6] The French have more protest involvement than most other established democracies, with nearly two-fifths of the population reporting participation at some point. These numbers reflect both French traditions of popular protest and the difficulties citizens often find in getting the attention of government. The Russian patterns are also striking. In 1990, only 4 percent of Russians reported participating in a protest, reflecting the communist government's repression of such activities.

BOX 4.1

The *Shangfang* System

In 1949, the communist government in China created the *Shangfang* system that allows individuals to formally petition the government to intervene on their behalf. This system was intended as a safety valve to allow disgruntled individuals to express their grievances, and as a method for the state to mobilize expression of support from the populace. The petitioners typically are concerned about personal problems or local issues, and this system allows them to bypass unresponsive local officials and petition Beijing. Sometimes they even travel to the capital to present their petition in person. The use of Shangfang has ebbed and flowed over time, but it illustrates how even authoritarian governments seek input from their citizens. In 2004, the government's petition office received more than 10 million petitions, ranging from a complaint over an eviction notice to protests about the effects of the Three Gorges Dam. However, only a miniscule fraction of these petitions receive a government response.

Source: Kevin O'Brien, "Rightful Resistance," *World Politics* 49 (1996): 31–55.

A decade later, nearly a quarter of Russians said they had participated in a legal demonstration—they are learning to express their grievances in a more democratic setting. The table also indicates that protest activities are less frequent in developing societies, such as Mexico and Nigeria.

Citizen participation thus reflects the way that people use the opportunities existing within a political system. In nations with active political parties and competitive elections, many people participate in the electoral process. In nations where such activities are limited, people may turn to group-based activity or protest in order to express their preferences, but it is more likely that they are politically inactive. As we noted in Chapter 3, a participatory political culture—of all forms—is a by-product of political modernization.

Cross-national research shows that better educated and higher social status individuals are more likely to use the various opportunities for participation. These individuals tend to develop attitudes that encourage participation, such as feelings of efficacy and a sense of civic duty.[7] They also possess the personal resources and skills that are useful in becoming politically active when duty calls or a need arises. Skill and confidence are especially important for demanding activities, such as organizing new groups or becoming a leader in an organization. This inequality in participation is less for easier activities, such as voting. The tendency for the better-off to be politically active is more evident in societies (such as the United States) with weak party organizations, weak working-class groups (such as labor unions), and less party attention to lower class interests. In nations with stronger working-class parties and labor unions, organizational networks encourage the participation of less affluent citizens.

Participation patterns are important for several reasons. For citizens to influence government policy, they first need to articulate their interests to the government. A wider choice of activities presumably increases the citizens' ability to express their interests and be heard. Moreover, the forms of action differ in their policy content and political pressure (see again Table 4.1). Finally, individuals differ in their level of political activity and the types of activities that they use. These differences in voice are likely reflected in policy outputs if the government responds to public pressures. In other words, those who are more active in articulating their interests are more likely to have their interests addressed by policymakers.

INTEREST GROUPS

Interest articulation can also occur through the actions of social or political groups that represent a set of people. Some groups are poorly organized and unfocused, and often short lived. Other groups have a permanent organizational base, often with professional staffs to provide expertise and representation. In addition, interest groups often participate in the political process, serving on government advisory bodies and testifying at parliamentary hearings. Interest groups vary in structure, style, financing, and support base, and these differences may influence a nation's politics, its economics, and its social life. We begin by defining four types of interest groups: anomic, nonassociational, institutional, and associational.

Anomic Groups

Anomic groups are spontaneous groups that suddenly form when many individuals react to an event that stimulates frustration, disappointment, or other strong emotions. They are flash affairs, rising and subsiding suddenly. Without previous organization or planning, frustrated individuals may suddenly take to the streets to vent their anger as news of a government action touches deep emotions or as a rumor of new injustice sweeps the community. Their actions may lead to violence, although not necessarily. Particularly where organized groups are absent or where they have failed to get adequate political representation, smoldering discontent may be sparked by an incident or by the emergence of a leader. It may then suddenly explode in relatively unpredictable and uncontrollable ways.

Some political systems, including both developed and developing nations, report a rather high frequency of violent and spontaneous anomic behavior.[8] This behavior often involves spontaneous public demonstrations or acts of violence, rather than the planned and orchestrated protests of institutionalized political groups. Other countries are notable for the infrequency of such disturbances, which may reflect either the limited opportunities for action or the nation's political culture.

In France, for example, protests have become part of the tradition of politics (see again Table 4.2). In the late 1960s, the French government nearly collapsed as a result of protests that began when university students stimulated a mass protest against the government. In 2006, another wave of mass protests nearly brought the economy to a standstill and forced the government to withdraw unpopular labor regulations. In a typical year, Paris might experience protests by students, shopkeepers, farmers, homemakers, government employees, environmentalists, women's groups, and a host of other interest groups. Protest is almost a national political sport in France.

Anger over the assassination of a popular political leader or other catastrophic event can also stimulate a public outburst. For instance, one commonly sees relatively spontaneous public demonstrations when one nation makes a hostile action toward another nation. Wildcat strikes (spontaneous strike actions by local workers, not organized actions by national unions), long a feature of the British trade union scene, also occur frequently in such European countries as France, Italy, and Sweden.

Sometimes anomic groups are a subset of individuals drawn from a larger social grouping, such as a racial or an ethnic group. For instance, in 1992 there was rioting and looting by some residents in minority neighborhoods of Los Angeles following the acquittal of police officers accused of excessive violence in the beating of an African-American suspect. Similarly, in 1992, riots broke out in Algeria when some Muslim fundamentalists protested the government's invalidation of the recent election. We treat these as anomic group actions because there is no structure or planning to the event, and the people involved disperse after the protest ends.

We must be cautious, however, about calling something an anomic political behavior when it really is the result of detailed planning by organized groups. For instance, the demonstrations against the World Trade Organization in Seattle in 1999 and Genoa in 2001 owed much to indignation but little to spontaneity (see Box 4.2).

Attacks on Globalization   BOX 4.2

In July 2001 tens of thousands of protestors arrived in Genoa to demonstrate at the G8 Summit Meeting. Hundreds of different groups came to protest at the meetings, and several of the more radical groups engaged in running battles with the police. Many of the most violent clashes involved what became known as the "Black Block." The Block was comprised of several loosely organized anarchist and radical groups, wearing trademark black clothing, black hoods, and gas masks. Confrontations with police often appeared choreographed in advance, coordinated by cell phones, and videotaped by sympathetic activists—and subsequently distributed on the Internet. Many other protest groups in Genoa were worried that the radical anarchist goals of the Block detracted attention from their policy concerns about the economic and social impacts of globalization. After two days of violent clashes, the summit ended. Damage ran into the tens of millions of dollars, 200 protestors were arrested, and one protestor was shot in a clash with police. In the end, the violence in the streets overshadowed both the elected politicians at the summit and the policy goals of the nonviolent groups in Genoa.

Source: BBC World News.

Nonassociational Groups

Like anomic groups, **nonassociational groups** rarely are well organized, and their activity is episodic. They differ from anomic groups because they are based on common interests and identities of ethnicity, region, religion, occupation, or perhaps kinship. Because of these economic or cultural ties, nonassociational groups have more continuity than anomic groups. Subgroups within a large nonassociational group (such as an ethnic minority or workers) may act as an anomic group, as in the 1992 Los Angeles riots, the 2005 Paris riots, and the Middle East protests against the Danish cartoons of Mohammed in 2006. Throughout the world, ethnicity and religion, like occupation, are powerful identities that can stimulate collective activity.

Two kinds of nonassociational groups are especially interesting. One is a large group that is not formally organized, although its members may perceive common interests. Many ethnic, regional, and occupational groups fit into this category. The members share a common interest or need, but there is no formal group to represent their interests.

It can be very difficult to organize such groups because although members share a common problem, none of them will undertake the effort to organize other members. This is commonly known as the **collective action problem**.[9] Moreover, if large collective benefits—for example, ending discriminatory legislation or cleaning up water pollution—are achieved, they will be shared even by those who did not work, the so-called free riders. This pattern of people waiting for the rewards without sharing the cost or risk of action affects other types of groups as well. For instance, students who might benefit from lower tuition fees are typically underrepresented because there is no organization to articulate their interests. Understanding the collective action problem helps us to see why some groups (including governments and revolutionary challengers) become organized and others do not, and under what circumstances the barriers to collective action are overcome.

A second type of nonassociational group is the small village, economic or ethnic subgroup whose members know each other personally. A small, face-to-face group has some important advantages and may be highly effective in some political situations. If its members are well connected or its goals unpopular or illegal, the group may remain informal or even inconspicuous. Such groups may undertake various actions, such as engaging in work stoppages, circulating student petitions to demand better support and training, requesting that a bureaucrat continue a grain tariff to benefit landowners, or asking a tax collector for favored treatment to benefit relatives. As the last example suggests, personal interest articulation may often have more legitimacy and perpetuate itself by invoking group or personal ties.

Institutional Groups

Institutional groups are formal and have other political or social functions in addition to interest articulation. Political parties, business corporations, legislatures, armies, bureaucracies, and churches often have separate political groups with special responsibility for representing a group's interests. Either as corporate bodies or as smaller groups within these bodies (legislative blocs, officer cliques, groups in the clergy, or ideological cliques in bureaucracies), such groups typically express the interests of their members. The influence of institutional interest groups is usually drawn from the strength of their primary organizational base—for instance, the size of their membership or their income. A group based on a governmental institution has direct access to policymakers.

In industrial democracies, bureaucratic and corporate interests use their resources and special information to affect policy. In the United States, for instance, the military industrial complex consists of the combination of the U.S. Department of Defense and defense industries that support military expenditures. Similarly, the farm lobby and the U.S. Department of Agriculture often advocate agricultural policies. Political parties are among the most active institutional participants in the policy process of most democracies. And as in most societies, government bureaucracies do not simply react to pressures from the outside, they also can act as independent forces of interest representation.

Nonpolitical institutional groups can also participate in the political process. In Italy, for example, the Roman Catholic Church has exerted significant influence on the government. In electoral politics, the Church used to ask Catholics to vote against the Communists. Less overtly, the Church has members of the clergy call on officeholders to express opinions on matters of concern to the Church. In Islamic countries, fundamentalist clergy pursue a similar role, prescribing what morals public policy should follow, actively lobbying governmental officials, and sometimes participating in the governing process.

In authoritarian regimes, which prohibit or at least control explicit political groups, institutional groups can still play a large role. Educational officials, party officials, jurists, factory managers, officers in the military services, and government bodies representing other social units had significant roles in interest articulation in communist regimes.[10] In preindustrial societies, which usually have fewer associational groups and with limited popular support, military groups, corporations, party factions, and bureaucrats often play prominent political roles. Even where the military does not seize power directly, the possibility of such action often forces close government attention to military requests.

Associational Groups

Associational groups are formed explicitly to represent the interests of a particular group, such as trade unions, chambers of commerce, manufacturers' associations, and ethnic associations. These organizations have procedures for formulating interests and demands, and they usually employ a full-time professional staff. Associational groups are often very active in representing the interests of their members in the policy process. For instance, in recurring debates about health care in the United States there is an enormous mobilization of pressure groups and lobbyists—from representatives of doctors and health insurance organizations to consumer groups and the like—seeking to influence legislation.

Associational interest groups—where they are allowed to flourish—affect the development of other types of groups. Their organizational base gives them an advantage over nonassociational groups, and their tactics and goals are often recognized as legitimate in society. Labor unions, for example, are often central political actors because they represent the mass of the working class; in the same way, business associations often speak for the corporate interests of the nation.

A special subset of associational groups consists of citizens who are united not by a common economic or individual self-interest but by a common belief in a political ideology or a policy goal.[11] The environmental movement, many women's groups, and other civic groups are examples of this kind of associational group. In some of these issue groups, the members may seldom interact directly and not even share common social characteristics (such as employment or ethnicity), but are bound together by their support of a political organization, such as Greenpeace or Amnesty International. On the organizational side, many of these new social groups have fluid and dynamic organizations, with frequent turnover in both leadership and membership. On the tactical side, they use a wide range of approaches, often discounting the value of partisan campaigning and conventional lobbying in favor of unconventional protests and direct actions.

Civic associations represent another way for citizens to articulate their policy goals by supporting groups that advocate their preferred policy positions. Such groups have proliferated in most advanced industrial democracies in the past generation, and they are now spreading to the developing world.

In summary, a social interest can manifest itself in many different groups. We can illustrate this point with examples of different groups that might involve members of the working class:

Anomic group: a spontaneous group of working-class individuals living in the same neighborhood

Nonassociational group: the working class as a collective

Institutional group: the labor department within the government

Associational group: a labor union

Distinguishing among the types of groups is important for several reasons. The nature of a group typically reflects the resources it can mobilize to support its political efforts. Perhaps one of the most important resources is an institutional structure that will sustain political efforts until the government responds to the group's interests. The nature of a group also may signify the tactics it uses to gain political access (see Table 4.3, page 99). Finally, since the articulation of interest is the first step in policy influence, the nature of groups suggests what types of interests are more likely to get a hearing in the political system and which interests may be underrepresented.

Civil Society

Political analysts have devoted increasing attention to whether an extensive network of interest groups and public participation in these groups creates a **civil society**— a society in which people are involved in social and political interactions free of state control or regulation. Community groups, voluntary associations, and even religious groups—as well as access to free communication and information through the mass media and the Internet—are important parts of a civil society.[12] Participation in associational and institutional groups can socialize individuals into the political skills and cooperative relations that are part of a well-functioning society. People learn how to organize, express their interests, and work with others to achieve common goals. They also learn the important lesson that the political process itself is as important as the immediate results. Thus, a system of active associational groups can lessen the development of anomic or nonassociational activity. Group activity can help citizens to develop and clarify their own preferences, provide important information about political events, and articulate the interests of citizens more clearly and precisely than parties and elections.[13] Thus, an active public involved in various interest groups provides a fertile ground for the development of democratic politics.

As political and economic conditions become interdependent across nations, there is also increasing attention directed toward the development of a global civil society. Individuals and groups in one nation are connected to groups with similar concerns in other nations, and jointly reinforce their individual efforts. Environmental groups in the Western democracies, for example, assist environmental groups in developing nations with the expertise and organizational resources to address the issues facing their country. National groups meet at international conferences and policy forums, and the network of social relations, as well as Internet connections, extends across national borders.[14] This is another sign of how the international context of domestic politics is growing worldwide.

One problem facing the nations of Eastern Europe and other newly democratizing nations is building a rich associational group life in societies where the government had suppressed or controlled organized groups.[15] The Communist Party and the government bureaucracy dominated the nations of Eastern Europe for over forty years. The process of building new, independent associational groups to articulate the interests of different citizens is underway and will be important to the democratic process. Similarly, many less economically developed nations need to create a civil society of associational groups to involve citizens in the political process and represent their interests if democratization is to succeed.

INTEREST GROUP SYSTEMS

The nature of the connection between interest groups and government policymaking institutions is another important feature of the political process. Different types of connections create different interest group systems. All modern societies have large numbers of interest groups, but their relationships with government can follow different models. Interest group systems are classified into three major groupings: pluralist, democratic neo-corporatist, and controlled.[16]

Pluralist interest group systems have several features involving both how interests are organized and how they participate in the political process:

- Multiple groups may represent a single societal interest.
- Group membership is voluntary and limited.
- Groups often have a loose or decentralized organizational structure.
- There is a clear separation between interest groups and the government.

For instance, not only are there different groups for different social sectors (such as labor, business, and professional interests), but there may be many multiple labor unions or business associations within each sector. These groups compete among themselves for membership and influence, and all simultaneously press their demands on the government. The United States is the best-known example of a strongly pluralist interest group system; Canada and New Zealand are also cited as examples. Despite its greater labor union membership and somewhat greater coordination of economic associations, Britain tends to fall on the pluralist side in most analyses, as do France and Japan.

Democratic **neo-corporatist interest group systems** are characterized by a much more organized representation of interests:

- A single peak association normally represents each societal interest.
- Membership in the peak association is often compulsory and nearly universal.
- Peak associations are centrally organized and direct the actions of their members.
- Groups are often systematically involved in making and implementing policy.

For instance, in a neo-corporatist system there may be a single peak association that represents all the major industrial interests; a pluralist system may have several different business groups that act autonomously. Equally important, interest groups in these systems often regularly and legitimately work with the government agencies and/or political parties as partners in negotiating solutions to policy problems.

The best-studied democratic neo-corporatist arrangements involve economic problems. Democracies with business and labor peak associations that negotiate with each other and the government have had better records than more pluralist countries in sustaining employment, restraining inflation, and increasing social spending.[17] In addition, there is also evidence that neo-corporatist systems are more effective in implementing other public policies, such as environmental protection.[18]

In many advanced industrial societies, however, membership in labor unions has decreased and some bargaining patterns have become less centralized. Thus, some countries that have relied on neo-corporatist patterns have adapted this system to these new consequences and applied corporatism in new ways.[19] In contrast, several nations in Eastern Europe had attempted to develop more corporatist structures to develop interest group politics, but the system of autonomous interest groups remained underdeveloped. The experience with neo-corporatist models in developing nations is even more varied.[20]

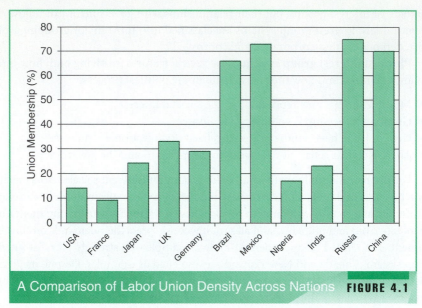

A Comparison of Labor Union Density Across Nations   **FIGURE 4.1**

Source: International Labor Organization, *World Labour Report 1997–1998,* The Statistical Annex, Table 1.2. (www.ilo.org). The figure plots union membership as a percentage of wage earners.

Because different sectors of a society may vary in their organized interest groups and in their government relations, we must be cautious about generalizing too much about interest group systems. Figure 4.1, however, shows the striking differences in organization of the labor movements across many of the nations in this book. Britain, the United States, France, and Japan are examples of more pluralist systems. Less than half the British labor force is unionized, but these unions are not as highly coordinated as those in corporatist countries. The member unions in the British Trades Union Congress have strong traditions of individual autonomy and are themselves relatively decentralized. Moreover, the influence of the labor unions on government policymakers has waned over the past few decades. In the United States and France, the labor movement is somewhat fragmented. These countries also lack a tradition of "social partnership" between government, unions, and employer associations. In the area of labor policy, at least, these are highly pluralist, not corporatist, interest group systems. However, corporatist-type arrangements among individual industries, trade associations, and governmental bureaucracies (without organized labor involvement) exist in Japan.

Germany is a closer fit to the neo-corporatist model. The most thoroughly corporatist interest group systems are in Austria, Finland, the Netherlands, Norway, and Sweden. These nations are characterized by a high level of union membership among the nonagricultural labor force, and a highly centralized and united labor movement. In addition, under the corporatist model interest groups such as labor unions often have special access to government. For instance, German labor unions have formal membership on many government commissions, special access to policy administration, and are very influential through informal channels of influence.

Mexico and Brazil are examples of another form of corporatist politics. Union membership in many Latin American nations is fairly high, and the trade unions and peasant associations are closely tied to political parties or religious interests. Usually, these groups mobilize support for the political parties or social institutions that dominate them, and are closely tied to the state when their party is in power. This system is changing in both Mexico and Brazil, as democratization encourages the unions to become more politically independent and influential.

Nigeria and India illustrate a pattern common in other developing democracies. Interest groups, such as unions, are often not well developed and have a limited mass membership. They are participants in the process, but without the mass membership or formal access that gives labor unions influence in established Western democracies of either the pluralist or corporatist model.

Finally, **controlled interest group systems** follow a different pattern:

- There is a single group for each social sector.
- Membership is often compulsory.
- Each group is normally hierarchically organized.
- Groups are controlled by the government or its agents in order to mobilize support for government policy.

The last point is the most important: Groups exist to facilitate government control of society. The best examples are the traditional communist systems in which the party penetrates all levels of society and controls all the permitted associational groups. For instance, Figure 4.1 shows that 70 percent of wage earners in China belong to a union.[21] Unions and other interest associations are subordinated to the Communist Party, and they are only rarely permitted to articulate the interests of their members. Russia also once followed this communist model, and the unions have large memberships as a result of this experience. Unions in Russia are struggling to gain autonomy from the state and play an influential role in the postcommunist system. But they have made limited progress.

These nations limit interest articulation to leaders of institutional groups, who can use their positions in political institutions as a base for expressing their demands. Numerous institutional interest groups can also emerge in these societies, especially from parts of the party and bureaucracy, such as the military, as well as informal nonassociational groups.

ACCESS TO THE INFLUENTIAL

To be effective, interest groups must be able to reach key policymakers through **channels of political access.** Otherwise, groups may express their members' interests yet fail to have an impact on policymakers. Political systems vary in the ways they respond to political interests. Interest groups vary in the tactics they use to gain access. Group tactics are partially shaped by the opportunities offered by the structure of policymaking, as well as by their own values and preferences.

There is a significant distinction between legitimate and constitutional channels of access (such as the mass media, parties, and legislatures) and illegitimate, coercive access channels. These two channels reflect the types of resources that groups can use to influence elites as well as the group's perceptions of which tactics will be most successful. Groups with substantial resources—money, members, or status—typically have an easier time working through legitimate constitutional channels. Groups with limited resources or legitimacy may feel they must act through coercive channels because they are not accepted by the political system. In democracies, groups tend toward legitimate channels because the system expects and allows group activity. In contrast, nondemocratic systems typically limit legitimate access, which might stimulate illegitimate or coercive activities.

Legitimate Access Channels

The legitimate channels of access can take many forms, and these are often seen in both democratic and nondemocratic systems. For instance, personal connections are an important means of reaching political elites in all societies—the use of family, school, local, or other social ties. An excellent example is the information network among the British elite based on old school ties originating at Eton, Harrow, or other "public" schools, or at Oxford and Cambridge universities. Similarly, in Japan many alumni of the University of Tokyo Law School hold top positions among the political and bureaucratic elites who interact because of these personal ties. Although personal connections are commonly used by nonassociational groups representing family or regional interests, they serve other groups as well. Face-to-face contact is one of the most effective means of shaping attitudes and conveying messages. Interests communicated by a friend or neighbor carry much more weight than a formal letter from a stranger. In modern nations, personal connections are usually cultivated with special care. In Washington, D.C., the business of advising interest groups and individuals on access to politicians is an increasingly lucrative profession (and, increasingly a target of government regulation and potential corruption). These activities are often carried on by former officeholders who use their personal governmental contacts for their lobbyist clients.

The **mass media**—television, radio, newspapers, and magazines—are another important access channel in democratic societies. The mass media, and the internet can mobilize support for interest group efforts, leading to donations of time and money, and encouraging sympathizers to support the group. Many interest groups thus hire skillful public relations specialists, purchase direct advertising, and seek favorable attention in the media. Interest groups encourage media reports on their needs as well as coverage of their views on specific policies. When a cause receives national media attention, the message to policymakers carries added weight if politicians know that millions of voters are interested in the issue. Moreover, groups believe that in an open society, "objective" news coverage has more credibility than sponsored messages. However, multiple conflicting messages and a lack of specific focus can limit the effectiveness of the mass media for many smaller groups.

The potential power of the media can be seen when the communist governments in Eastern Europe loosened control over the media in this late 1980s. This action gave a huge boost to democracy movements. For instance, when asked what caused the democratic revolution in Poland in the 1990s, Lech Walesa pointed to a television and said "that did." Media reports on the failures in communist government policy and the contrasting lifestyles in the West undermined the legitimacy of the regimes. As democratic protests spread across Eastern Europe, stories of successful protests in other parts of the country, or in other countries, enhanced the confidence of demonstrators. Citizen protests encouraged by mass media reports helped convince the ruling groups that their support had vanished.

Political parties are another important access point. Democratic political parties often rely on interest groups for financial and voter support, and act as representatives of these interests within government. In a nation like Germany, the various components of the party organization, particularly parliamentary committees, are important channels for transmitting demands to the cabinet and the party in power. In some cases, other factors limit the role of parties as interest representatives. For instance, highly ideological parties with a hierarchical structure, such as most communist parties, are more likely to control affiliated interest groups than to communicate the interest groups' demands. Decentralized party organizations, like those in the United States, may be less helpful than individual legislators in providing access.

Legislatures are another common target of interest group activities (see Box 4.3). Standard lobbying tactics include making appearances before legislative committees and providing information to individual legislators. In the United States, political action committees raise campaign contributions for individual members of Congress and usually receive some political attention in exchange. In Britain and France, the strong party discipline in the legislature lessens the importance of individual members of Parliament (MPs) as access channels for interest groups. In contrast, in the United States the combination of loose party discipline and a decentralized legislative system makes the individual members of the Congress major targets of group efforts.

Government bureaucracies are also a major access point in most political systems. Contacts with the bureaucratic agencies may be particularly important where the bureaucracy has policymaking authority or where interests are narrow and directly involve few citizens. A bureaucrat sympathetic to a group may try to respond to its demands without leaving bureaucratic channels, by exercising administrative discretion. A government official may also give public consideration to an issue or frame an issue in a way that receives a sympathetic hearing by policymakers. The bureaucracy may be an especially important access point in nondemocratic systems because other legitimate channels of citizen access do not exist.

Lobbying Behind the Scenes

BOX 4.3

British beer companies use a variety of means to support their industry. For example, the industry contributed funds to Labour MPs who recently voted for longer opening hours for British pubs. They also provide travel support for MPs who are favorable to the industry. A group of MPs who support the industry formed the All-Party Parliamentary Beer Group (APBG). The group's announced goal is "to promote the wholesomeness and enjoyment of beer and the unique role of the pub in UK society." The parliamentary group campaigned to have beer taxes reduced, conducted hearings on whether the government overregulates British pubs, and supported the extension of pub hours. The group hosts a series of functions at Westminster, giving industry chiefs the opportunity to meet MPs and showcase their products. The parliamentary group also selects a "beer drinker of the year," who receives an award at their annual dinner. The parliamentary group receives direct financial support from breweries, and the secretary for the group is paid by the alcohol industry.

Visit the APBG website: www.publications.parliament.uk/pa/cm/cmparty/memi140.htm.

Government officials may consider protest demonstrations, strikes, and other forms of dramatic and direct pressure on government as legitimate or illegitimate tactics, depending on the political system. Protests may be either spontaneous actions of an anomic group or a planned use of unconventional channels by an organized group. In democratic societies, demonstrations often mobilize popular support—or electoral support—or media attention for the group's cause. The mass demonstrations on immigration reform in 2006 are examples of efforts to shape and influence the U.S. public debate on legislation being considered by Congress. On a regular basis, the Mall in Washington, D.C., hosts other groups protesting other policy issues. In nondemocratic societies, such demonstrations are more hazardous and often represent more extreme dissatisfaction that cannot find voice through conventional channels of access.

Lawful protest can be a tactic of society's powerless, those who do not have access or resources to influence policymakers through conventional channels. As a political tactic, protest activity is especially attractive to young people and minority groups, who are not among the elite. Protests are also a favored tactic of groups whose ideological commitments focus on challenging the established social and political order. Yet, protests are increasingly used as a means of interest articulation by organized and accepted interests who feel that dramatic actions can heighten support for their cause. Protests can supplement other channels, especially in gaining the attention of the mass media in an age when television comes to every household. Thus we find doctors in New Delhi, farmers in Japan, and "gray panthers" (the elderly) in Germany using a tactic that once was limited to the poor and minorities.[22]

Coercive Access Channels and Tactics

Most scholars see the level of collective violence as closely associated with the character of a society and the circumstances in the nation. In his studies of civil strife, Ted Robert Gurr argued that feelings of relative deprivation motivate people to act aggressively. Gurr defined relative deprivation as a "discrepancy between people's expectations about the goods and conditions of life to which they are entitled, on the one hand, and, on the other, their value capabilities—the degree to which they think they can attain these goods and conditions."[23]

Feelings of relative deprivation are a source of frustration, discontent, and anger. The more such discontent and anger persist, the greater the chance of collective violence. People also tend to turn to violence if they believe it is justified and if they believe it will lead to success. If they think that their government is illegitimate and that the cause of their discontent is justified, they will more readily turn to political violence. To this end, it is the responsibility of the government and its institutions to provide peaceful alternatives to violence as a means of change.

This general description of political violence should not overlook the differences among the types of violent political activities. A riot, for example, involves the spontaneous expression of collective anger and dissatisfaction by a group of citizens. Though riots have long been dismissed as aberrant and irrational action by social riffraff, modern studies have shown that rioters vary greatly in their motivation, behavior, and social background.[24] Most riots seem to follow some fairly clear-cut patterns, such as confining destruction or violence to particular areas or targets. Relative deprivation appears to be a major cause of riots, but the release of the frustrations is not as aimless as is often supposed.

Although the 2005 riots in Paris, were triggered by the accidental deaths of two teenagers, most analysts see their deaths as only a proximate cause, a "spark" that ignited already volatile factors. Gangs of minority youth burned thousands of automobiles, damaged shops, and attacked police who attempted to quell the violence. The French president and then the Parliament declared a state of emergency in reaction to the violent protests, establishing a curfew and limiting civil liberties. Even though much of the mayhem seemed poorly related to effective political action, it was a cry for attention. Youth from immigrant families had high levels of unemployment and felt that social and economic discrimination was limiting their life chances. Even in a democracy, the government sometimes overlooks the needs of its own citizens and allows such frustrations to explode into violence.

While deprivation may help fuel the discontent, strikes and obstructions are typically carried out by well-organized associational or institutional groups. For instance, violent protests in Seattle and Genoa against the World Trade Organization and globalization involved highly organized activities among some of the more radical groups participating in the protests (see again Box 4.2).

Historically, labor unions used the general strike to pressure the government or employers on fundamental issues. The influence of strikes and obstructions has varied, however, depending on the legitimacy of the government and coercive pressure from other groups. A massive truckers' strike helped bring down the government in Chile in 1972–1973, but student-inspired boycotts in Korea in the 1980s had only a modest impact on the government. Most spectacularly, the strikes, obstructions, and demonstrations in Eastern Europe in 1989 and 1990, like the earlier people's power movement in the Philippines, had massive success against regimes that had lost legitimacy.

Finally, **political terror tactics**—including deliberate assassination, armed attacks on other groups or government officials, and mass bloodshed—are sometimes used by radical groups. The tragedies in Northern Ireland; the suicide bombings by Palestinians in Israel; and the attacks of jihadist terrorists in New York City, Madrid, London, Bali, and other cities demonstrate the use of such tactics. The use of terrorism typically reflects the desire of some group to change the rules of the political game or to destroy a political system, rather than to gain political access.

The use of political terror is more often likely to produce negative consequences rather than construct positive policy change. Massive deadly violence may destroy a democratic regime, leading to curtailment of civil rights or even military intervention when many people and leaders feel that any alternative is preferable to more violence. For example, democratically elected governments justified their suppression of democratic institutions in Peru in 1992 and India in 1975 in response to the violent actions of terrorists. An authoritarian, repressive response often promises quick results against terrorists; however, small-group terrorism usually fails when confronted by united democratic leadership.[25] In a democratic society, violence often forfeits the sympathy that a group needs if its cause is to receive a responsive hearing. The current conflict between the West and jihadist terrorists has renewed the debate on how democratic governments should balance the need for security against the preservation of civil liberties.

POLICY PERSPECTIVES ON INTEREST ARTICULATION

As we pointed out in Chapter 2, we need to examine the structures performing political functions from both process and policy perspectives. In order to understand the formation of policies, we need to know which groups articulate interests and their policy preferences. Many associational interest groups specialize in certain policy areas. The concerns of other interest groups, such as anomic or institutional groups, may be less easily discerned, but they are equally important for the policy process.

Table 4.3 provides examples of legitimate and coercive interest articulation for different types of interest groups. Each case provides an example of the differences in legitimate access channels, such as informal meetings by Mexican business leaders lobbying their government to Greenpeace testifying before European Parliament committees. Similarly, coercive acts range from spontaneous outbursts by anomic groups to Hamas using terror tactics on the West Bank. This framework also helps us to think about how a single interest group might pursue its goals through multiple channels, including protests, representation by institutional groups, and lobbying by associational groups. For instance, honeybee farmers in the United States have

TABLE 4.3

Process and Policy Perspectives on Interest Articulation

Examples of Interest Articulation

Types of Interest Groups	Channel of Access	
	Legitimate Channel	**Coercive Channel**
Anomic groups	Russian workers strike to protest price increases	Iranians attack Danish embassy to protest cartoons depicting Mohammed
Nonassociational groups	Mexican business leaders discuss taxes with president	Minorities in France riot in 2005 over their social conditions
Institutional groups	U.S. Department of Agriculture advocates subsidies for honey production	Indonesian army supports democracy movement to overthrow Suharto regime (1997)
Associational groups	Greenpeace lobbies the European Parliament to ban genetically modified foods	Palestinian Hamas launches terror attacks on Israel

lobbied their representatives in Congress to maintain federal price supports, and they have also used their allies in the U.S. Department of Agriculture to support their position (will honeybee protests be next?). This table presents examples from many nations in order to suggest the varied possibilities that exist in each nation. If we were studying interest articulation patterns in one nation, we could build a table showing the structures, policies, and channels involved during a particular period.

INTEREST GROUP DEVELOPMENT

One consequence of modernization is a widespread belief that the conditions of life can be altered through human action. Modernization normally involves education, urbanization, rapid growth in public communication, and improvement in the physical conditions of life. These changes are closely related to increases in political awareness, participation, and feelings of political competence. Such participant attitudes encourage more diverse and citizen-based interest articulation.

At the same time, modernization produces an increasing diversity of life conditions and a specialization of labor as people work in many types of jobs—a process that leads to the formation of large numbers of special interests. The interdependence of modern life, the exposure provided by mass communications, and a larger policy role of government further multiply political interests. These interests are organized into different interest groups. Thus, the diversity of interest groups is another by-product of modernization.

Successful democratic development leads to the emergence of complex interest group systems that express the needs of groups and individuals in the society. Yet, this process is by no means automatic. The problems of organizing large groups for collective action are huge. Societies vary widely in the extent to which people engage in associational activity. One factor explaining participation is the level of trust shared among members of the society. Robert Putnam and his colleagues found that an active associational life in Northern Italian communities was associated with widespread trust in others. Furthermore, these qualities of the political culture were related to economic growth and a participant political life.[26] Ronald Inglehart has shown similar continuity in social trust across nations.[27] Alternatively, modernization may weaken traditional structures in some societies, but then fail to develop effective associational groups in their place because of restrictive social attitudes. A nation's ability to achieve either stability or democracy will be hindered as a result.

In other cases, authoritarian parties and bureaucracies may control associational groups and choke off the channels of political access. Eastern Europe offers a situation in which forty years or more of authoritarian domination suppressed autonomous interest groups. Eventually, the processes of economic modernization pressured these authoritarian systems to allow more open organization and expression of political interests. In addition, social change led to an expansion of interest articulation activity and a need for associational groups to provide regular and organized expression for citizens' interests.

The recent development of organized interest groups in Eastern Europe should not, however, lead us to conclude that every conceivable group now has equal standing. Using the American experience as an example, the articulation of interests is frequently biased toward the goals of the better-off, who are also often better organized.[28] It is often pointed out that the American Association of Retired Persons (AARP) is an effective group that is not counterbalanced by a "Young Taxpayers Group," and that the traditional labor-management competition leaves consumers underrepresented.

We might test the breadth of citizen representation by evaluating systems in terms of their inclusiveness: what proportion of the population is represented to what degree in national-level politics? South Africa under apartheid illustrates the extreme case where the majority was prevented outright from forming associational groups. In the Third World, competing interests in the capital rarely involve the interests of rural peasants; sometimes peasant organizations are brutally suppressed, while urban middle- and upper-class groups can petition authorities. It seems to be no coincidence that the bias in group inclusion appears greatest where the gaps in income and education are widest. We previously suggested that, pushed to the extreme, those excluded from the process may engage in anomic activity or resort to violence, a conclusion supported by statistical studies of inequality and violence.[29] Even in less extreme cases, the presence of different levels of political awareness means that every interest group system is somewhat biased. Democratization involves not only the provision of competitive elections but also the reduction of the bias in interest representation.

Another challenge faces the patterns of interest articulation and representation in advanced industrial democracies. There are claims that participation in associational groups is decreasing in the United States, and perhaps in other established democracies.[30] For instance, memberships in labor unions and formal church engagement have steadily trended downward in most Western democracies over the past several decades. Some scholars argue that this trend represents a growing social isolation in developed nations, as people forsake social and political involvement for the comfort of their favorite chair and their favorite television program. However, other researchers argue that we are witnessing a change in how citizens organize and express their interests, such as through public Interest groups, Internet networks, and blogging.[31] Even in nations such as India and China, millions of people are now using the Internet to learn about politics and how they can articulate their interests.

What can be said for certain is that democratic politics rests on a participatory public that uses individual and group methods to express and represent its interests. Thus, developing an active social and political life is an important standard for measuring the political development of a nation.

REVIEW QUESTIONS

- How do the different forms of citizen action vary in their potential influence on policy makers?
- What are the main types of interest groups?
- How does a "civil society" differ from a noncivil society?
- What are the key differences among pluralist, neo-corporatist, and controlled interest group systems?
- What are the consequences when an interest group works through legitimate channels of influence rather than coercive channels?
- What factors increase the diversity of interest groups and their efforts to influence the political process?

KEY TERMS

anomic groups

associational groups

channels of political access

civil society

collective action problem

controlled interest group
  systems

institutional groups

interest articulation

mass media

neo-corporatist interest
  group systems

nonassociational groups

pluralist interest group
  systems

political terror tactics

protests

SUGGESTED READINGS

Dahl, Robert A. *Polyarchy: Participation and Opposition.* New Haven, CT: Yale University Press, 1971.

———. *Democracy and Its Critics.* New Haven, CT: Yale University Press, 1989.

Dalton, Russell J. *Citizen Politics: Public Opinion and Political Parties in Advanced Industrial Democracies,* 4th ed. Washington, DC: CQ Press, 2005.

Denardo, James. *Power in Numbers: The Political Strategy of Protest and Rebellion.* Princeton, NJ: Princeton University Press, 1985.

Hirschman, Albert. *Exit, Voice, and Loyalty.* Cambridge: Harvard University Press, 1970.

Howard, Marc Morjé. *The Weakness of Civil Society in Post-Communist Europe.* New York: Cambridge University Press, 2003.

Keck, Margaret, and Kathryn Sikkink. *Activists Beyond Borders: Advocacy Networks in International Politics.* Ithaca, NY: Cornell University Press, 1998.

Lichbach, Mark. *The Rebel's Dilemma.* Ann Arbor: University of Michigan Press, 1994.

Meyer, David, and Sidney Tarrow, eds. *The Social Movement Society: Contentious Politics for a New Century.* Lanham, MD: Rowman & Littlefield, 1998.

Norris, Pippa. *Democratic Phoenix: Reinventing Political Activism.* New York: Cambridge University Press, 2003.

Olson, Mancur. *The Logic of Collective Action.* Cambridge: Harvard University Press, 1965.

Putnam, Robert. *Bowling Alone: The Collapse and Revival of American Community.* New York: Simon & Schuster, 2000.

Putnam, Robert D., ed. *Democracies in Flux: The Evolution of Social Capital in Contemporary Society.* Oxford: Oxford University Press, 2002.

Richardson, Jeremy J., ed. *Pressure Groups.* New York: Oxford University Press, 1993.

Rootes, Christopher. *Environmental Movements: Local, National, and Global.* London: Frank Cass, 1999.

Shi, Tianjian. *Political Participation in Beijing.* Cambridge: Harvard University Press, 1997.

Tarrow, Sidney. *The New Transnational Activism.* New York: Cambridge University Press, 2005.

Thomas, Clive. *Political Parties and Interest Groups: Shaping Democratic Governance.* Boulder, CO: Lynn Rienner, 2001.

Van Deth, Jan et al. *Social Capital and European Democracy.* New York: Routledge, 1999.

Verba, Sidney, Norman H. Nie, and Jae-on Kim. *Participation and Political Equality.* Cambridge: Cambridge University Press, 1978.

Verba, Sidney, Kay Schlozman, and Henry Brady. *Voice and Equality.* Cambridge: Harvard University Press, 1996.

Wattenberg, Martin. *Where Have All the Voters Gone?* Cambridge: Harvard University Press, 2003.

Wiarda, Howard J. *Corporatism and Comparative Politics: The Other Great "ism."* Armonk, NY: Sharpe, 1997.

ENDNOTES

1. This framework draws on Sidney Verba, Norman N. Nie, and Jae-on Kim, *Participation and Political Equality* (Cambridge: Cambridge University Press, 1978), ch. 2.

2. See, for example, the range of activities of Beijing residents described in Tianjin Shi, *Political Participation in Beijing* (Cambridge: Harvard University Press, 1997).

3. Dietlind Stolle, Marc Hooghe, and Michele Micheletti, "Politics in the Supermarket: Political Consumerism as a Form of Political Participation," *International Political Science Review* 26 (2005): 245–70.

4. Pippa Norris, *Democratic Phoenix: Reinventing Political Activism.* (New York: Cambridge University Press, 2003) Verba, Nie, and Kim, *Participation and Political Equality.*

5. Citizen interest group activity includes membership in groups working on local community issues, environmental interests, humans rights issues, women's issues, and the peace movement.

6. Russell Dalton, *Citizen Politics,* 4th ed. (Washington, DC: CQ Press, 2006, 2002), ch. 4; Norris, *Democratic Phoenix,* ch. 10.

7. See Verba, Nie, and Kim, *Participation and Political Equality;* and Barnes, Kaase, et al., *Political Action* (Beverly Hills: Sage Publications, 1979).

8. See the evidence in J. Craig Jenkins and Kurt Schock, "Political Process, International Dependence, and Mass Political Conflict: A Global Analysis of Protest and Rebellion, 1973–1978," *International Journal of Sociology* (2004) 33:41–63.

9. Studies of these problems were stimulated by the now classic work of Mancur Olson, *The Logic of Collective Action* (Cambridge: Harvard University Press, 1965). See also Mark Lichbach, *The Rebel's Dilemma* (Ann Arbor: University of Michigan Press, 1994); Mancur Olson, "Dictatorship, Democracy, and Development," *American Political Science Review* 87, no. 3 (Sept. 1993): 567–76; Todd Sandler, ed., *Collective Action: Theory and Applications* (Ann Arbor: University of Michigan Press, 1992).

10. See G. F. Skilling and F. Griffiths, eds., *Interest Groups in Soviet Politics* (Princeton, NJ: Princeton University Press, 1971); the essays by Frederick C. Barghoorn and Skilling in Robert A. Dahl, *Regimes and Oppositions* (New Haven, CT: Yale University Press, 1973); and Roman Kolkowicz, "Interest Groups in Soviet Politics," *Comparative Politics* 2, no. 3 (April 1970): 445–72.

11. Christopher Rootes, ed., *Environmental Movements: Local, National, and Global* (London: Frank Cass, 1999); Amrita Basu, ed., *The Challenges of Local Feminism: Women's Movements in Global Perspective* (Boulder, CO: Westview, 1995).

12. Jean Cohen and A. Arato, *Civil Society and Political Theory* (Cambridge: MIT Press, 1992); M. Walzer, ed., *Toward a Global Civil Society* (Oxford: Berghahn Books, 1995).

13. See Table 4.1; John Pierce et al., *Citizens, Political Communication, and Interest Groups: Environmental Organizations in Canada and the United States* (Westport, CT: Praeger, 1992).

14. Sidney Tarrow, *The New Transnational Activism* (New York: Cambridge University Press, 2005); Margaret Keck and Kathryn Sikkink, *Activists Beyond Borders: Advocacy Networks in International Politics* (Ithaca: Cornell University Press, 1998).

15. Marc Morjé Howard. *The Weakness of Civil Society in Post-Communist Europe* (New York: Cambridge University Press, 2003); Russell Dalton, "Civil Society and Democracy," in Russell Dalton and Doh Chull Shin, eds. *Citizens, Democracy, and Markets Around the Pacific Rim* (Oxford: Oxford University Press, 2006).

16. Philippe Schmitter, "Interest Intermediation and Regime Governability," in Suzanne Berger, ed., *Organizing Interests in Western Europe* (New York: Cambridge University Press, 1981), ch. 12; Arend Lijphart and Markus Crepaz, "Corporatism and Consensus Democracy in 18 Countries," *British Journal of Political Science* 21, no. 2 (April 1991): 235–46; Wyn Grant, ed., *The Political Economy of Corporatism* (New York: St. Martin's Press, 1985).

17. On the relative success of the corporatist systems in economic performance, see Miriam Golden, "The Dynamics of Trade Unionism and National Economic Performance," *American Political Science Review* 87, no. 2 (June 1993): 439–54; Arend Lijphart, Ronald Rogowski, and R. Kent Weaver, "Separation of Powers and Cleavage Management," in R. Kent Weaver and Bert A. Rockman, *Do Institutions Matter? Government Capabilities in the United States and Abroad* (Washington: Brookings Institution, 1993), 302–44.

18. Lyle Scruggs, "Institutions and Environmental Performance in Seventeen Western Democracies," *British Journal of Political Science* 29 (1999): 1–31.

19. Oscar Molina and Martin Rhodes, "Corporatism: The Past, Present and Future of a Concept," *Annual Review of Political Science* 2 (2002): 305–31.

20. Howard Wiarda, ed. *Authoritarianism and Corporatism in Latin America—Revisited* (Gainesville: University Press of Florida, 2004), Julius E. Nyang'Oro and Timothy M. Shaw, *Corporatism in Africa: Comparative Analysis and Practice* (Boulder, CO: Westview Press, 1990).

21. We should also note that most Chinese work and live in rural areas and are not wage earners. The figure is based on the share of the labor force that receives a regular salary, which in China means

urban workers. But India has a comparable labor structure, and many fewer Indian wage earners are unionized.

22. Norris, *Democratic Phoenix*.

23. Ted Robert Gurr, "A Comparative Study of Civil Strife," in Hugh David Graham and Ted Robert Gurr, eds., *The History of Violence in America* (New York: Bantam Press, 1969), 462–63.

24. See Pippa Norris, Stefaan Walgrave, and Peter van Aelst, "Does Protest Signify Disaffection? Demonstrators in a Postindustrial Democracy," In Mariano Torcal and Jose Ramón Montero, eds., *Political Disaffection in Contemporary Democracies: Social Capital, Institutions and Politics* (London: Routledge, 2006): 279–307; Mark Baldassare, ed., *The Los Angeles Riots: Lessons for the Urban Future* (Boulder, CO: Westview, 1994).

25. On violence and democratic survival, see G. Bingham Powell, Jr., *Contemporary Democracies: Participation, Stability, and Violence* (Cambridge: Harvard University Press, 1982), ch. 8; see also the contributions to Juan J. Linz and Alfred Stepan, eds., *The Breakdown of Democratic Regimes* (Baltimore: Johns Hopkins University Press, 1978).

26. Robert D. Putnam, *Making Democracy Work: Civic Traditions in Modern Italy* (Princeton, NJ: Princeton University Press, 1993).

27. Ronald Inglehart, *Culture Shift in Advanced Industrial Societies* (Princeton, NJ: Princeton University Press, 1990), 34–36; see also Almond and Verba, *Civic Culture*, ch. 11.

28. Jeffrey M. Berry, *The Interest Group Society* (New York: Longman, 1997).

29. Many of these studies are reviewed by Mark I. Lichbach, "An Evaluation of 'Does Economic Inequality Breed Political Conflict' Studies," *World Politics* 41 (1989): 431–70. More recent references and analyses appear in T. Y. Wang et al., "Inequality and Political Violence Revisited," *American Political Science Review* 87, no. 4 (Dec. 1993): 979–93.

30. Robert Putnam, *Bowling Alone: The Collapse and Revival of American Community* (New York: Simon & Schuster, 2000); Robert Putnam, ed., *Democracies in Flux: The Evolution of Social Capital in Contemporary Society* (Oxford: Oxford University Press, 2002).

31. Cliff Zukin et al., *A New Engagement? Political Participation, Civic Life, and the Changing American Citizen* (New York: Oxford University Press, 2006); Russell Dalton, *The Good Citizen* (Washington, DC: CQ Press, 2007) ch. 4.

INTEREST AGGREGATION AND POLITICAL PARTIES

Interest aggregation is the activity in which the political demands of individuals and groups are combined into policy programs. For example, in developing an economic policy program, politicians often have to balance farmers' desires for higher crop prices, consumers' preferences for lower prices and taxes, and environmentalists' concerns about water pollution and pesticides. Who prevails in such balancing acts depends in part on political institutions, which is the subject of Chapter 6. But interest aggregation depends also on political skills and resources, such as votes, campaign funds, political offices, media access, or even armed force.

How interests are aggregated is a key feature of the political process. The aggregation process determines which interests are heard, and what individuals and groups are allowed to participate. Interest aggregation can also help create a balanced government program out of competing policy goals. How stable and effective governments are also depend on their patterns of interest aggregation.

Interest aggregation can occur in many ways. An influential party leader or military dictator may have a considerable personal impact. Yet, large states usually develop more specialized organizations for aggregating interests. Political parties are just such organizations, and they play an important role in interest aggregation in democratic as well as in many nondemocratic systems. Each party (or its candidates) stands for a set of policies and tries to build a coalition of support for this program. In a democratic system, two or more parties compete to gain support for their alternative policy programs. In an authoritarian system, a single party or institution may try to mobilize citizens' support for its policies. In either type of system political parties may play a major role. In authoritarian systems the process is frequently covert and controlled, and the process is top-down rather than bottom-up. In other words, parties mobilize interests to support the government, rather than responding to demands by regular citizens or social interests.

It is important to remember that political parties may perform many different functions, and that different structures may aggregate interests. For instance, in addition to aggregating interests, parties frequently shape the political culture as they strive to build support for their ideologies, issue positions, and candidates. Parties recruit voters and select would-be officeholders. They articulate interests of their own and transmit the demands of others. Governing parties are also involved in making public policy and even in overseeing its implementation and adjudication. Yet, the distinctive and defining goal of a political party—its mobilization of support for policies and candidates—is especially related to interest aggregation. In this chapter we compare the role of parties in interest aggregation to those of other structures.

PERSONAL INTEREST AGGREGATION

One way to bring political interests together in policymaking is through personal connections. Virtually all societies feature **patron-client networks**—structures in which a central officeholder, authority figure, or group provides benefits (patronage) to supporters in exchange for their loyalty. It was the defining principle of feudalism. The king and his lords, the lord and his knights, the knight and his serfs and tenants—all were bound by ties of personal dependence and loyalty. The American political machines of Boss Tweed of New York or Richard Daley, Sr., of Chicago were similarly bound together by patronage and loyalty. Personal networks are not confined to relationships cemented by patronage only. The president of the United States, for instance, usually has a circle of personal confidants, a "brain trust" or "kitchen cabinet," bound to their chief by ideological and policy propensities as well as by ties of friendship.

The patron-client network is so common in politics that it resembles the cell in biology or the atom in physics—the primitive structure out of which larger and more complicated political structures are composed. Students of politics in all countries report such networks. When interest aggregation is performed mainly within patron-client networks, it is difficult to mobilize political resources behind unified policies of social change or to respond to crises. This is because political decisions depend on ever-shifting agreements among many factional leaders (patrons). Patron-client politics thus typically means a static political system.

Contemporary research on patron-client relationships was pioneered in studies of Asian politics, where this structure runs through the political processes of countries such as the Philippines, Japan, and India.[1] But parallels exist in Europe, the Middle East, Latin America, and most regions of the world. Patron-client relationships affect recruitment to political office, interest aggregation, policymaking, and policy implementation. Yet as Table 5.1 shows, patron-client networks are a particularly important means of aggregating political interests in poorer countries.

INSTITUTIONAL INTEREST AGGREGATION

In modern societies, as citizens become aware of larger collective interests and have the resources and skills to work for them, personal networks tend to be regulated, limited, and incorporated within broader organizations. Interest groups with powerful

	Structures Performing Interest Aggregation in Selected Contemporary Nations*				**TABLE 5.1**

		Extensiveness of Interest Aggregation by Actor			
Country	**Patron-Client Networks**	**Associational Groups**	**Competitive Parties**	**Authoritarian Parties**	**Military Forces**
Brazil	Moderate	Moderate	Moderate	—	Moderate
Britain	Low	High	High	—	Low
China	Moderate	Low	—	High	High
France	Low	Moderate	High	—	Low
Germany	Low	High	High	—	Low
India	High	Moderate	Moderate	—	Low
Iran	High	Moderate	Low	—	Moderate
Japan	Moderate	High	High	—	Low
Mexico	Moderate	Moderate	Moderate	—	Low
Nigeria	High	Low	Moderate	—	Moderate
Russia	Moderate	Low	Moderate	—	Moderate
United States	Low	Moderate	High	—	Low

*Extensiveness of interest aggregation rated as low, moderate, or high. Rating refers to broad-level performance issue areas and at different times. Blank implies that such actors do not exist.

resources can easily cross the subtle dividing line between interest articulation and aggregation. Associational groups (see Chapter 4) often support political contenders such as political parties. But they can occasionally wield sufficient resources to become contenders in their own right. For instance, the political power of the labor unions within the British Labour Party historically rested on the unions' ability to develop coherent policy positions and mobilize their members (who were formally represented in the party) to support those positions. As we discussed in Chapter 4, interest group systems of democratic corporatism empower both labor and business groups to get actively engaged in making economic policies. These arrangements include continuous political bargaining among organized labor, business interests, political parties, and government representatives. Such corporatist systems interconnect organizations that in other political systems play very different, often antagonistic, roles. Table 5.1 illustrates how associational groups tend to play a larger role in democratic politics that accept the independence of interest groups and their attempts to influence government policy.

Institutional groups, like bureaucratic agencies and military factions, can also be important interest aggregators. Indeed, the bureaucracy performs this function in most societies. Although established primarily to implement public policy, the bureaucracy may negotiate with interest groups to identify their preferences or to mobilize their support. Government agencies may even be "captured" by interest groups and used to support their demands. Bureaucrats often create client support networks to expand their organizations or to enhance their ability to solve problems in their areas of expertise. Military organizations, with their special control of physical force, can also be powerful interest aggregators. We shall have more to say about their role later in this chapter.

COMPETITIVE PARTY SYSTEMS AND INTEREST AGGREGATION

In many contemporary political systems, parties are the primary structures of interest aggregation. Political parties are *groups or organizations that seek to place candidates in office under their label.* In any given society, there may be one party, two parties, or as many as ten or twenty. We refer to the number of parties, and the relationships among them, as properties of the **party system.** The most critical distinction runs between **competitive party systems,** which primarily try to build electoral support, and noncompetitive or **authoritarian party systems,** which seek to direct society. This distinction does not depend on the closeness of electoral victory, or on the number of parties. It depends instead on the ability of political parties to freely form and compete for citizen support, and on this competition for citizen support as the key to government control. Thus a party system can be competitive even if one party wins most of the votes in a certain area, or even dominates several consecutive national elections, as long as other parties can challenge its dominance at the polls.

The role of competitive parties in interest aggregation depends not only on the individual party but also on the structure of parties, electorates, electoral laws, and policymaking institutions. Typically, interest aggregation in a competitive party system takes place at several stages: within the individual parties, as the party chooses candidates and adopts policy proposals; through electoral competition; and after the election through bargaining and coalition building with other parties in the legislature or executive.

Political parties have been around as long as there have been elections and representative assemblies, but modern democratic parties began developing in Europe and the Americas from about the mid-nineteenth century. They have since emerged in all societies that have adopted free and fair elections and democratic government. Parties differ in their purposes and organization. Some have elaborate policy platforms, whereas others are little more than vehicles for ambitious politicians to get elected (or even to enrich themselves). Some parties are highly structured mass organizations, whereas others are loose, *personalistic* groups dominated by their leaders (see Box 5.1).

The first parties were typically *internally created,* their founders were politicians who already held seats in the national assembly or other political offices. These parties were often committed to broad constitutional principles (such as republican government, universal suffrage, or separation of church and state), but otherwise they often had only loose policy programs and little organization outside the legislature. They often had colorful names which said little about their policies, such as Whigs and Tories in Britain, Whites ("Blancos") and Reds ("Colorados") in several

BOX 5.1

Personalistic Parties

Political parties are typically formal organizations with officers, members, statutes, and official policy programs. Sometimes, however, parties can be much looser *personalistic* movements built around one political leader, or a small group of leaders. Personalistic parties are particularly common in new democracies. In Russia, for example, President Putin has been able to form a party (United Russia) with a strong personal following. But even India and France have highly personalistic parties. In India, the Congress Party has been dominated by the families of its most important founders, Gandhi and Nehru. In France, most presidents have come out of the Gaullist movement, which has had many names but has been dominated from the start by President Charles de Gaulle and later by some of his followers. Personalistic parties commonly do not have a very clear policy program. They are often susceptible to clientelistic politics and sometimes become vehicles for purely personal ambitions and rent seeking.

Shmuel Flatto-Sharon offers a blatant but extreme example. Flatto-Sharon is a French businessman of Jewish background. In 1977 he fled to Israel because the French authorities wanted to prosecute him for embezzling $60 million. To avoid extradition, he decided to run for election to the Knesset (the Israeli national assembly), which would give him immunity from prosecution. He formed a party, which he ran as a one-man operation—it had no other candidates or officers. Flatto-Sharon refused to identify himself as left, right, or center. He appealed for Jewish solidarity, arguing that Israel should not allow him to be imprisoned in a gentile country (France). He also promised a free television set to all Israeli households (this was before television sets became inexpensive and commonplace). And he promised to pay anyone who voted for him. Remarkably, he won two parliamentary seats, even though as his party's only candidate he could not fill the second seat. In 1981, however, Flatto-Sharon lost his bid for reelection. He was convicted of bribery for his vote-buying scheme and sent to jail in Israel, but never extradited to France.

Latin American countries, Hats and Caps in Sweden, or for that matter Democrats and Republicans in the United States. Some of the descendents of these parties have kept their original names; others now call themselves Liberals (such as the previous Whigs) or Conservatives (such as the previous Tories).

During the late nineteenth century and early twentieth century, a series of other types of parties emerged, as the democratic countries industrialized and urbanized, and as larger and larger segments of the adult population gained the right to vote. The growth of the industrial working class led to the formation of socialist, social democratic, communist, and other workers' parties. Farming interests gained representation through agrarian parties, and other parties emerged to represent religious communities (such as Catholics or Hindus) or ethnic or linguistic minorities. In countries that were not independent, parties of national independence often became a dominant force. All of these parties were typically *externally created*—they organized outside parliament before they became a force inside those institutions. They often had much stronger mass membership organizations than their older competitors, and they often also had (and continue to have) closer ties to specific interest groups. Thus, social democrats and communists tended to have strong ties to labor unions, agrarian parties to farmers' organizations, and many Christian Democratic parties (at least Catholic ones) to the Vatican and religious organizations.

Most of these parties still exist and continue to play a leading role. They have settled into stable *party families* of Social Democrats, Conservatives, Christian Democrats, Liberals, Nationalists, etc., which often maintain close contacts across national boundaries. The party systems of most countries show a great deal of stability, and many of the most important parties of the early twenty-first century were also the dominant parties a hundred years ago. Yet, two important new types of parties have emerged in the past thirty or forty years, particularly in advanced industrial countries. One is the "new left," or Green parties, that in many countries emerged in the 1960s or 1970s. These parties tend to champion international peace and disarmament, ecological and environmental protection, gender equality, a large welfare state, and minority rights. They are often more supportive of alternative life styles than traditional working-class parties of the left (such as Social Democrats). The other important type of new party is the "populist right." These parties tend to be critical of existing parties and political leaders, whom they see as elitist, corrupt, and out of touch. They favor strict law-and-order policies but criticize what they see as "politically correct" government interventionism. They dislike the distortions that the welfare state sometimes creates, such as policies that make it unattractive to work and easy to live off of welfare benefits (see Chapter 7). And they typically oppose large-scale immigration (see Box 5.2).

The party systems of most democratic countries reflect a mix of these various party families. But no two party systems are exactly alike, and not all party families are represented in all countries. The variations in party systems reflect differences in demographics, economic development, and political histories. They also depend on differences in electoral systems, as we shall discuss below.

Elections

In democracies, political parties live and die by their performance in political elections. The act of voting, and giving support to a political candidate, party, or policy proposal, is one of the simplest and most frequently performed political acts. By aggregating these votes, the citizens can make a collective decision about their future leaders and public policies. Elections are one of the few devices through which diverse interests can be expressed equally and comprehensively.[2]

The simple act of voting can have profound implications. The voters' choice of parties and candidates helps aggregate political interests. Electoral outcomes determine who manages the affairs of government and makes public policy. And parties generally fulfill their electoral promises when they gain control of government.[3]

Parties Just for Fun

BOX 5.2

Some political parties seem to have no other purpose than to make fun of politics and politicians. One example is Britain's Official Monster Raving Loony Party (OMRLP) formed in 1983. Its founding leader was musician David Sutch, who called himself Screaming Lord Sutch. Sutch and the other founders were apparently inspired by the television series Monty Python's Flying Circus. The OMRLP has never won any seat in Parliament, but has captured a few seats in local British government. Sutch died in 1999 and was replaced as party leader by Alan "Howling Laud" Hope. In 2005, the party ran on a platform of abolishing the income tax, inviting the rest of Europe to adopt the British currency, retraining "stupid traffic cops" as clergy, and introducing a ninety-nine-pence coin to "save on change." These proposals may be political long-shots, but one of the party's early goals, for British pubs to stay open all day, has actually been achieved.

In Denmark, comedian Jacob Haugaard has since 1979 several times con-tested parliamentary elections as a candidate for the Association of Deliberate Work Avoiders. In 1994, he won election to the Danish Parliament. His election platform included demands for disability pensions for people who lack a sense of humor, tail-winds on all Danish bike paths, more generous Christmas presents, more renais-sance furniture at IKEA, and more whales in Danish waters. Haugaard also promised his voters free beer, and he used the public funds his party received from the Danish government to fulfill this campaign commitment (he bought beer and hot dogs for his supporters after the election).

When leftist governments come to power in Europe, they tend to expand the size and efforts of the government; whereas conservative parties generally slow the growth of government programs and promote private enterprise. Republicans and Democrats in the United States also have been fairly responsible in keeping their promises. However, parties that want radical change or have not recently been in office often find it difficult to implement their programs when they eventually come to power. When, for example, the German Greens came to power in 1998 as part of a coalition government, they had to modify their promise to shut down Germany's nuclear power plants immediately. Instead they negotiated a phase-out over many years. But by and large, parties try hard to implement their programs, and citizens can therefore influence interest aggregation and policymaking through their role in selecting elites.

When they aggregate interests and make policy, party leaders are often caught between the demands of their party activists and the voters. Party activists often want policies that are more radical than those that most voters prefer. At any rate, activists will typically insist more vigorously that the party program should be implemented, whereas ordinary voters are often happier when governments try to compromise and listen to opinions outside their own parties. There is a broad and ongoing debate about the extent to which democracy requires political parties to be internally democratic. Advocates of participatory democracy strongly support this idea, as do parties such as the European Greens. On the other hand, the famous Austrian economist Joseph A. Schumpeter argued that vigorous competition *between* parties is what matters for a healthy democracy and that democracy within parties is irrelevant or even harmful.[4] (See also Box 5.3.)

Elections often have other functions as well (see also Chapter 4). The communist nations of Eastern Europe and elsewhere utilized elections to legitimize their governments. They routinely reported turnout that exceeded 98 percent of the electorate. But the outcome was given in advance. Until 1990, voters in the Soviet Union were given only one candidate to vote for, and this person was always a nominee of the Communist Party. Voter participation was very high in these nations because the government pressured people to participate and express their symbolic support for the regime, not because the elections actually decided anything. Elections played a role in socializing and shaping citizens' attitudes, but had little to do with interest articulation or aggregation.[5]

In most democratic countries, voters can freely choose whether or not to vote. Some democratic countries, though, require citizens to vote and impose penalties on

The Iron Law of Oligarchy   BOX 5.3

Can political parties be the main vehicles of democratic representation if they do not govern themselves democratically? This has been a main concern among students of modern political parties. In 1911, the young German sociologist Robert Michels published a study of the German Socialist Party in which he formulated the "iron law of oligarchy," which states that all modern organizations tend towards oligarchy (rule by the few) rather than democracy. "Who says organization says oligarchy," Michels famously observed. He identified several forces that push organizations such as political parties towards oligarchy. One is the need for specialization and differentiation that exists in all large, modern organizations. A second cause of oligarchy lies in the fact that most ordinary members do not have the time or resources to hold their leaders accountable and that they often crave strong leadership. A third reason is that parties foster leaders who live "off" politics rather than "for" politics. They exploit their leadership positions to advance their own ambitions for wealth or power, often to the detriment of their followers. (In contemporary terms, we would refer to such self-interested pursuit of power as rent seeking.) Michels' study was particularly troubling because he found these tendencies even in a party, the German Socialist Party, with which he sympathized and which was considered particularly strongly committed to democratic ideals.

Source: Robert Michels, *Political Parties* (New York: Free Press, 1962).

those who do not. Voting choices reflect a mix of motivations.[6] Many citizens try to judge the parties' policy promises. For others, elections are a simple referendum on government performance. They vote to throw the rascals out if times are bad, and to reelect them if times are good. In other cases, elections can be dominated by the charisma of a strong leader or the incompetence of a weak one. In each case, however, elections aggregate these diverse concerns to make a collective decision on the composition of government.

Electoral Systems

The rules by which elections are conducted are among the most important structures that affect political parties. We refer to these rules as the **electoral system.** They determine who can vote, how people vote, and how the votes get counted. The rules that determine how voter choices are translated into election outcomes, how votes are converted into seats, are especially important. In the United States, Britain, and many countries influenced by Britain (such as India and Canada), the legislative election rules divide the country into many election districts. In each district, the candidate who has more votes than any other—a *plurality*—wins the election in the district. This simple, **single-member district plurality (SMDP) election rule** is often called "first past the post," a horse-racing term, because the winner need only finish ahead of the others but not win a majority of the votes. This system seems obvious and natural to Americans, but it is rarely used in continental Europe or in Latin America. Another version of single-member district elections is the **majority runoff** (or **double-ballot**) system used in France and in presidential elections in Russia. In this system, voting happens in two stages, normally separated by a couple of weeks. In the first round, it takes a majority of all votes (50 percent + 1) to win. The winning candidate, then, has to win not just more votes than any other candidate, but more votes than all other candidates combined. If there is no majority winner in the first round, then only a smaller number of candidates (in French and Russian presidential elections the top two) make it into the second round, in which whoever gets the largest number of votes is elected.

In contrast to the single-member district system, most democracies use some form of **proportional representation (PR)** in multimember districts. In these systems the country is divided into a few large districts, which may elect as many as twenty or thirty members apiece. These districts are often the states or provinces that make up the country. In the Netherlands and Israel, the entire country is a single electoral district with more than 100 members. The competing parties offer lists of candidates for the slots in each district. The number of representatives a party wins depends on the overall proportion of the votes it receives, though no system is perfectly proportional. A party receiving 4 percent of the vote would be awarded approximately 4 percent of the legislative seats. Sometimes parties must achieve a minimum threshold of votes, usually 3 to 5 percent nationally, to receive any seats at all. If so many parties compete that a lot of them fall below this threshold, many voters may be left unrepresented, as happened in Russia in 1995.

In order to compete effectively, parties must formulate appealing policy programs and nominate attractive candidates for office. They must anticipate the offerings of their competitors and the preferences of the voters. The procedure that parties use to develop policy positions varies greatly from country to country and from party to party. In the United States the national party conventions held at each presidential election formalize the party's policy positions, both by adopting a party platform and by selecting a slate of candidates. In other countries, parties have more regular congresses, and centralized party organizations issue party programs (also known as platforms or manifestos).[7] Whatever the system, a successful program must both spell out policy positions that are popular with the voters and aggregate interests within the party.

Parties must also offer candidates for office. In the United States, voters directly select these candidates through **primary elections.** But primaries are an unusually open form of candidate selection. In most other countries with **single-member district (SMD)** elections, party officials select the candidates, either locally or nationally. In proportional representation elections, the party draws up a list of candidates for each district. In **closed-list PR systems,** the elected representatives are then simply drawn from the top of this list, in declining order, and ordinary voters have no say about their candidates. In **open-list systems,** on the other hand, voters can give preference votes to individual candidates, and these votes are counted when it is decided which candidates will represent the party in that district. Besides adopting programs and selecting candidates, parties also attempt to publicize them and mobilize electoral support through rallies, media advertising, door-to-door campaigning, and other activities.

Patterns of Electoral Competition

In democratic party systems, the electoral system is a major determinant of the patterns of electoral competition. Two famous political science theories help us understand this connection: Duverger's Law and Downs' median voter result. **Duverger's Law,** which is named after the French political scientist Maurice Duverger, is one of the best-known theories in political science.[8] It states that there is a systematic relationship between electoral systems and party systems, so that plurality single-member district election systems tend to create two-party systems in the legislature, while proportional representation electoral systems generate multiparty systems. Duverger identified two mechanisms behind this regularity. He called them the mechanical effect and the psychological effect. The **mechanical effect** is to be found in the way that different electoral systems convert votes into seats. In single-member district systems, parties get no representation unless they finish first in at least one district. Therefore, smaller parties that run second, third, or fourth across many districts receive little or no representation. In the 2001 election in Britain, for example, the Liberal Democratic Party (Britain's third largest party) received 18 percent of the votes, but only 8 percent of the seats in Parliament. The **psychological effect** lies in the fact that both voters and candidates anticipate the mechanical effect. Therefore, voters do not throw their support behind "hopeless" parties and candidates. Instead, they may support their second-best (or even third-best) option in order to keep a party that they strongly dislike from winning. And knowing that the voters will not support them, minor party candidates are reluctant to run. Giving your support to a party or candidate that is not your first choice in order to avoid an even worse outcome is known as **strategic voting.** Duverger argues that strategic voting tends to work to the advantage of parties that are already large and to the disadvantage of small ones. In U.S. elections, it has been fairly common for third-party candidates to run well in the polls until close to the election date, when voters realize that these candidates are not going to win. Their support then often declines rapidly.

Anthony Downs examined the effects of the number of parties on their policy positions. He showed that in two-party systems in which the parties are competing along a left-right (or other) policy dimension and are interested only in winning elections, and where all voters choose the party closest to their policy preferences, the parties will moderate their policies so as to try to win the support of the median voter (the voter who is at the midpoint of the policy spectrum, with as many other voters to the right as to the left). Downs' contribution is known as the **median voter result.** According to this theory, two-party systems will exhibit a centrist pull or "convergence." In systems with only two parties, parties have to try to win a majority, so targeting the "center" of the electorate is critical. In PR systems with many political parties, however, no one group has much chance of winning a majority, and parties can survive with much less support. Therefore, there is not the same centrist pull and parties may instead spread themselves out across the policy spectrum.[9]

Figure 5.1 offers a comparative "snapshot" of parties and voters in several democratic countries. It shows where party supporters in each country placed themselves on a left-right scale in public opinion surveys in the early 2000s, with one identified as Left (or liberal in the United States) and 10 identified as Right (or conservative in the United States). Note that although the left-right placements reflect the relative positions of party supporters in their respective societies, the meaning of left, right, and center can be different in different societies. The height of the columns above the scale shows what percentage of the electorate voted for each party. The two countries at the top of the figure, the United States and Britain, use SMDP electoral systems, whereas France uses a majority runoff system, Mexico a mixed system, and Germany in practice a PR system. According to Duverger, we should expect the United States and Britain to have only two serious parties and the others more. Following Downs, we should expect the two-party systems to be centrist and clustered in policy space and the multiparty systems to be more dispersed.

By and large, Figure 5.1 supports both Duverger and Downs. In the countries at the top of the figure, especially in the United States, there are only two large parties. Moreover, the parties are fairly close to the center. Democrats are somewhat to the left and Republicans somewhat to the right, with a lot of overlap. The left-right "gap" between the average party supporters, although larger than it was twenty years ago, is still fairly small. In France, toward the bottom of the figure, many parties receive voter support. There is a very large distance between the left-most party (the Communists)

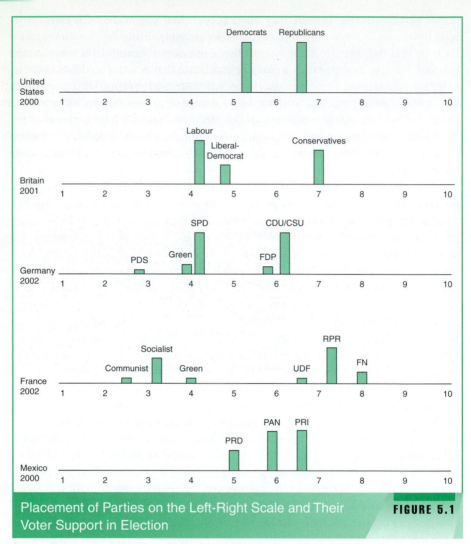

Placement of Parties on the Left-Right Scale and Their Voter Support in Election

FIGURE 5.1

Source: Party positions from the self-placements of party voters. The height of the bar represents the percentage of the total vote won by that party in the legislative election identified on the left.

and right-most party (the National Front), and even between the two largest parties (Socialists and RPR.) Britain and Germany fall between these more extreme cases. As Duverger would predict, Britain looks more like the United States, but the parties are farther apart and the smaller Liberal Democratic Party falls between the two major ones. Mexico shows that even systems with proportional representation and more than two parties (though only three significant ones) can have convergent and centrist electoral politics. Yet, in the most recent years, for example in the 2006 presidential election, the Mexican parties have seemed to pull apart and become less centrist.

Table 5.2 presents additional information on the electoral and party systems of the twelve countries in this book. It displays data on the **effective number of parties**

TABLE 5.2

Elections—Lower House of National Legislature

Country	Electoral System	Effective Number of Parties—Vote Shares	Effective Number of Parties—Seat Shares	How Are Individual Candidates Selected?
Brazil	PR open list	10.63	9.30	Candidate preference vote
Britain	SMD plurality	3.56	2.45	Nominated by local constituency association
China	No contested elections	No contested elections	No contested elections	No contested elections
France	SMD majority run-off	3.37	2.25	Nominated by local constituency association
Germany	Mixed system: SMD plurality + PR closed list	3.75*	3.44*	National party + state party conventions
India	SMD plurality	7.5	6.55	Nominated by local constituency association
Iran	MMD majority run-off	No available data	2.66	Must be approved by Council of Guardians
Japan	Mixed system: SMD plurality + PR closed list	3.72	2.26	National party
Mexico	Mixed system: SMD plurality + PR closed list	3.60	3.02	Nominated by local constituency association + national party
Nigeria	SMD plurality	2.62	2.34	Nominated by local constituency association
Russia	PR closed list	4.71 (under previous electoral system with SMD plurality + PR closed list)	3.18	National party
United States	SMD plurality	2.17	2.00	Primary elections

Note: Data from the most recent national elections, as of October 1, 2006.

MMD = Multimember district

SMD = Singlemember district

PR = Proportional representation

*Calculated using proportional representation results.

Sources: Arend Lijphart, *Patterns of Democracy* (New Haven: Yale University Press, 1999), www.Electionguide.org; www.Wikipedia.org.

in each country. This measure takes into account both the overall number of parties and their relative sizes. For example, if there are two parties and they are exactly the same size, the effective number of parties is 2.0. If, however, one party has 80 percent of the votes and the other 20 percent, the effective number of parties is just below 1.5.[10] The effective number of parties can be calculated for either votes or seats, as we have done in Table 5.2. If Duverger's Law is correct, then the effective number of parties should be lower in countries that have SMDP electoral systems than in those that have other systems (particularly PR). Table 5.2 shows that this is largely true, as three of the four countries that have the lowest effective number of parties do indeed have SMDP elections. At the same time, India is an exception; it has a large number of parties despite an SMDP electoral system. But a closer look at India shows that even though the country has many parties overall, most electoral districts feature only two serious parties.[11] Thus, India helps us understand one limitation of Duverger's Law, which is that while SMDP systems tend to sustain only two parties in each election district, these two parties need not be the same throughout the country.

Table 5.2 also gives us a measure of the mechanical effect in Duverger's Law, the consequences of the counting rules themselves. By comparing the effective number of parties among the voters (vote shares) with the effective number of parties in the national assembly (seat shares), we can see how much the electoral system helps the large parties and disfavors the small ones. This bias exists in all countries and electoral systems, as the numbers in the column for seat shares are consistently lower than those in the column for vote shares. Duverger's Law suggests that this difference should be greater in "first past the post" (SMDP) systems than elsewhere, but it is not clear that our data bear that out.

Competitive Parties in Government

If a competitive party wins control of the legislature and the executive, it will (if unified) be able to pass and implement its policies. Sometimes this control emerges directly from the electoral process, as a single party wins a majority of the vote. But in many countries the election laws help the largest party gain a governing majority even if it does not enjoy majority support among the voters. Thus, less than 50 percent of the vote may be converted into more than 50 percent of the legislative seats. Such "artificial" or "manufactured" legislative majorities have been the rule in countries with "first past the post" (SMDP) electoral systems, such as Britain.[12]

For example, since 1974 either the Conservative Party or the Labour Party has consistently won a majority of seats in the British House of Commons, even though neither party has ever been supported by a majority of the voters in any of these elections. Margaret Thatcher's Conservative Party won a solid majority in the House of Commons in 1983 and 1987 with only about 42 percent of the vote. With almost exactly the same level of support, Tony Blair and the Labour Party won nearly two-thirds of the seats in 1997 and 2001. In 2005, Labour's share of the vote fell to about 35 percent, but the party still got a solid majority of the seats. In all these elections, the quarter of the electorate supporting the smaller British parties received only a handful of parliamentary seats.

In other countries, multiparty elections do not yield single-party majorities, but party coalitions formed before the election may still offer the voters a direct choice of future governments. Before the election, a group of parties may join forces, agree to coordinate their election campaigns, or agree to govern together if they jointly win a parliamentary majority. When such coalitions form, as they have in many (but not all) elections in France and Germany, it is almost like a two-party system. Voters can clearly identify the potential governments and reward or punish the incumbents if they so choose. They thus have the ability to choose the direction of government policy through their party choice.

When elections do not create a majority party, and there is no preelectoral coalition, the political parties and their leaders must negotiate a new government after the election. This is common in many multiparty parliamentary systems, such as the Netherlands and Italy.[13] In these nations interests are not aggregated through elections, because the election does not determine the government. Instead, the aggregation of interests occurs in government when a coalition is negotiated. (See also Chapter 6, and Figure 6.2.)

The aggregation of interests at the executive rather than electoral level can have both costs and benefits. On the one hand, when elite party coalitions determine government policy, voters may feel that the government is not accountable to them. And because interest aggregation occurs among political elites, different elite coalitions can form on different issues. This can be confusing to citizens (and even informed observers). It may be difficult for voters to assign clear responsibility for government policy, and it may seem unfair that the electoral losers sometimes get to decide. This situation lessens the value of the vote as an instrument to shape future policy or to punish parties responsible for bad policy choices in the past.

On the other hand, there may be benefits for minority interests when all parties, not just the election winners, are represented in policymaking. All citizens hold minority opinions on some issues, and some are in the minority on many issues. If even minority representatives can influence policy between elections, they may feel that they have more political protection. Finally, even governments that win a majority of votes typically do not have majority support for all of their policy proposals. So there may be benefits for the nation as a whole when even the winners have to negotiate the different parts of their programs. Such bargaining may even increase the likelihood that policies reflect different majorities on different issues. The value of elections as instruments of representation may increase when interests are aggregated within a government coalition, though the value of elections as instruments of accountability may diminish.[14]

Cooperation and Conflict in Competitive Party Systems

Competitive party systems can be classified by the number of parties as well as by the patterns of competition or cooperation among them. **Majoritarian two-party systems** are either dominated by just two parties, as in the United States, or they have two dominant parties and election laws that usually create legislative majorities for one of them, as in Britain. In **majority-coalition systems,** parties establish preelectoral coalitions so that voters know which parties will attempt to work together to form a government. Germany and France have in most elections been in this category. Purely **multiparty systems** have election laws and party systems that virtually ensure that no single party wins a legislative majority and no tradition of preelection coalitions. Interest aggregation then depends on a coalition of parties bargaining and coming to agreement after the election.

The degree of antagonism or polarization among the parties is another important party system characteristic. In a **consensual party system,** the parties commanding most of the legislative seats are not too far apart on policies and have a reasonable amount of trust in each other and in the political system. These are typically party systems like those shown toward the top of Figure 5.1 Bargaining may be intense and politics exciting, but it seldom threatens the system itself. In a **conflictual party system,** the legislature is dominated by parties that are far apart on issues or are antagonistic toward each other and the political system, such as the Russian party system in the 1990s.

Some party systems have both consensual and conflictual features. Arend Lijphart has used the term **consociational** (or **accommodative**) to describe party systems in which political leaders are able to bridge the intense differences between antagonistic voters through power-sharing, broad coalitions, and decentralization of sensitive decisions to the separate social groups.[15] A consociational system can enable a deeply divided nation to find a way to peaceful democratic development. In Austria and Lebanon after World War II, suspicious and hostile groups—the socialists and Catholics in Austria, and the Christians and Muslims in Lebanon—worked out a set of consociational understandings that made stable government possible. Austria's accommodation was based on a two-party system and Lebanon's on many small, personalistic religious parties. Austria's consociationalism was largely successful, but the Lebanese experiment was not. After 1975, the country fell victim to civil war.

South Africa also adopted consociational practices in its transition to democracy. Leaders of the major political parties of the white minority and two major segments of the black majority negotiated (with great difficulty) arrangements for a democratic transition. The "Interim Constitution" guaranteed a share in power and government—cabinet posts—to all parties winning over 5 percent of the vote. Later, this feature was abandoned.

As the contrasting examples of Austria and Lebanon suggest, consociational practices (and the ability even to agree to attempt them) offer deeply divided democracies hope but no guarantees of long-term success. One critical aspect of consociationalism is that many important decisions are taken by small groups of politicians behind closed doors. If these politicians are able to work together more constructively than their supporters, then consociationalism can be a happy solution. But if the politicians are intransigent or self-interested, it may not be the best option.

The number of parties does not always tell us much about the degree of antagonism. The United States and Britain are relatively consensual majoritarian party systems. They are not perfect two-party systems because minor parties exist in both countries, especially in Britain. Yet, one or the other of the two major British parties usually wins majority control and governs through disciplined party voting. In the United States, the degree of consensus changes from election to election because of the shifting programs of presidential candidates. Moreover, the looser cohesion of American parties and the frequency of divided government lead to postelection bargaining that is similar to consensual multiparty systems.

But not all majoritarian party systems are consensual. Austria between 1918 and 1934 is the best example of a conflictual majoritarian party system. Antagonism between the Socialist Party and the other parties was so intense that in the mid-1930s it produced a brief civil war. The Austrian experience also illustrates how party systems can change. After World War II, the leaders of the two major parties negotiated an elaborate coalition agreement of mutual power sharing—checks and balances— to contain the country's conflicts. After some twenty years of the consociational "Grand Coalition," party antagonism had greatly declined.

Consensual multiparty systems are found in Norway and Sweden, among other countries. France (1946—1958), Italy (1945–1992), and Weimar Germany (1919–1933), on the other hand, are historical examples of conflictual multiparty systems, with powerful communist parties on the left and conservative or fascist movements on the right. Cabinets had to form out of centrist movements, which were themselves divided on many issues. This resulted in instability, poor government performance, and loss of citizen confidence in democracy. These factors contributed to the collapse of the French Fourth Republic, to government instability and citizen alienation from politics in Italy, and to the overthrow of democracy in Weimar Germany.

New democracies, especially those divided by language or ethnicity, sometimes face similar challenges. Some of the emerging party systems in Central and Eastern Europe have fallen into the pattern of conflictual, multiparty competition. For instance, in the 1995 parliamentary elections in Russia, forty-three parties appeared on the ballot—ranging from unreformed communists on the left to nationalist parties on the right—and seven parties won representation in Parliament. But later elections greatly reduced the number of parties.

Thus, although the number of parties affects political stability, the degree of antagonism among parties is more important. Two-party systems are stable and effective, but they may be dangerous if society is too deeply divided. Multiparty systems consisting of relatively moderate parties can often offer stability and fairly effective performance, especially if the parties are willing to commit themselves to preelectoral coalitions. Pure multiparty systems without preelectoral coalitions are more prone to ineffectiveness, but some have worked well over long periods. Where social groups and parties are highly antagonistic, however, collapse and civil war are ever-present possibilities, regardless of the number of parties. When crises develop, the most critical factor is typically how committed party leaders are to working together to defend democracy. Sometimes party leaders in a multiparty, representational setting are more accustomed to such cooperation.[16]

AUTHORITARIAN PARTY SYSTEMS

Authoritarian party systems can also aggregate interests. They deliberately attempt to develop policy proposals and to mobilize support for them, but they do so in a completely different way from competitive party systems. In authoritarian party systems, aggregation takes place within the party or in interactions with business groups, unions, landowners, and institutional groups in the bureaucracy or military. Although there may be sham elections, the citizens have no real opportunity to shape aggregation by choosing between party alternatives.

Authoritarian party systems can be distinguished according to the degree of top-down control within the party and the party's control over other groups in society. At one extreme is the **exclusive governing party,** which insists on almost total control over political resources. It recognizes no legitimate interest aggregation by groups within the party. Nor does it permit any free activity, much less opposition, from interest groups, citizens, or other government agencies. In its most extreme form, sometimes called totalitarianism, it penetrates the entire society and mobilizes support for policies developed at the top. Its policies are legitimated by a political ideology, such as communism or national socialism (Nazism) that claims to know the true interests of the citizens, regardless of what the citizens themselves believe.[17] At the other extreme is the **inclusive governing party,** which recognizes and accepts at least some other groups and organizations, but may repress those that it sees as serious challenges to its own control.

Exclusive Governing Parties

In a purely totalitarian society, there is only one party with total top-down control of society, and no autonomous opposition parties or interest groups. Totalitarian single-party systems can be impressive vehicles of political mobilization. A clear ideology provides legitimacy and coherence, and the party penetrates and organizes society in the name of that ideology and in accordance with its policies. But totalitarianism is difficult to sustain. Although the ruling communist parties of the Soviet Union before 1985, of Eastern Europe before 1989, and of North Korea, Vietnam, and Cuba today resemble this model, few parties have long maintained such absolute control. China is an interesting mixed case. While the Chinese government has withdrawn from the direct administration of much of the economy, it still does not recognize the legitimacy of any opposition groups. The ruling party permits, within bounds, some interest articulation by individuals, but not mass mobilization against government policy.[18]

Not all exclusive governing parties are totalitarian, however. Many leaders committed to massive social change—for example national independence from colonialism—have used the exclusive governing party as a tool for mass mobilization. Such exclusive governing parties may experience more internal dissent than is commonly recognized. Within the party, groups may unite around such interests as their region or industry, or behind leaders of different policy factions. Beneath the supposedly united front, power struggles may erupt in times of crisis. Succession crises are particularly likely to generate such power struggles, as at the death of Stalin in the Soviet Union and Mao Zedong in China. The Chinese Communist Party has several times had to rely on the army, even on coalitions of regional army commanders, to sustain its control.

It is difficult to build an exclusive governing party as an agent for social transformation. The seduction of power regularly leads to rent seeking or other abuses of power that are not checked by competitive democratic politics and that may distort the original party objectives. The exclusive governing parties in some African states also had limited capacity to control society. Furthermore, the loss of confidence in Marxist-Leninist ideology and in the Soviet model led all eight of the African regimes that had once invoked it to abandon that approach by the early 1990s.

As exclusive governing parties age, many enter a stage in which they maintain control but place less emphasis on mobilization. Some, such as North Korea, may degenerate into vehicles for personal rule and exploitation by the ruler's family and supporters.[19] Finally, as shown by the collapse of communism in the former Soviet Union and Eastern Europe, if and when the party leaders lose faith in the unifying ideology, it may be difficult to maintain party coherence.

Inclusive Governing Parties

Among the preindustrial countries, especially those with notable ethnic and tribal divisions, the more successful authoritarian parties have been *inclusive*. These systems recognize the autonomy of social, cultural, and economic groups and try to incorporate them or bargain with them, rather than control and remake them. The more successful African one-party systems, such as Kenya and Tanzania, permitted aggregation around personalistic, factional, and ethnic groups within a decentralized party.

Inclusive party systems have sometimes been labeled *authoritarian corporatist systems*. Like the democratic corporatist systems (see Chapter 4), some of these systems encourage the formation of large organized interest groups that can bargain with each other and the state. Unlike the democratic corporatist systems, however, these authoritarian systems provide no political resources directly to the populace. Independent protest and political activity outside of official channels are suppressed. The party leaders permit only limited autonomous demands within the ranks of the party and by groups associated with it.

The inclusive authoritarian systems may permit substantial amounts of autonomous interest aggregation, which may take many forms. The party typically tries to gather various social groups under the general party umbrella and negotiate with outside groups and institutions. Some inclusive parties have attempted aggressive social change. Others have primarily been arenas for interest aggregation. Many inclusive party governments permit other parties to offer candidates in elections, as long as these opposition candidates have no real chance of winning. Indeed, one interesting feature of politics in the last thirty years or so, along with the increasing number of liberal democracies, has been the growth of **electoral authoritarianism.** This is where there is a facade of democracy providing "some space for political opposition, independent media, and social organizations that do not seriously criticize or challenge the regime."[20] The Mexican PRI was long a successful example of an inclusive governing party featuring electoral authoritarianism (see Box 5.4).

The fact that some inclusive authoritarian parties have been impressively durable does not necessarily mean that they are strong or successful. In many countries these parties coexist in uneasy and unstable coalitions with the armed forces and the civilian bureaucracy. In some countries the party has become window dressing for a military regime or personal tyranny. Seldom have these parties been able to solve the economic or ethnic problems that face their country.

These political systems were often created in a struggle against colonialism, and as colonialism becomes more distant, they may implode. As memories of the

---

Mexico's PRI   BOX 5.4

One of the oldest and the most inclusive authoritarian parties was the Partido Revolucionario Institucional (PRI) in Mexico. For more than fifty years the PRI dominated the political process and gave other parties no realistic chances of winning elections. The PRI attained this dominance after President Lázaro Cárdenas turned it into a "big-tent" coalition in the 1930s; it was also careful to control the counting of the ballots. It did not have to fear electoral competition, at least until the 1990s. The PRI incorporated many social groups, with separate sectors for labor, agrarian, and middle-class interests. The party dealt with its opponents in carefully designed ways. While some political dissidents were suppressed, others were deliberately enticed into the party. The party also gave informal recognition to political factions grouped behind such figures as former presidents. Various Mexican leaders mobilized their factions within the PRI and in other important groups not directly affiliated with it, such as big business interests. Bargaining was particularly important every six years when the party had to choose a new presidential nominee, since the Mexican Constitution limits presidents to one term. This guaranteed some turnover of elites. In recent decades, however, rising discontent made it difficult to aggregate interests through a single party. The urban and rural poor who had not shared in Mexico's growth joined with reformers to demand a more fully democratic system. An armed uprising of peasant guerrillas in early 1994 shocked the political establishment and led to promises of genuine democratic competition. Legislative elections in 1997 were more open than earlier contests, and ended the seventy-year rule of the PRI, which then lost the presidency to the National Action Party (PAN) in 2000. After that election, the PRI has quickly diminished as a political force, even though it still controls many state and local governments. In 2006, its candidate ran a distant third in Mexico's presidential election.

independence struggle fade and the leaders die off or retire, the ties of ideology and experience that hold these parties together weaken. These developments, in conjunction with the worldwide expansion of democracy, have led to a general loss of legitimacy for the single-party model. In some cases (as in Tanzania), they have adjusted by permitting real party competition. More frequently, they have resorted to electoral authoritarianism with varying degrees of manipulation to provide a veneer of domestic and international legitimacy. In more than a few cases, they have turned to naked coercion, with the military serving as final arbiter.

THE MILITARY AND INTEREST AGGREGATION

After independence, most of the nations of the Third World adopted at least formally democratic governments. But in many countries these civil governments lacked effectiveness and authority, which often led to their breakdown and replacement by **military governments.** The military had instruments of force and organizational capacity, and in the absence of a strong constitutional tradition, it was an effective contender for power. Even under civilian rule, the military had substantial political influence and often constituted a significant power contender. In Brazil, for example, the military played a crucial role in interest aggregation even under the civilian government prior to the coup of 1964. After that intervention, it was the dominant actor for the next twenty years. In many other countries, the military has long been a similarly important interest aggregator.

The military's virtual monopoly on coercive resources gives it great potential power. Thus, when aggregation fails in democratic or authoritarian party systems, the military may emerge by default as the only force able to maintain orderly government. If the legitimacy of the government is weak and the social order threatens to break down, a united military may be the only force that can sustain political cohesion. The military may also intervene for more self-interested reasons, such as protecting its autonomy or budgets from civilian interference. About two-fifths of the world's nations have confronted military coup attempts at some time, and in about a third of the nations these coups were at least partially successful in changing leaders or policy. Fewer than half of these coup attempts, however, focused on general political issues and public policy. Most coups seemed motivated by the professional interests of the military.

What happens after the military intervenes can vary. The soldiers may support the personal tyranny of a civilian president or a dominant party. Or the armed forces may use their power to further institutional or ideological objectives. Military rulers may try to create military and/or bureaucratic versions of authoritarian corporatism, linking organized groups and the state bureaucracy with the military as final arbiter. They may undertake "defensive" modernization in alliance with business groups or even more radical modernization. In Latin America almost all the corporatist versions of authoritarian aggregation have had a strong military component and only rarely a dominant authoritarian party.

The major limitation of the military in interest aggregation is that its internal structures are not designed for interest aggregation. The military is primarily organized to have an efficient command structure. It is not set up to aggregate internal differences, to build compromise, to mobilize popular support, or even to communicate with social groups outside the command hierarchy. Nor do military regimes have the legitimacy in the international community that elections provide. Thus the military lacks many of the advantages held by party systems. These internal limitations may be less serious when the military is dealing with common grievances and putting pressure on—or seizing power from—unpopular authorities. The same limitations become a major problem, however, when a military government needs to stake out its own course and mobilize support for it. For these reasons military governments frequently prove unstable and are often forced to share power with other institutions, or they simply voluntarily withdraw from politics.

TRENDS IN INTEREST AGGREGATION

As we have previously noted, the democratic trend in the world has gained momentum since the end of the 1980s. Figure 5.2 classifies the world's regimes by their degree of freedom at four points: the end of the 1970s, the end of the 1980s, the late 1990s, and 2005–2006. The percentages should be viewed as estimates, often based on limited information. But the figure provides a rough idea of the importance of competitive interest aggregation across the world.

In 1978 fewer than one-third of the world's almost 200 independent countries were classified as free. These regimes, which tended to have competitive party systems as their predominant interest aggregation structures, were dominant in Western Europe and North America (including the Caribbean), not uncommon in Latin America and Asia, but rare in Africa and the Middle East. Nearly as many countries had some versions of a single-party regime, and about 40 percent were classified as not free. In slightly less than a quarter of all countries the military dominated interest aggregation, either formally (military governments) or in practice (military-dominated civilian governments). The military-dominated regimes accounted for about a third or more of the countries in Africa and Latin America. Single-party systems were the main form in Eastern Europe and relatively common in Africa and Asia and accounted for most of the remaining unfree countries.

A decade later, the trend was away from single-party governments. Across the world they declined from 30 to 24 percent of the world's nations, although still accounting for nearly 40 percent of African nations. As we already know, the decline of exclusive governing party regimes is even more striking. The proportion of military governments actually increased slightly, from 23 to 26 percent of the world's countries. There was a minor democratic trend toward competitive party and electoral systems, with more than one-third of the world's governments now classified as free.

The trend toward democracy took off more dramatically beginning in 1989 in Eastern Europe, and with new pressures for democracy in the developing world.

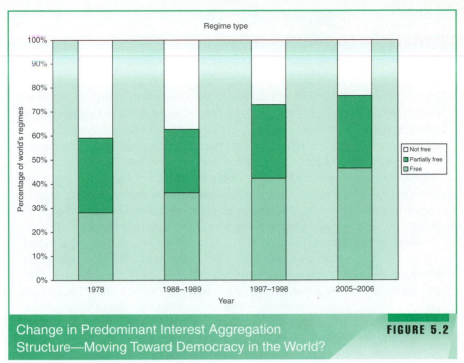

Change in Predominant Interest Aggregation Structure—Moving Toward Democracy in the World?

FIGURE 5.2

Source: Adapted from Raymond D. Gastil, *Freedom in the World 1979, 1988–1989, 1997–1998* (New York: Freedom House, 1979, 1989, 1998), and other data from www.freedomhouse.org.

By the late 1990s, for the first time in world history there were more free than unfree states. The collapse of communism in Europe and elsewhere was in large part responsible, but the number of military dictatorships also declined. The declining acceptance of authoritarian governments, as well as the withdrawal of Soviet support, contributed to this trend, especially in Africa. Many African nations moved toward a more democratic and free system during the 1990s. Yet a few authoritarian party systems with exclusive governing parties are still around, such as China and Cuba. Most of the remaining unfree states are in the Middle East, Central Asia, and Africa. Many African nations still feature some variety of the "electoral authoritarianism" discussed above, with severe constraints on civil freedom and electoral opposition. A few remain unabashed authoritarian systems (as in Zimbabwe) or are mired in deadly civil war (as in Sudan and Somalia) (see Box 5.5).

Perhaps in deference to the decline in the legitimacy of authoritarianism, the military throughout the world is now more likely to dominate from behind the scenes than through direct rule. Latin America also has experienced the genuine replacement of military regimes by competitive party regimes in such important countries as Argentina, Brazil, Chile, and Uruguay. Although the era of confidence in the military as a solution to development seems to have passed, military domination remains likely when other types of government are unsuccessful.

Trying to Make Democracy Work

BOX 5.5

Nigeria is in many ways typical of the rough road to democracy that many developing countries have traveled. The Nigerian military government, which had ousted an ineffective civilian government in 1983, responded to the democratization wave of the early 1990s by introducing careful and measured reforms. It initiated state-level elections in1991 and federal legislative elections in 1992. Finally, after presidential elections scheduled for June 1993, the transition to civilian rule would be complete. But the military kept strict control of the electoral process and disqualified politicians who had held office under previous civilian regimes (because they were considered to be tainted by corruption). Voters were left with a choice of only two parties, both created by the government. Voting turnout was low because many voters became cynical about the process. These doubts were confirmed when the military annulled the presidential election, even before the results were announced, and installed an interim government instead. In November 1993, Defense Minister General Sani Abacha launched a military coup which overturned the interim government, banned all political activity, dissolved the legislature, dismissed the elected state governments, and thus ended Nigeria's cautious experiment with elections. In 1998, President Abacha suddenly died of a heart attack, and the reform process could begin anew. In spring 1999, the military government held a presidential election. The victor was a former army general, Olusegun Obasanjo, who went on to try to implement democratic reforms. He was reelected four years later. But continuing ethnic and religious violence, corruption, and abuses of power have made the Nigerian transition to democracy fragile.

Where there has been "backsliding" on the road to democracy, the military has often played a part. So we cannot assume that the democratizing trend will continue relentlessly. Multiparty regimes that seem unable to cope with economic and social problems often lose their legitimacy. Such is now the challenge facing parts of Eastern Europe, as well as much of the Third World. In many of these countries, competitive party systems exist, but citizens have very little trust in them and often consider them to be corrupt. And military coups continue to occur, as in Thailand and Fiji in the fall of 2006.

SIGNIFICANCE OF INTEREST AGGREGATION

How interests are aggregated is an important determinant of what a country's government does for and to its citizens. Successful public policy depends on effective interest aggregation. One importance function of interest aggregation is to narrow policy options, so that the desires and demands of citizens are converted into a few policy alternatives. Many possible policies are eliminated in the process. Those that remain typically have the backing of significant sectors of society. For instance, even though such policies have been adopted in other nations, there has never been a "serious" proposal that the United States government take over the country's steel industry, because no powerful group has ever favored it.

In democratic countries, competitive party systems narrow down and combine policy preferences. Through elections, voters throw their support behind some of these parties and thus shape party representation in the legislature. Even at the legislative stage, further consolidation and coalition building takes place. At some point, however, most policy options have been eliminated from consideration. Either no party backed them or the parties supporting them fared badly in the elections.

In noncompetitive party systems, military governments, and monarchies, aggregation works differently, but with the similar effect of narrowing policy options. On some issues, aggregation virtually determines policy, as when a military government or a faction of an authoritarian party can decide the government's program. In other cases the legislative assembly, military council, or party politburo may contain several factions that must negotiate over policy. The narrowing of policy choices also affects the influence and access of social interests.

But politics shapes its environment as well as reflecting it. Interest aggregation often alters the polarization that the political culture projects into policymaking. That is one reason why politics is so fascinating. Well-organized and well-led political parties might, at least for a while, be able to dominate politics and limit the strength of extremist groups in the legislature. Conversely, well-organized extremists might be able to appeal to the fears and prejudices of some groups and get their support at the polls, thus gaining more legislative strength in an otherwise consensual country.

Aggregation ultimately affects the government's adaptability and stability. Authoritarian interest aggregation tends to create political power structures that do not reflect popular opinion. In highly divided and conflict-ridden societies, rulers may portray such lack of representation as a virtue. Leaders of military coups often justify their overthrow of party governments by claiming to depolarize politics and rid the nation of conflict it cannot afford. Similarly, heads of authoritarian parties typically claim that their nation must concentrate all its energies and resources on common purposes and that party competition would be too polarizing.

In contrast, most proponents of democratic interest aggregation argue that the best hope for accommodating conflicting social and political interests lies in free and fair electoral competition, followed by negotiation among those groups that gain the voters' favor. Democracy thus leads policymakers to act as the people wish. In a polarized political culture, the division and uncertainty that interest aggregation implies may be seen as a high price to pay for citizen control. As the frequent instability in authoritarian governments indicates, however, it may be easier to do away with the appearance of polarization than with the reality. Competing demands may find their way to the surface anyway, and the citizens may end up without either freedom and participation or stability.

REVIEW QUESTIONS

- What structures other than political parties aggregate interests?
- What is Duverger's Law? Which two effects does it imply?
- What is the median voter result, and why does it pertain only to two-party systems?
- What are the differences between totalitarian parties and other single-party systems?
- Why do many countries turn to military governments, and why are military governments often short-lived?

KEY TERMS

accommodative party systems

authoritarian party systems

closed-list PR systems

competitive party systems

conflictual party system

consensual party system

consociationalism

double-ballot (runoff) elections

Duverger's Law

effective number of parties

electoral authoritarianism

electoral system

exclusive governing party

inclusive governing party

institutional groups

interest aggregation

majoritarian two-party systems

majority-coalition systems

majority runoff

mechanical effect

median voter result

military governments

multiparty systems

open-list systems

party system

patron-client networks

plurality election rules

primary elections

proportional representation (PR)

psychological effect

single-member district (SMD)

single-member district plurality (SMDP) election rule

strategic voting

SUGGESTED READINGS

Cox, Gary W. *Making Votes Count: Strategic Coordination in the World's Electoral Systems.* Cambridge: Cambridge University Press, 1997.

Dalton, Russell J., and Martin P. Wattenberg. *Parties Without Partisans: Political Change in Advanced Industrial Democracies.* New York: Oxford University Press, 2000.

Decalo, Samuel. *Coups and Army Rule in Africa,* 2nd ed. New Haven, CT: Yale University Press, 1990.

Downs, Anthony. *An Economic Theory of Democracy.* New York: Harper & Row, 1957.

Farrell, David. *Electoral Systems: A Comparative Introduction.* New York: St. Martin's Press, 2001.

Farrell, David, Ian Holliday, and Paul Webb, eds. *Political Parties in Democratic States.* Oxford: Oxford University Press, 2002.

Jackson, Robert H, and Carl G. Rosberg. *Personal Rule in Black Africa.* Berkeley: University of California Press, 1982.

Kitschelt, Herbert. *The Transformation of European Social Democracy.* New York: Cambridge University Press, 1994.

Laver, Michael, and Norman Schofield. *Multiparty Government.* New York: Oxford University Press, 1990.

Lijphart, Arend. *Electoral Systems and Party Systems.* New York: Oxford University Press, 1994.

———. *Patterns of Democracy.* New Haven, CT: Yale University Press, 1999.

Linz, Juan J. *Totalitarian and Authoritarian Regimes.* Baltimore: Johns Hopkins University Press, 2002.

Mainwaring, Scott. *Rethinking Party Systems in the Third Wave of Democratization.* Stanford, CA: Stanford University Press, 1999.

Michels, Robert. *Political Parties.* New York: Free Press, 1962.

Nordlinger, Eric A. *Soldiers in Politics: Military Coups and Governments.* Englewood Cliffs, NJ: Prentice-Hall, 1976.

Powell, G. Bingham, Jr. *Contemporary Democracies: Participation, Stability, and Violence.* Cambridge: Harvard University Press, 1982.

———. *Elections as Instruments of Democracy.* New Haven, CT: Yale University Press, 2000.

Riker, William H. *Liberalism Against Populism.* San Francisco: W. H. Freeman, 1982.

Strøm, Kaare, Wolfgang C. Müller, and Torbjörn Bergman, eds. *Cabinets and Coalition Bargaining: The Democratic Life Cycle in Western Europe.* Oxford: Oxford University Press, 2008.

ENDNOTES

1. See, for example, Luis Roniger and Ayse Gunes-Ayata, eds., *Democracy, Clientelism, and Civil Society* (Boulder, CO: Lynne Rienner, 1994); S. Eisenstadt and L. Roniger, *Patrons, Clients, and Friends* (Cambridge: Cambridge University Press, 1984); Lucian W. Pye, *Asian Power and Politics* (Cambridge: Harvard University Press, 1985); and Martin Shefter, "Patronage and Its Opponents," in *Political Parties and the State* (Princeton, NJ: Princeton University Press, 1994).

2. Unfortunately, elections cannot solve all the problems of aggregating interests fairly. For example, giving each citizen one vote does not take into account the varying intensities with which different people may hold their opinions. Moreover, economists and political scientists have found that when there are three or more alternatives in any decision, there is no fair way to aggregate votes to select a single, best outcome ("Arrow's Paradox"). See Duncan Black, "On the Rationale of Group Decision Making," *Journal of Political Economy* 56 (1948): 23–34; and Kenneth Arrow, *Social Choice and Individual Values* (New Haven, CT: Yale University Press, 1951). For an accessible discussion of some political implications, see William H. Riker, *Liberalism Against Populism* (San Francisco: W. H. Freeman, 1982); and Kenneth A. Shepsle and Mark S. Bonchek, *Analyzing Politics: Rationality, Behavior, and Institutions* (New York: Norton, 1997), Part II.

3. Hans-Dieter Klingemann, Richard Hofferbert, and Ian Budge, eds., *Parties, Policy, and Democracy* (Boulder, CO: Westview, 1995); Michael, Gallagher, Michael Laver, and Peter Mair, *Representative Government in Western Europe*, 4th ed. (New York: McGraw-Hill, 2005); and Richard Rose, *Do Parties Make a Difference?* (Chatham, NJ: Chatham House, 1984), ch. 5.

4. Joseph A. Schumpeter, *Capitalism, Socialism, and Democracy* (New York: Harper, 1943).

5. However, in Communist China semicompetitive elections for village leadership positions since 1987 has in some areas brought the opinions of local leaders and ordinary citizens closer together. See Melanie Manion, "The Electoral Connection in the Chinese Countryside," *American Political Science Review* 90 (1996): 736–48.

6. See Russell J. Dalton, *Citizen Politics: Public Opinion and Political Parties in Advanced Industrial Democracies*, 4th ed. (Washington, DC: Congressional Quarterly Press, 2005).

7. Ian Budge, David Robertson, and Derek Hearl, eds., *Ideology, Strategy, and Party Change: Spatial Analyses of Post-War Election Programmes in 19 Democracies* (New York: Cambridge University Press, 1987); Richard Katz and Peter Mair, eds., *How Parties Organize: Change and Adaptation in Party Organizations in Western Democracies* (Thousand Oaks, CA: Sage, 1994).

8. Maurice Duverger, *Political Parties: Their Organization and Activity in the Modern State*, [1954] trans. Barbara and Robert North (New York: Wiley, 1963). For a more contemporary contribution, see Gary W. Cox, *Making Votes Count* (Cambridge: Cambridge University Press, 1997).

9. Anthony Downs, *An Economic Theory of Democracy* (New York: Harper & Row, 1957).

10. The effective number of parties is calculated as follows: first calculate the proportion of seats (or votes) held by each party. Square each of these proportions and then add them all up. Finally, divide one by the sum of all the squared proportions. See Markku Laakso and Rein Taagepera, "'Effective' Number of Parties: A Measure With Application to West Europe," *Comparative Political Studies* 12 (1979): 3–27.

11. See Pradeep Chhibber and Kenneth Kollman, *The Formation of National Party Systems* (Princeton, NJ: Princeton University Press, 2004).

12. For analyses of the consequences of election laws, see Douglas Rae, *The Political Consequences of Election Laws* (New Haven, CT: Yale University Press, 1967); and Arend Lijphart, *Electoral Systems and Party Systems: A Study of Twenty-seven Democracies, 1945–1990* (Oxford: Oxford University Press, 1994).

13. On government coalitions, see especially Michael Laver and Norman Schofield, *Multiparty Government: The Politics of Coalition in Europe* (New York: Oxford University Press 1990); and Kaare Strøm, Wolfgang C. Müller, and Torbjörn Bergman, eds., *Cabinets and Coalition Bargaining: The Democratic Life Cycle in Western Europe* (New York: Oxford University Press, 2008).

14. On elections and the representation of votes and preferences, as well as the trade-off with accountability, see G. Bingham Powell, Jr., *Elections as Instruments of Democracy* (New Haven, CT: Yale University Press, 2000), chs. 5–10.

15. See Arend Lijphart, *Democracy in Plural Societies* (New Haven, CT: Yale University Press, 1977); and Arend Lijphart, *Patterns of Democracy* (New Haven, CT: Yale University Press, 1999).

16. See Lijphart, *Patterns of Democracy*; G. Bingham Powell, Jr., *Contemporary Democracies* (Cambridge: Harvard University Press, 1982), chs. 8 and 10; and Juan J. Linz and Alfred Stepan, eds., *The Breakdown of Democratic Regimes* (Baltimore: Johns Hopkins University Press, 1978).

17. Juan Linz, *Totalitarian and Authoritarian Regimes* (Boulder, CO: Lynne Rienner, 2000); Amos Perlmutter, *Modern Authoritarianism: A Comparative Institutional Analysis* (New Haven, CT: Yale University Press, 1981), especially 62–114.

18. See Melanie Manion, "Politics in China," Chapter 13 below; for the earlier period, see, for example, Franz Schurman, *Ideology and Organization in Communist China* (Berkeley: University of California Press, 1966).

19. Juan Linz calls these "sultanistic" regimes; see *Totalitarian and Authoritarian Regimes* (Boulder, CO: Lynne Rienner, 2000), 151–157; Houchang Chehabi and Juan Linz, ed., *Sultanistic Regimes* (Baltimore: Johns Hopkins University Press, 1998); and Robert H. Jackson and Carl G. Rosberg, *Personal Rule in Black Africa* (Berkeley: University of California Press, 1982).

20. Larry Diamond, "Thinking About Hybrid Regimes," *Journal of Democracy* 13 (2002): 26; and the articles by Andreas Schedler; Steven Levitsky and Lucan Way; and Nicolas van de Walle in the same issue.

GOVERNMENT AND POLICYMAKING

Policymaking is the pivotal stage in the political process, the point at which bills become law or edicts are issued by the rulers. Later, policies are implemented and enforced. To understand public policy, we must know how decisions are made. Where is power effectively located in different political systems? What does it take to change public policy: a simple majority vote in the legislature or approval also by an independently elected executive? Or is it a decree issued by the military commanders or the party central committee? Or is it merely the whim of the personal dictator?

This chapter focuses on decision rules and on the policymaking role of government agencies, such as legislatures, chief executives, bureaucracies, and courts. Government agencies are at the core of policymaking. While parties, interest groups, and other actors may be very active in articulating and aggregating interests, government officials do most of the actual initiation and formulation of policy proposals. Interest group demands for tax relief or for the protection of endangered species cannot succeed unless they are transformed into policy by government officials according to some accepted decision rules. They cannot be effective until these policies are appropriately implemented by other officials.

Yet, government action does not flow in one direction only. The interaction between government and citizens is a two-way process. It includes an upward flow of influence and demands from the society, as well as a downward flow of decisions from the government. (See Figure 2.2 in Chapter 2.)

CONSTITUTIONS AND DECISION RULES

A constitution establishes the basic rules of decisionmaking, rights, and the distribution of authority in a political system. We sometimes use the term "constitution" to refer to a specific document laying out such principles—for example, the one adopted by the Founders of the United States in 1787. But a constitution need not be embodied in a single document. In fact, it rarely is. We should therefore think of a constitution as a set of rules and principles, whether it is a specific written document,

133

a set of customs or practices, or, as is usually the case, both. Even a military or party dictatorship typically sets procedures for having decrees proposed, considered, and adopted.

Written constitutions are particularly important in political systems based on the *rule of law.* This means that government should take no action that has not been authorized by law and that citizens can be punished only for actions that violate an existing law. Under the rule of law, the constitution is the supreme body of laws.

A constitution thus contains a set of **decision rules**—the basic rules governing how decisions are made. Policymaking is the conversion of social interests and demands into authoritative public decisions. Constitutions establish the rules by which this happens. They confer the power to propose policies on specific groups or institutions. They may give others the right to amend, reject, or approve such proposals, or to implement, police, or adjudicate them. They may specify how many resources are needed to make policies, as well as what these resources are.

Decision rules affect political activity because they determine what political resources are valuable in influencing decisions and how to acquire and use these resources. For example, in a federal and decentralized system such as the United States, a pressure group may have to approach both the legislative and the executive branches, and it may have to be active both at the state and the federal levels. If instead decisions are made by decree from the commander of the armed forces or the central committee of a single-party state, groups will need to influence these crucial policymakers.

Different decision rules have different attractions. More inclusive rules about policymaking—such as those that require the cooperation of several institutions or the support of over 50 percent of voters—can protect against hasty decisions. They can also prevent decisions that disadvantage large minorities (perhaps close to half) of the voters. At the same time, more inclusive rules can give a minority the power to block proposals favored by a majority. The more inclusive the voting rules are, as the percentage to approve approaches unanimity, the less likely it is that any decision can be made at all. Less inclusive decision rules make it easier to reach a policy, but many interests may be ignored.

Both the government as a whole and its institutions have decision rules. Decision rules may be simple or complex and apply to different circumstances. For example, the U.S. Congress has many different decision rules that apply under different circumstances, such as a simple majority in each house to pass a bill initially, but a two-thirds majority to override a presidential veto. The British House of Commons uses a much smaller set of rules (mainly simple majority rule). Decision rules may be more or less formal and precise. Most legislatures have formal and precise decision rules, whereas cabinets at the head of the executive branch often have informal and flexible rules.

Within any given branch of government or other political institution, numerous rules affect the policymaking process. In most modern assemblies the decision rules about voting are *egalitarian,* which is to say that each member has the same voting power. Simply speaking: one person, one vote. That is hardly ever true in government departments (ministries), however. Or in dictatorships. There, decisionmaking is *hierarchical*. Everybody is supposed to defer to his or her superior. In a pure hierarchy, only the vote of a person at the very top (for example, the minister) counts. Such a decision rule makes it easy to respond quickly in a policymaking emergency, but few interests or ideas may be taken into account.

Even when decisions are made through equal voting, the inclusiveness of the decision rules still shapes the outcomes. Many institutions operate through simple majority voting: in a choice between two options, whichever option gets the larger number of votes wins. Alternatively, more inclusive rules—such as "qualified" majorities of three-fifths, two-thirds, or even three-fourths—are sometimes required for particularly consequential decisions. For example, the U.S. Constitution requires two-thirds majorities in both houses of Congress in order to amend the Constitution or override a presidential veto. The most inclusive voting rule is unanimity, which means that any one member can block any decision.

It is important that decision rules in a democracy be transparent and stable. If they are not, citizens will not know what to expect from government. That may in turn cause them to be less trusting and less willing to invest or make other commitments. It may also lead to serious conflicts, and ultimately government may break down and issues be decided by force. The importance of having predictable decision rules was suggested by Thomas Jefferson in his introduction to the first Manual of the House of Representatives: "A bad set of rules is better than no rules at all."

Making Constitutions

Making a constitution is a fundamental political act: it creates or transforms decision rules. Most current constitutions were formed as the result of some break, often violent, with the past—war, revolution, or rebellion against colonial rule. New decision rules were made to accommodate new internal or external powers. Thus, the defeated powers and the successor states of World Wars I and II all adopted new constitutions or had new constitutions imposed on them.

Britain is unusual in having not a formal written constitution but only a long accepted and highly developed set of customs and conventions, buttressed by important ordinary statutes. This reflects the British record of gradual, incremental, and (on the whole) peaceful political change. Nevertheless, the major changes in British decision rules—such as the shift of power from the Crown to Parliament in the seventeenth century, and the Reform Acts of 1832 and 1867, which established party and cabinet government and vastly extended the right to vote—followed on periods of civil war or unrest.

Perhaps the most significant exception to the association between disruptive upheavals and constitution creation is the peaceful development over the last fifty years of the constitution of the European Union, whose growing powers are altering the decision rules affecting about 460 million Europeans in twenty-seven countries. While there has been no violence associated with the formation and growth of the EU, its origins lie in the bitter lessons of World Wars I and II.

The decades since World War II have seen much constitutional experimentation. Not only the defeated powers, but many new states—such as India and Nigeria, which achieved independence with the breakup of colonial empires—introduced new political arrangements. Some of the new states in the developing areas, such as Nigeria, have subsequently changed their form of government several times. In the last two decades the worldwide trend toward democracy, the end of the Cold War, and the dissolution of the Soviet Union have produced a new round of constitutional design. The recent constitutional crafting in Eastern Europe, Russia, and the other Soviet successor states as well as in South Africa and elsewhere have reignited old debates about the virtues and faults of different constitutional arrangements, or about the very wisdom of constitutional engineering.[1]

DEMOCRACY AND AUTHORITARIANISM

The most important distinction in policymaking is between democratic and authoritarian systems. **Democracy** means "government by the people." In small political systems, such as local communities, "the people" may share directly in debating, deciding, and implementing public policy. In large political systems, such as contemporary states, democracy must be achieved largely through indirect participation in policymaking. Policymaking power is delegated to officials chosen by the people.

Elections, competitive political parties, free mass media, and representative assemblies are political structures that make some degree of democracy, some "government by the people," possible in large political systems. Competitive elections give citizens a chance to shape policy through their selection and rejection of key policymakers. Such indirect democracy is not complete or ideal. Moreover, the democratic opportunities in less economically developed societies are often meaningful to educated elites or to those living near the centers of government, but less relevant to the average citizen in the countryside. But the more citizens are involved and the more influential their choices, the more democratic the system.

In **authoritarian regimes,** in contrast, the policymakers are chosen by military councils, hereditary families, dominant political parties, and the like. Citizens are either ignored or pressed into symbolic assent to the government's choices.

The basic decision rules of political systems—both democratic and authoritarian—differ along three important dimensions:

1. the separation of powers among different branches of government;
2. the geographic distribution of authority between the central (national) government and lower levels, such as states, provinces, or municipalities; and
3. limitations on government authority.

We shall discuss these dimensions in order, beginning with the separation of authority between executive and legislative institutions.

SEPARATION OF GOVERNMENT POWERS

The theory of **separation of powers** between different institutions of government has a long and venerable history going back at least to the work of Locke and Montesquieu.[2] Separation of powers, they argued, has the virtue of preventing the injustices that might result from an unchecked executive or legislature. Madison and Hamilton elaborated this theory in *The Federalist*,[3] which described and defended the institutional arrangements proposed by the U.S. Constitutional Convention of 1787.

Political theorists in the course of the nineteenth and first part of the twentieth centuries drew upon the two successful historical cases of representative democracy—Britain and the United States—to create the "classic" separation of powers theory. This theory argued that there are essentially two forms of representative democratic government: the presidential and the parliamentary.

The **democratic presidential regime** provides two separate agencies of government—the executive and the legislative—separately elected and authorized by the people. (See Table 6.1, column 3.) Each branch is elected for a fixed term; no one branch can by ordinary means unseat the other; and each has specific powers under the constitution. Ultimate power to authorize legislation and approve budgets

Distinguishing Features[a]	Parliamentary Democracies	Presidential Democracies
Title of chief executive	Prime minister (head of government)	President (head of state and government)
Selection of assembly	By citizens in competitive election	By citizens in competitive election
Selection of chief executive	By assembly after election or removal	By citizens in competitive election
Removal of chief executive before fixed term?	By assembly: (No) confidence vote	Fixed terms
Dismissal of assembly before fixed term?	Prime minister may call for early election[b]	Fixed terms
Authority to legislate	Assembly only	Assembly plus president (e.g., veto)
Party relations in assembly and executive	Same parties control both; cohesive party voting	Different party control possible; less cohesive party voting

TABLE 6.1 Distinguishing Features of Parliamentary and Presidential Democracies

[a]These define the pure parliamentary and presidential types; as discussed in the text, many constitutional systems, especially in Eastern Europe, "mix" the features of the two types.

[b]Some constitutional systems that are parliamentary in all other ways do not allow for early legislative elections. All parliamentary democracies provide for legislative elections after some maximum time (from three to five years) since the last election.

in modern democracies resides with the legislature, whose relationships with the executive are then critical for concentration or dispersal of power. Different presidential regimes provide their presidents with a variety of different powers over government appointments and policymaking. For example, some presidents have the authority to veto legislation or to make policy by executive decree under some conditions.[4] In the United States, both the legislature and executive (Congress and the presidency) have large and significant roles in policymaking. In some other democratic presidential systems, such as Brazil, the president may have such a variety of constitutional powers (including the power to make laws through "emergency" decrees) that he or she can reduce the role of the legislature. But coordination between the separate institutions of executive and legislature must somehow be achieved to make policy.

The **parliamentary regimes,** in contrast, make the executive and legislative branches interdependent. (See Table 6.1, column 2.) First of all, only the legislative branch is directly elected. The prime minister and his or her cabinet (the collective leadership of the executive branch) emerge from the legislature. The cabinet is chaired by the prime minister, who is the head of government and selects the other cabinet members.[5] Typically, neither branch has a fixed term of office. The cabinet can be voted out of office at any time, and most often this is true of the legislature (the parliament) as well.

The critical feature that makes this possible is the **confidence relationship** between the prime minister and the parliamentary majority. In a parliamentary system, the prime minister and his or her cabinet must at all times enjoy the confidence of the parliamentary majority. Whenever the parliamentary majority for whatever reason votes a lack of confidence, the prime minister and all the other cabinet members have to resign. At the same time, the prime minister typically has the power to dissolve parliament and call new elections at any time. These two powers—the parliamentary majority's dismissal power and the prime minister's dissolution power—make the two branches mutually dependent. This structure induces agreement between them by forcing each branch to be acceptable to the other.

Prime ministers in parliamentary democracies lead precarious political lives. Unlike presidents in presidential systems, prime ministers can be voted out of office at any time, and for any reason, by a parliamentary majority. There are two ways in which this can happen. One is when parliament passes a motion expressing a lack of confidence in the prime minister—a no-confidence motion. The other possibility is when parliament defeats a motion expressing confidence in the prime minister—a confidence motion. No-confidence motions are typically introduced by the parliamentary opposition in the hope of bringing down the prime minister. Confidence motions, on the other hand, are normally introduced by prime ministers themselves.

Since one possible result of a confidence motion is being kicked out of office, it may seem like a form of Russian roulette. In reality, however, the confidence vote can be a powerful weapon in the hands of the prime minister. It is typically attached to a bill (a policy proposal) the prime minister favors, but the parliamentary majority does not. By attaching a confidence motion to the bill, the prime minister forces the

BOX 6.1

The Confidence Vote in Britain

British prime ministers can resort to the confidence motion in order to bring rebellious party members into line. Usually, the mere threat of a confidence motion is sufficient. But in 1993, Conservative Prime Minister John Major faced a parliamentary crisis over the ratification of the Maastricht Treaty, which expanded the powers of the European Union. Major had only a slim majority in the House of Commons. Many "Euro-skeptics" in his own party were opposed to the Maastricht Treaty. About twenty of these Conservative dissidents voted with the Opposition and helped defeat the Maastricht Treaty in the House of Commons.

Immediately after this embarrassing defeat, however, Major introduced a confidence motion on his Maastricht policy. He announced that if he lost this vote, he would dissolve the House of Commons and hold new elections. Many of the Conservative dissidents feared that their party would do poorly in such an election and that they might personally lose their seats. Prime Minister Major's confidence motion passed by a vote of 339 to 299, and the House of Commons approved the Maastricht Treaty.

Thus, the confidence vote, which is generally available to prime ministers in parliamentary systems, helps explain why party discipline tends to be stronger in parliamentary than in presidential systems.

members of parliament to choose between the bill and the fall of the cabinet. This can be a particularly painful choice for dissident members of the prime minister's own party. If they vote for the bill, they may bring down their own government, and perhaps immediately have to face the voters to boot (see Box 6.1). Thus, the possibility of a confidence motion actually helps explain why party discipline tends to be stronger in parliamentary than in presidential systems.

Thus parliamentary democracies do not experience the form of divided government that is common under presidentialism, when the party that controls the presidency does not control the legislature, or vice versa. Instead, the chief executive (prime minister and cabinet) becomes the agent of the parliamentary majority. In most parliamentary systems the cabinet consists largely of members of parliament. Conflicts between parliament and the executive are less likely to occur and decisionmaking tends to be more efficient than under presidentialism. Since the same party (or parties) controls both branches of government, the cabinet tends to dominate policymaking, and the legislature may be less influential than under a presidential constitution.

Not all democracies fit neatly into the presidential or parliamentary category. Some, such as France, are often characterized as mixed, or **"semipresidential."** In some of these mixed types, the president and the legislature are separately elected (as in presidential systems), but the president then has the power to dissolve the legislature (as in parliamentary systems). In such systems, the cabinet may be appointed by the president (as under presidentialism), but subject to dismissal by the legislature (as under parliamentarism). A variety of arrangements exist for such shared control. Their consequences are often sharply affected by which party or coalition controls the presidency and legislature. Many of the new constitutions of the emergent democracies of Eastern Europe and Asia are of this mixed type.

Reading across Figure 6.1, we see political systems classified by the separation of policymaking powers between executive and legislative institutions, from concentrated to dispersed. The vertical dimension of the table shows geographic division of power, which is discussed in the next section. In authoritarian governments on the left of the figure, executive, legislative, and judicial power are typically concentrated. Two of the twelve countries discussed in this book—China and Iran—have authoritarian governments not chosen in competitive elections. Britain, Germany, Japan, and India are parliamentary systems in which executive and legislative powers are concentrated in cabinets responsible to the popularly elected lower houses of parliament. At the extreme right of Figure 6.1 are pure presidential systems, such as Brazil, Mexico, and the United States. Nigeria seems to be in transition to a presidential democracy. In between, we find mixed systems, such as France and Russia.

In the debate over the best system of representative democracy, many political theorists traditionally favored the British-style parliamentary system. This version of parliamentarism—coupling plurality voting rules that usually create clear single-party majorities in parliament with a cabinet and prime minister responsible to

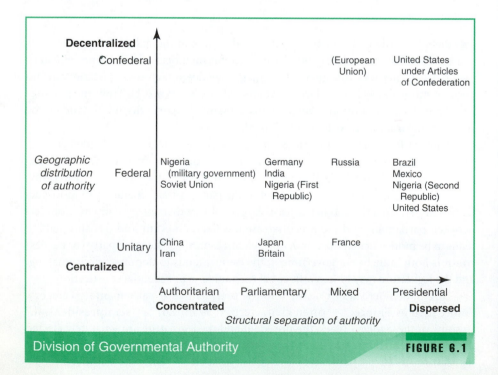

		Concentrated ← Structural separation of authority → Dispersed			
Decentralized Confederal				(European Union)	United States under Articles of Confederation
Geographic distribution of authority	Federal	Nigeria (military government) Soviet Union	Germany India Nigeria (First Republic)	Russia	Brazil Mexico Nigeria (Second Republic) United States
Centralized	Unitary	China Iran	Japan Britain	France	
		Authoritarian **Concentrated**	**Parliamentary**	**Mixed**	**Presidential** **Dispersed**

Structural separation of authority

Division of Governmental Authority   **FIGURE 6.1**

parliament—can result in fairly stable governments responsible to the public will. Parliamentarism coupled with proportional representation—as in Germany and France between the two world wars—seemed more crisis prone. Such crises occurred because of the emergence of large extremist political parties, which resulted in cabinet instability and even breakdown. However, the Scandinavian countries demonstrated that parliamentary systems with proportional representation can be quite stable when ideological conflict between the political parties remains moderate. Moreover, dominating parliamentary majorities, as in Northern Ireland, can sometimes threaten minority groups and intensify conflict.[6] In comparison to both versions of parliamentary government, the U.S. presidential system has often been criticized for periodically producing divided government, which could result in stalemate or "gridlock."

The third wave of democratization reopened these parliamentary-presidential debates. Advocates of parliamentarism, particularly of the proportional variety, argue that it provides a consensual framework in which different economic, ethnic, and religious groups can find representation and negotiate their differences. Parliamentary systems also have the flexibility to change governments between elections if the people disapprove of actions of the executive. Since many of the current transitional democracies are deeply divided, a parliamentary, proportional representation system may be particularly suitable. Presidentialism, they argue, is more susceptible to social conflict and democratic breakdown. Under conditions of divided government, a confrontation between the two legitimately elected institutions representing the people can tear a political system apart. Or, a strong president can use executive powers to repress competition.

Other scholars point out that practical politics is producing presidential systems with significant executive power.[7] Even in the domain of the former British empire (such as in Nigeria) and in most of Eastern Europe and the Soviet successor states, the constitutions provide for powerful presidents. Latin America has been dominated by presidential regimes for more than a century. A 1993 referendum in Brazil reaffirmed its commitment to presidentialism. Presidentialism also offers the citizens a more direct choice of chief executive, and it puts more effective checks on the power of the majority in the legislature.

GEOGRAPHIC DISTRIBUTION OF GOVERNMENT POWER

Another distinction between governmental structures is the geographic division of power: confederal systems at one extreme, unitary systems at the other extreme, and **federal systems** in the middle. (See the vertical dimension of Figure 6.1.) The United States under the Articles of Confederation was confederal. Ultimate power rested with the states. The central government had authority over foreign affairs and defense but depended on financial and other support from the states. Under the Constitution of 1787, the U.S. government changed from confederal to federal, which is to say that both central and state governments had separate spheres of authority and the means to implement their power. Today, the United States,

Germany, Russia, India, Nigeria, Mexico, and Brazil are federal systems in which central and local units each have autonomy in particular spheres of public policy. These policy areas and powers are, however, divided among central and local units in varying ways. Britain, France, China, Japan, and Iran are unitary systems with power and authority concentrated in the central government. Regional and local units have only those powers specifically delegated to them by the central government, which may change or withdraw these powers at will.

Most of the world's states are unitary. In fact, only eighteen states are federal, or fewer than one in ten. Although the federal states are relatively few in number, they tend to be large and politically important. Thus, federal states account for more than one-third of the world's population and 41 percent of its land area. In general, the larger and the more diverse a state is, the more likely it is to be federal.

Federalism is commonly thought to have several advantages. In culturally divided societies, it may help protect ethnic, linguistic, or religious minorities, particularly if they are geographically concentrated. It may serve as a check on overly ambitious rulers and thus protect markets and citizen freedoms. Moreover, federalism may allow subunits (such as states) to experiment with different policy programs. Governments may thus learn from the experiences of others. In addition, citizens may be free to "vote with their feet" and choose the policy environment that best fits their preferences.

While federalism promotes choice and diversity, however, it does so at the expense of equality. Federalism allows local governments to pursue different policies. One implication is that citizens may get systematically different treatments and benefits from different local governments. Unitary governments may also be in a better position to redistribute resources from richer regions to poorer regions, if that is desirable.

In comparing confederal, federal, and unitary systems, we must distinguish between formal and actual distributions of power. In unitary systems, in spite of the formal concentration of authority at the center, regional and local units may acquire power that the central government rarely challenges. In federal systems, centralized party control may overcome apparent regional autonomy. Thus, the real differences between federal and unitary systems may be considerably less significant than their formal arrangements suggest.

Mexico is an example of the discrepancy between formal and actual federalism. Until recently the Partido Revolucionario Institucional (PRI) had centralized control in this formally federal system. Recent developments in Mexico, with oppositional parties winning ground in some states and the PRI power monopoly under challenge, have produced some "real" federalism to go along with the formalities.

LIMITATIONS ON GOVERNMENT POWER

Unlike authoritarian regimes, democracies are characterized by some legal or customary limitation on the exercise of power. Systems in which the powers of various government units are defined and limited by a written constitution, statutes, and custom are called **constitutional regimes.** Civil rights—such as the right to a fair trial and freedom to speak, petition, publish, and assemble—are protected against government interference except under specified circumstances.

The courts are crucial to the limitations on governmental power. As illustrated in Table 6.2, governments may be divided into those, at one extreme, in which the power to coerce citizens is relatively unlimited by the courts, and those, at the other extreme, in which the courts not only protect the rights of citizens but also police other parts of the government to see that their powers are properly exercised. The United States, Germany, and India are systems in which high courts rule effectively on challenges that other parts of the government have exceeded the powers allocated by the constitution. This practice of **judicial review** is authorized to various degrees in about half of the world's democracies and seems to be growing in popularity. But judicial review is often weakened by lack of independence of the appointment or tenure of judges, as in Japan, or by their ineffectiveness in overcoming executive power, as in Russia.

Some other constitutional regimes have independent courts that protect persons against the improper implementation of laws and regulations, but cannot legally overrule the assembly or the political executive, as in Britain. The substantive rights of people in these systems are protected by statute, custom, self-restraint, and political pressure—which are also essential to the effectiveness of courts even where judicial review is authorized. In authoritarian systems, policymakers do not usually allow courts to constrain their use and abuse of power, even where brave judges attempt to rule against them.

Arend Lijphart characterizes only four of the thirty-six democratic systems he examines as having "strong" judicial review: Germany, India, the United States, and Canada after 1982.[8] The Supreme Court of India is most similar to the U.S. Supreme Court, having successfully overruled the prime minister and assembly by declaring over 100 national laws and ordinances to be unconstitutional.[9] The German Constitutional Court also has a substantial impact on national and state policymaking, both through its rulings and through government's anticipation of those rulings.

TABLE 6.2

Judicial Limitation of Governmental Authority

Unlimited		*Limited*
Nonindependent Courts	**Independent Courts**	**Judicial Review**
China	Britain	United States
Iran		India
Nigeria		Germany
		France
		Brazil
		Japan
		Russia

About a quarter of Lijphart's democracies had either strong or medium-strength judicial review. In both France and Germany, new legislation may be challenged in court by opposition members of parliament even before it takes effect, a process called "abstract" judicial review. Lijphart classified a little over half of his democracies as having "weak judicial review," with the powers of courts constrained by very limited constitutional authority (as in Sweden) or limited independence of government-appointed judges (as in Japan). In the remaining democracies, including Britain, courts enjoyed no power of judicial review of legislation, although, as suggested in Table 6.2, they may still protect individuals from government abuse not specifically authorized by law.

In many of the new democracies of Eastern Europe judicial review was proclaimed in the constitution, but proved harder to implement in practice. There have been striking successes in constraining governments in some countries, as in Bulgaria, but failures in others, such as Albania and Belarus. In Nigeria, the courts long retained a striking degree of judicial independence under a succession of otherwise undemocratic military regimes, but were shown little respect under the Abacha regime of the mid-1990s, which established special military tribunals to prosecute its perceived enemies.

China, in contrast, after explicit rejection of any limits on "mass justice" from the late-1950s to the 1970s, has gradually attempted to introduce a very limited "rule by law." This is seen by Chinese rulers as a way to encourage stability and economic growth and control corruption. However, the practice falls far short of the promise of limitation on governmental authority.

All written constitutions provide for amending procedures. Most framers of constitutions have recognized that basic decision rules must be adaptable, because of potential ambiguities, inefficiencies, changes in citizen values, or unforeseen circumstances. But if amendments are too easy to make, they may jeopardize important constitutional protections. Therefore, many constitutions provide that certain arrangements may not be amended (for example, the provision in the U.S. Constitution granting each state equal representation in the Senate).

Amending procedures vary widely, ranging from the complex to the simple. Perhaps the simplest case is that of the United Kingdom, where an ordinary parliamentary statute may alter the constitution. In some cases, constitutional amendments must be approved by a popular vote. The U.S. Constitution has the most difficult formal procedure.

One of the main points of Figure 6.1 and Tables 6.1 and 6.2 is that constitutions may concentrate or disperse government power along several dimensions.[10] There are necessary trade-offs involved in making such constitutional choices. Probably no one who favors democracy and individual liberties would argue for extreme centralization of power in an omnipotent dictator, as in Thomas Hobbes's *Leviathan* (see Chapter 1). However, constitutional democracies that concentrate power to a somewhat lesser degree, such as the British system, have some important advantages. Their governments tend to be effective and efficient, and by relying on majority rule, they tend to treat all citizens equally. No small group can hold up a decision favored by a solid majority. On the other hand, constitutions that disperse power, like more inclusive decision rules, have their own advantages. They are more likely to check potential abuses of power, such as the tyranny of a majority, and policies will tend to be more stable over time.

CHECKING THE TOP POLICYMAKERS

One challenge of government is to control the excesses of top political leaders. In many authoritarian systems, there is no legal and institutionalized way to remove the top political leaders if they become unpopular or overstep whatever bounds they may face. Moreover, authoritarian leaders can usually change or simply ignore the constitution when it restricts their desires. Democracies have various procedures for keeping the leaders in check, but the procedures vary among the types of systems. In parliamentary systems, chief executives can be removed virtually at any time through a vote of no confidence if they lose the support of a parliamentary majority. In Germany, for example, Social Democratic Party Chancellor Helmut Schmidt was ousted by Helmut Kohl of the Christian Democratic Party in October 1982.

Democratic presidential systems fall somewhere in between. Unlike prime ministers under parliamentary constitutions, presidents have fixed terms of office. Most presidential systems provide for the removal of presidents before their term is up, but typically only if they are guilty of serious criminal or other wrongdoing. This procedure is called **impeachment.** Impeachment typically involves three components: (1) impeachable offenses are usually identified as presenting unusual danger to the public good or safety; (2) the penalty is removal from office (sometimes with separate criminal penalties); and (3) impeachment cases are decided by the legislature, but require more than ordinary majorities and may also involve the judiciary in some way. The positive value of impeachment is that it provides a way of legally mobilizing political power against a threat to the constitutional or legal order. At the same time, the danger is that it can be used for mere partisan or personal goals.

In the U.S. system, impeachment procedures can be used against the incumbents in top offices, even the president (as in the cases of Presidents Nixon and Clinton) or a Supreme Court justice, if their activities stray too far beyond legal bounds. No U.S. president has yet been convicted by the Senate and removed from office, although that fate has befallen other federal officials, such as judges.

Impeachment is associated with constitutions having powerful presidencies with fixed terms of office, such as those in the United States, Brazil, South Korea, and the Philippines. Impeachment rules have also been adopted in the constitutions of semi-presidential regimes, such as Russia, and even in purely parliamentary regimes.

In the long run, the ultimate control of democratic order is periodic and competitive elections. This need to achieve and regularly renew their mandates is the fundamental device that leads politicians to respond to the needs and demands of citizens. It is deeply imperfect. It may be difficult to tell when elected officials are incompetent, deceitful, or just unlucky. The complexities of policymaking may baffle the attempt of even trained observers to assign responsibility for successes or failures. The multiplicity of political issues may leave citizens torn between their candidate choices. Or, none of the choices may seem very palatable. Yet, deeply imperfect as it is, this remarkable

Impeachment in Latin America   BOX 6.2

Brazil, Mexico, and many other Latin American nations with strong presidents have impeachment rules and traditions. These were often modeled on the U.S. Constitution. In Mexico, the president, the state governors, and federal judges are subject to impeachment. Brazil has an impeachment process similar to that of the United States, except that it takes a two-thirds vote in the lower house of the assembly to charge the president and other high civil officers with impeachable offenses. A two-thirds vote is also required in the Senate to convict. The clause was invoked in 1992 when Brazil's President Fernando Collor was impeached on charges of large-scale corruption. He resigned before trial in the Senate. Impeachment procedures also forced presidents from office in Venezuela in 1993 and Paraguay in 1999.

recruitment structure gives every citizen some influence on the policymaking process. For this reason, we consider it the most significant democratic structure.

ASSEMBLIES

Legislative **assemblies** have existed for thousands of years. Ancient Greece and Rome had them, as did many other ancient societies. Indeed, the Roman Senate has given its name to modern assemblies in the United States and many other countries.

Almost all contemporary political systems have assemblies, variously called senates, chambers, diets, houses, and the like. Assemblies are also known as "legislatures" (regardless of what role they actually play in legislating) or as "parliaments" (mainly in parliamentary systems). Their formal approval is usually required for major public policies. They are generally elected by popular vote, and hence are at least formally accountable to the citizenry. Today, more than 80 percent of the countries belonging to the United Nations have such governmental bodies. The almost universal adoption of legislative assemblies suggests that in the modern world a legitimate government must formally include a representative popular component.

Assembly Structure

Assemblies vary in their size—from less than 100 to more than 1,000—and their organization. They may consist of one (in which case they are called unicameral) or two (bicameral) chambers. Most democracies, and some authoritarian systems, have bicameral (two-chamber) assemblies. Federal systems normally provide simultaneously for two forms of representation: often representation in one chamber is based on population and representation in the second chamber is based on geographic units. Even in unitary systems (such as France or Japan), **bicameralism** is common, but the purpose of the second chamber is to provide a check on policymaking rather than to represent subnational units. The bicameral U.S. Congress grew out of both federalism and the desire to separate the power of the federal government.

The U.S. system, in which the two chambers have roughly equal powers, is unusual. In most bicameral systems, one chamber is dominant, and the second (such as the Russian Council of the Federation or the French Senate) has more limited powers that are often designed to protect regional interests. While representatives in the dominant chamber are popularly elected, those in the second chamber are sometimes chosen by the regional governments (as in Germany) or in other indirect ways. The prime minister in most parliamentary systems is responsible only to the more popularly elected chamber, which therefore has a more important position in policymaking than the second chamber. (See the discussion of the vote of confidence procedure earlier in this chapter and in Box 6.1.) In such systems members of the prime minister's cabinet are usually chosen from the majority party or parties' leadership in this chamber.

Assemblies also differ in their internal organization in ways that have major consequences for policymaking. There are two kinds of internal legislative organization: party groups and formal assembly subunits (presiding officers, committees, and the like). There is often an inverse relationship between the strength of parties versus other subunits (such as committees). The stronger parties are, the weaker are committees, and vice versa. British members of Parliament vote strictly along party lines much more consistently than members of the U.S. Congress. As in most parliamentary systems, British members of Parliament rarely vote against the instructions of their party leaders. Because cabinets generally hold office only as long as they can command a parliamentary majority, deviating from the party line means risking the fall of the government and new elections.

In presidential systems, the president and the legislators are independently elected for fixed terms of office. Thus the fate of the governing party is less directly tied up with voting on legislative measures. In U.S. legislatures, party discipline operates principally on procedural questions, such as committee assignments or the selection of a presiding officer. On substantive policy issues, Democratic and Republican legislators are freer to decide whether or not to vote with their party leaders.

All assemblies have a committee structure, some organized arrangement that permits legislators to divide up their labor and to specialize in particular issue areas. Without such committees, it would be impossible to handle the large flow of legislative business. As we have seen, however, the importance of committees varies. In some legislatures—such as those in the United States, Japan, and Germany—committees are very influential. This is partially because they are highly specialized, have jurisdictions that match those of the executive departments, and have large staff resources. Strong committees tend to have a clear legislative division of labor that matches the executive branch, allowing for specialized oversight of executive activity. They are often arenas in which the opposition can be influential. British committees are much weaker than their opposite numbers in the United States, since they have small staffs, are dominated by the governing party, and get appointed for one bill at a time. Hence, they cannot accumulate expertise in a particular policy area. German and Japanese committees are stronger than those of Britain but weaker than their American counterparts.[11]

Assembly Functions

Assembly members deliberate, debate, and vote on policies that come before them. Most important policies and rules must be considered and at least formally approved by these bodies before they have the force of law. Assemblies typically also control public spending decisions, so that control of the purse strings (budgeting) is one of their major functions. In addition, some assemblies have important appointment powers, and some (like the British House of Lords in criminal cases) may serve as a court of appeals. Although laws typically need assembly approval, in most countries legislation is actually formulated elsewhere, usually by the political executive and the upper levels of the bureaucracy.

When we compare the importance of assemblies as policymaking agencies, the U.S. Congress, which plays a very active role in the formulation and enactment of legislation, is at one extreme. The other extreme is represented by the National People's Congress of the People's Republic of China, which meets infrequently and does little more than listen to statements by party leaders and rubber-stamp decisions made elsewhere. Roughly midway between the two is the House of Commons in Britain. There, legislative proposals are sometimes initiated or modified by ordinary members of Parliament, but public policy is usually initiated and proposed by members of the Cabinet (who are, to be sure, chosen from the members of the parliamentary body). The typical assembly provides a deliberating forum, formally enacts legislation, and sometimes amends it.

Assemblies should not be viewed only as legislative bodies. All assemblies in democratic systems have an important relationship to legislation, but not necessarily a dominant role. Their political importance is based not just on this function, but also on the great variety of other political functions they perform. Assemblies can play a major role in elite recruitment, especially in parliamentary systems where prime ministers and cabinet members typically serve their apprenticeships in parliament. Legislative committee hearings and floor debates may be important sites for interest articulation and interest aggregation, especially if there is no cohesive majority party. Debates in assemblies can be a source of public information about politics and thus contribute to the socialization of citizens generally and elites in particular.

Representation: Mirroring and Representational Biases

Contemporary legislative assemblies, especially in democratic systems, are valued particularly because they represent the citizens in the national policymaking process. It is not obvious, however, what the ideal linkage between citizens and government officials should be. Some argue that government officials should mirror the characteristics of the citizens as far as possible. This principle, also known as *descriptive representation*, is held to be particularly important with respect to potentially conflictual divisions (such as race, class, ethnicity, gender, language, and perhaps age).

However, descriptive representation is not the only concern in recruiting public officials. The limits of mirroring were inadvertently expressed by a U.S. senator.

In defending a U.S. Supreme Court nominee who was accused of mediocrity, the senator lamely contended, "[E]ven if he were mediocre, there are a lot of mediocre judges and people and lawyers. They are entitled to a little representation, aren't they?"[12] Most people would probably not argue that government officials should mirror the general population in their abilities to do their jobs. Instead, we generally want political elites to be the best possible *agents* for their constituents. In this view, government officials should be selected for their ability to serve the interests of the citizens, whether or not they share the voters' background characteristics.

For politicians to be good agents, they need to have similar *preferences* to the citizens they represent *and* they need the appropriate *skills* to do their jobs. In democracies, political parties are the most important mechanism by which the preferences of citizens and leaders get aligned. As far as skills are concerned, education and experience are the most important factors. Political and governmental leadership—particularly in modern, technologically advanced societies—requires knowledge and skills that are hard to acquire except through education and training. Natural intelligence or experience may, to a limited degree, take the place of formal education.

Hence, it might be a good thing for government officials to be better informed, more intelligent, more experienced, and perhaps better educated than the people who they serve. Just as medical patients tend to look for the most capable physician rather than the one who is most like them, so, one could argue, citizens should look for the best qualified officeholder. In this view, selecting government officials, including representative policymakers, is like delegating to experts. It may be a hopeful sign that citizens in many modern democracies are increasingly willing to select leaders who do not share their background characteristics.

As in the case of so many other political choices, there is no obvious or perfect way to choose between mirroring and expert delegation. This is an old debate, and in many situations it is necessary to make a trade-off between the two. And different offices may require different considerations. Most people would, for example, probably put a higher emphasis on mirroring in their local assembly than in a regulatory agency overseeing nuclear technology.

The bad news is that political elites, even democratically elected members of legislative assemblies, hardly ever mirror the citizens they represent on any of the standard social characteristics. Even in democracies such as the United States, Britain, and France, political leaders tend to be of middle- or upper-class background or unusually well-educated and upwardly mobile individuals from the lower classes. There are exceptions. In some countries, trade unions or leftist political parties may serve as channels of political advancement for people with modest economic or educational backgrounds. These representatives acquire political skills and experience by holding offices in working-class organizations. Thus the Labour Party delegation in the British House of Commons and the Communist delegation in the French National Assembly have included substantial numbers of workers. And during the long domination of the executive by the Norwegian Labor Party (1935–1981), none of its prime ministers had even completed secondary school. But these are rare and vanishing examples. In most contemporary states, the number of working-class people in high office is small and declining.

Women have also been poorly represented in political leadership positions in most countries. History certainly offers examples of strong and influential female rulers, such as Queen Elizabeth I of England (who ruled from 1558 to 1603). Yet in most countries women did not have the right to vote until well into the twentieth century and have not held many political leadership positions.

That situation has changed significantly in the last twenty-five years. In 1980, women on average held fewer than 10 percent of the parliamentary seats in the advanced industrial democracies. By 1990, that figure was up to about 15 percent, and by 1997 women had surpassed 20 percent. Women have also held the chief executive office in a growing number of countries, particularly in Europe and Asia. (See Box 6.3.) Angela Merkel, for example, became chancellor of Germany in 2005.

But women's advancement has been uneven, and their representation remains low in the developing world. In many Northern European countries, such as Sweden,

Women as Chief Executives

BOX 6.3

From about 1970 on, women have gained chief executive office in a growing number of countries. Interestingly, many of them have been from Asian and Middle Eastern countries, where women's roles in public life traditionally have been limited. Sinmavo Bandaranaike of Sri Lanka (1960–1965 and 1970–1977), Indira Gandhi of India (1966–1977 and 1980–1984), and Golda Meir of Israel (1969–1974) were among the pioneers. In the 1980s and 1990s, women also came to power in the Philippines, Pakistan, Bangladesh, and again in Sri Lanka. In Burma, Nobel Peace Prize winner Aung San Suu Kyi won the elections of 1990 but the military prevented her from taking office.

Women have also made inroads in leadership positions in Europe and North America, though they are still few and far between in Africa and Latin America. The first female leader in a major European country was Prime Minister Margaret Thatcher of Britain (1979–1990). Her strong and decisive leadership made her one of Europe's most influential politicians in the 1980s. Women have come to power in other western countries as well. Ireland and Iceland have had female presidents. Canada, France, and Switzerland have had brief stints with female prime ministers. Angela Merkel is chancellor of Germany. In Norway, Gro Harlem Brundtland held the prime ministership for a total of about ten years between 1981 and 1996. Brundtland, a physician and environmentalist, later headed the World Health Organization.

The career paths of Asian women leaders have tended to differ from those in Europe. Many of the former have come from prominent political families, such as the Gandhi family in India and the Bhuttos in Pakistan. In several cases, they have been the widows or daughters of important political leaders. In Europe, women leaders are more likely to have made independent political careers, and they can rely on stronger women's interest groups.

women by the late 1990s accounted for 30 to 40 percent of the legislators and a similar proportion of cabinet members. But in Russia, Mexico, Brazil, and Japan, women still accounted for fewer than one legislator in ten in the 1990s.[13]

Political elites also tend to be unrepresentative with respect to age. In many countries, legislators (much less chief executives) under age 40 are a rarity, whereas a large proportion of leading politicians are past normal retirement age. Japan is an extreme example. In 1990, there were about eight legislators over age 60 for every one member under age 40. In many countries, university graduates—and often lawyers and civil servants in particular—are vastly overrepresented, whereas ethnic, linguistic, and religious minorities are often underrepresented. Representational biases are thus numerous and pervasive. And while women's representation is increasing, class biases are getting worse.

POLITICAL EXECUTIVES

In modern states, the executive branch is by far the largest, the most complex, and typically the most powerful branch of government. It is not easy to describe executives in simple ways, but it is sensible to start at the top. Governments typically have one or two **chief executives,** officials who sit at the very top of the often-colossal executive branch. Such executives have various names, titles, duties, and powers. They are called presidents, prime ministers, chancellors, secretaries general, or even leader (in Iran.) There are even a few kings who still have genuine power. Titles may mislead us as to what functions these officials perform, but they tend to be the main formulators and executors of public policy.

Structure of the Chief Executive

Democratic governments typically feature either a single chief executive (in presidential systems) or a split chief executive of two offices: a largely ceremonial head of state (who represents the nation on formal occasions) and a more powerful head of government, (who determines public policies). Table 6.3 distinguishes among executives according to the bases of their power to affect policymaking. In the left column we see the chief executives in authoritarian systems, whose power ultimately rests on coercion. The middle and right columns show the chief executives in democratic countries. The middle column shows executives whose power rests primarily on their partisan influence in the legislature, which is the case of the prime ministers in most parliamentary systems. The right column includes chief executives whose ability to influence legislation resides in powers directly granted them by the constitution, rather than partisan connection alone. Strong presidents may be able to veto legislation, for example, issue legal decrees, or introduce the budget. They usually have the power to appoint and dismiss members of the cabinet.

Reading down the table, we see the distinction between executives with effective power over policy, purely ceremonial roles, or both effective and ceremonial power. Political executives are effective only if they have genuine discretion in the enactment and implementation of laws and regulations, in budgetary matters, or in important government appointments. Where they do not have these powers, they are symbolic or ceremonial. In presidential systems, the ceremonial and effective roles are almost always held by the same person, the president, as we see in both authoritarian and democratic systems at the bottom of Table 6.3. In parliamentary democratic systems, and in some authoritarian systems, the two roles are separated between the "head of state," who is primarily a ceremonial official, and a "head of government," who makes and implements the decisions. The British, German, Indian, and Japanese prime ministers appear in column two at the top right of the table, while their ceremonial counterparts appear at the center right.

These distinctions are not absolute. Some constitutions, such as the German, give substantial formal powers to their prime ministers. At the same time even largely ceremonial presidents can exert important influence if the parties are divided or by exercising special constitutional powers (or both, as has recently happened in India). Moreover, partisan influence in the legislature is useful even to the strongest democratic presidents. Still, it is usually easy to determine the primary sources of legislative power, even where the formal names may be misleading.

Bases of Legislative Power of Chief Executives

TABLE 6.3

Authoritarian	Democratic: Partisan Influence	Democratic: Constitutional Powers
Effective		
General Secretary, China	British Prime Minister	
	French Prime Minister	
	German Chancellor	
	Indian Prime Minister	
	Japanese Prime Minister	
	(Russian Prime Minister)	
Ceremonial		
Chinese President		British Queen
		German President
		Indian President
		Japanese Emperor
Ceremonial and Effective		
Iranian Leader	French President	Brazilian President
		Mexican President
		Nigerian President
		Russian President
		U.S. President

As noted earlier, a few countries, such as France and Russia, have both significant presidents and prime ministers. The balance of power between them depends on the constitutional powers of the president and on the partisan division in the legislature. In Russia, the constitutional powers of veto and decree of the president are very great, and the legislature has seldom been unified against him; the prime minister is mostly just another administrator, with little effective power. In France, however, the president's formal powers are much weaker; when the legislature is unified under opposition parties it has elected a prime minister who has effectively dominated policymaking, greatly reducing the president's political influence.

In China the chairman of the Communist Party is the most powerful political figure and the effective chief executive. The Chinese president is the head of state, which is a purely ceremonial role, without associated powers. However, in recent years the same individual (Jiang Zemin and now Hu Jintao) has held both offices, and also a key role as chairman of the party military commission. A third role was the premier, or head of government, which was a largely administrative position.

Monarchies are much more rare at the beginning of the twenty-first century than they were at the beginning of the twentieth. Some monarchs, such as the king of Saudi Arabia and some other Arab monarchs, still exercise real power. Most contemporary monarchs, however, have little or no actual political influence. Monarchs like the British queen or the Scandinavian kings are principally ceremonial and symbolic officers with very occasional political powers. They are living symbols of the state and nation and of their historical continuity. Britain's queen may bestow honors or peerages (appointments to the nobility) with a stroke of her scepter, but these are recommended by the prime minister. The Japanese monarchy has also traditionally been dignified and exalted and played an important role as a national symbol. In contrast, the Scandinavian and Low Country monarchies are more humdrum. Because members of these royal families occasionally use more humble means of transportation, these dynasties are sometimes called "bicycle monarchies." In republican democracies with parliamentary systems, presidents perform the functions that fall to kings and queens in parliamentary monarchies. Thus German presidents give speeches on important anniversaries and designate prime ministers after elections or when a government has resigned.

A system in which the ceremonial executive is separated from the effective executive has a number of advantages. The ceremonial executive symbolizes unity and continuity and can be above politics. The U.S. presidency, which combines both effective and ceremonial functions, runs the risk that the president will use his ceremonial and symbolic authority to enhance his political power or that his involvement in politics may make him a less effective symbolic or unifying figure.

Recruitment of Chief Executives

Historically, finding generally acceptable ways to select the individuals to fill the top policymaking roles has been critical to political order and stability. A major accomplishment of stable democracies is regulating the potential conflict involved in

Recruitment of Chief Executive

TABLE 6.4

Country	Chief Executive Structure	Recruitment Structures	How Often Has This Type of Government Survived Succession?[b]
Brazil	President	Party and voters	Often
Britain	Prime minister	Party, House of Commons, voters	Very often
China	Party secretary[a]	Party and military	Often
France	President/Prime minister	Party, (Assembly) voters	Often
Germany	Chancellor	Party, Bundestag, voters	Often
India	Prime minister	Party, Lok Sabha, voters	Often (one interruption)
Iran	Leader, President	Religious elites, voters	Once
Japan	Prime minister	Party, Diet, voters	Often
Mexico	President	Party and voters	Twice
Nigeria	President	Military, party, voters	Never
Russia	President	Party and voters	Once
United States	President	Party and voters	Very often

[a]"Party secretary" refers to that position or to a similar one as head of party in a communist regime.

[b]"Often" means that at least three successions have taken place under that type of government.

leadership succession and confining it to the mobilization of votes instead of weapons. When we refer generally to "recruitment structures," we are thinking of how nations choose their top policymakers and executives. Table 6.4 shows the recruitment structures in the countries selected for this book.

The most familiar structures are the presidential and parliamentary forms of competitive party systems. In presidential systems, as in Brazil and the United States, parties select candidates for nomination, and the electorate chooses among them. Russia and France have directly elected presidents but also give an important role to the prime minister, who is appointed by the president but can be removed by the legislature.

Mexico appears similar to other presidential systems. But for half a century the Partido Revolucionario Institucional (PRI) had such control over the electoral process that the voters merely ratified the party's presidential nominee. That nomination itself was announced by the outgoing president after complex bargaining between party factions and other powerful groups. Mexico seemed to be moving to give the voters an honest role in choosing between alternative candidates, but until the remarkable July 2000 election many voters remained skeptical that a non-PRI president could really come to power. As the table shows, Mexico now seems a newly democratic presidential system, with parties nominating candidates and voters genuinely choosing among them, as in the very close election of 2006.

In both presidential and parliamentary democracies the tenure of the chief executive is limited, directly or indirectly. In the presidential system this is usually directly, through fixed terms of office for the chief executive. In the parliamentary system there is a maximum term for the parliament, which then indirectly also limits the life of the cabinet, since the prime minister is accountable to the new parliamentary majority and can be removed by it.

Table 6.4 also illustrates the role of noncompetitive parties and military organizations in China, the military in Nigeria, and nonelected religious elites in Iran. The important role played by political parties illustrates the great need to mobilize broad political support behind the selection of chief executives. The frequent appearance of parties also reflects, no doubt, the modern legitimacy of popular sovereignty: the promise that the rulers' actions will be in the interest of the ruled.

Authoritarian systems rarely have effective procedures for leadership succession. The more power is concentrated at the top, the riskier it is to transfer it from one person to the next. Very often, authoritarian leaders do not dare to relinquish their power, and leadership succession occurs only when they die or are overthrown. In communist regimes, the Communist Party selected the general secretary (or equivalent), who was the controlling executive force. Individual succession was not a simple matter. These systems did not limit the terms of incumbents, who were difficult to oust once they had consolidated their supporters into key party positions. Nonetheless, they always had to be aware of the possibility of a party coup of the type that ousted Nikita Khrushchev from the Soviet leadership in 1964. As a system, however, the Soviet leadership structure seemed quite stable until the dramatic 1991 coup attempt against Gorbachev. Although he was briefly restored to power, the events surrounding the coup stripped the Soviet presidency of power, and legitimacy passed to the presidencies and legislatures of the fifteen constituent republics, most importantly to President Boris Yeltsin of Russia. Russia managed its first democratic transition surprisingly smoothly, from Yeltsin to his chosen successor Vladimir Putin, who was elected as the new president in April 2000 and reelected in 2004.

The poorer nations show substantially less stability, and the regimes have usually had less experience at surviving succession crises.[14] Nigeria is typical. It experienced a succession of military coups and governments from 1966 until 1979, then introduced a competitive presidential system, which was overthrown by a military coup shortly after its second election in 1983. The military government again moved toward civilian rule in the early 1990s but then annulled the 1993 presidential election before the results were announced. The military rulers finally allowed a return to civilian rule in 1999.

Many African nations experienced repeated coups. Military governments, stable or unstable, have also been common in Latin America and the Middle East, although they are now more likely to dominate in coalition or from behind the scenes.

(See Chapter 5.) The Chinese Communist Party has remained in power for fifty years but has suffered several periods of internal strife, and the army has been involved in recruitment at all levels. India's democracy, having persisted through assassinations and other crises, has been an exception to the rule among poorer nations. It has provided a number of democratic successions with a single interruption (authoritarian emergency rule that postponed elections for several years) in the 1970s.

The Cabinet

In many political systems, the **cabinet** is the most important collective decisionmaking body. Its power can be particularly great in parliamentary systems, where its formation is closely linked to selection of the prime minister. It typically contains the leaders (often called "ministers" or "secretaries of state") of all the major departments (sometimes called "ministries") into which the executive branch is divided. The cabinet meets frequently, often several times per week. It is typically selected and led by the head of government: the president in presidential systems and the prime minister in parliamentary ones. In some parliamentary systems, the entire cabinet is collectively responsible to the legislature. The prime minister may be little more than "first among equals," especially under conditions of multiparty coalition governments. In other parliamentary systems, such as Germany, the constitution confers much more authority on the prime minister.[15]

How does the cabinet get selected? In presidential systems, selecting cabinet members is typically a presidential prerogative, though sometimes (as with the U.S. Senate), the legislature has to give its approval. The president can typically also dismiss cabinet members at will, whereas the legislature's ability to do so is most often severely limited.

In parliamentary systems, in contrast, the process is very different, since the prime minister and his or her cabinet need to maintain the confidence of the parliamentary majority. Therefore, cabinet formation depends on the result of parliamentary elections and on the composition of parliament. If a competitive party wins a parliamentary majority by itself, it will (if unified) be able to form a cabinet of its own members and can then pass and implement its policies. Sometimes the election directly determines who controls the majority. This will always be the case in pure two-party systems, where one party or the other will always have a parliamentary majority. It can also happen in multiparty systems, whenever one party gets more seats than all its competitors combined. But the more parties there are, the less likely it is that one of them will have a majority on its own. We call the outcome in which one party controls a parliamentary majority by itself a majority situation. Whenever majority situations occur in parliamentary systems, the majority party almost always forms a *majority single-party cabinet* by itself.

Far more often, no party wins a majority of votes. In most multiparty countries, the typical election result is that no party has a parliamentary majority by itself—a minority situation. Most commonly under such circumstances, several parties (two, three, or as many as six or seven) join forces and form a *coalition cabinet* in which they are all represented. Sometimes, parties anticipate this need to form coalitions before the election. They may then make a formal agreement with one another and inform the voters that they intend to govern together if they collectively get enough votes. The allied parties may thus encourage their voters to support the coalition partners' candidates where their own party's candidates seem weak and often take advantage of special provisions of voting laws. Many German and French governments have come to power in this fashion. In such cases, the voters can have a direct voice in the choice of the future cabinet, much as they do in two-party systems. Voters are thus given a major role in choosing the direction of government policy.

But parties often do not make such preelection commitments. Even when they do, they often fail to get the support they would need to control a parliamentary majority. If no party or preelection coalition wins control of the legislature through the election, then parties may bargain after the election, or between elections, to form a new cabinet. In the Netherlands, such bargaining took four months after the 2003 election. In Germany, about three weeks of bargaining was necessary to form a "grand coalition" of the two largest parties after the 2005 parliamentary election.

Whether bargaining takes place before or after the elections, the parties in parliamentary systems typically have a lot of options concerning the composition of the cabinet. In minority situations, the result can be either a minority government or a majority coalition of several parties. In some cases, a single party decides that it can form a minority cabinet alone, often because the other parties disagree too much among themselves to offer any alternative. Figure 6.2 illustrates these various possibilities. In the minority case, the parties in the cabinet must continually bargain with other parties to get policies adopted and even to remain in office. In majority coalitions, bargaining will take place primarily among coalition partners represented in the cabinet. In both of these circumstances, the power of the prime minister may depend on the bargains he or she can strike with leaders of other parties.

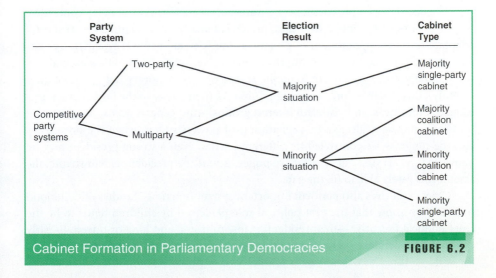

Cabinet Formation in Parliamentary Democracies   FIGURE 6.2

These complications illustrate two of the problems of combining parliamentary government with electoral systems of proportional representation. Such systems tend to produce minority situations, which do not give the voters a very clear choice about who will control the executive branch. Instead, the parties may determine this behind closed doors after the election. Sometimes, the results are paradoxical, as when parties that have just lost votes in the elections are able to negotiate their way into a governing coalition. The second problem is that under minority situations, cabinets are sometimes unstable. Italy, for example, has had on average more than one change of government per year since World War II. Yet, such problems need not always emerge. In Germany, for example, cabinets have been quite stable, and the voters have generally been given fairly clear options ahead of elections.

Functions of the Chief Executive

Typically, the chief executive is the most important structure in policymaking. The executive normally initiates new policies. Depending on the division of powers with the legislature and the partisan balance, the executive also has a substantial part in their adoption. In presidential systems, the president very often has veto powers. Thus the chief executive not only has the first word in policymaking, he or she also typically has the last word. In parliamentary systems, on the other hand, the chief executive is less likely to be able to exercise a veto.

The political executive also oversees policy implementation and can hold subordinate officials accountable for their performance. The central decisions in a foreign policy crisis are generally made by the chief executive: the president (George W. Bush in the Iraq War) or the prime minister (Tony Blair in the Iraq War). Political initiatives and new programs typically originate in the executive. A bureaucracy without an effective executive tends to implement past policies, rather than to initiate new ones. Without politically motivated ministers, bureaucracies tend toward inertia.

The decision of a president, prime minister, cabinet, or central party committee to pursue a new foreign or domestic policy is usually accompanied by structural adaptations—the appointment of a vigorous minister, an increase in staff, the establishment of a special cabinet committee, and the like. Where the political executive is weak and divided, as in Fourth Republic France or contemporary Italy (at least until recently), this dynamic force is missing. Initiative then passes to the bureaucracy, legislative committees, and powerful interest groups—and general needs, interests, and problems may be neglected. In a separation-of-powers system when the presidency and the congress are controlled by different parties, even a strong president may be hampered in carrying out an effective policy. And if the president is hamstrung, the assembly is rarely able to fill the gap.

Chief executives also perform important system functions. Studies of childhood socialization show that the first political role perceived by children tends to be the chief political executive—the president, prime minister, and king or queen. In early childhood the tendency is to identify the top political executive as a parent figure. As the child matures, he or she begins to differentiate political from other roles, as well as to differentiate among various political roles (see Chapter 3). The conduct of the chief executive affects the trust and confidence that young people feel in the whole political system and they carry that with them into adulthood. The role of the chief executive in recruitment is obviously important, appointing the cabinet and other officials. The political executive also plays a central role in communication, in explaining and building support for new policies, or in improving performance in various sectors of the society and economy.

THE BUREAUCRACY

Modern societies are dominated by large organizations, and the largest contemporary organizations are government **bureaucracies,** or their systems of public administration. These agencies, by which we mean all the members of the executive branch below the top executive (president/monarch, prime minister, and cabinet) are generally in charge of implementing government policy. The size of government bureaucracies increased over the course of the twentieth century. This is partly due to the efforts of governments to improve the health, productivity, welfare, and security of their populations. It may also be partly due to the tendency for government agencies, once they have been established, to seek growth for its own sake. In reaction to this tendency, and as part of the concern about government inefficiencies, there has been a recent movement to reduce government budgets and to downsize the bureaucracy (see Chapter 7).

Structure of the Bureaucracy

The most important officials in bureaucracies are the experienced and expert personnel of the top **civil service.** The British "government," which we can think of as its top executive positions, consists of approximately 100 "frontbench" members of Parliament, some twenty of whom serve in the Cabinet, with the remainder named as ministers, junior ministers, and parliamentary secretaries. This relatively small group of political policymakers oversees some 3,000 permanent members of the **higher civil service,** largely recruited directly from the universities. They spend their lives as an elite corps, moving about from ministry to ministry, watching governments come and go, and becoming increasingly important as policymakers as they rise in rank. Below the higher civil service are a huge body of more than half a million permanent public employees, ordinary civil servants, organized into about twenty government departments and a number of other agencies. The total number of British civil servants rose from 100,000 in 1900 to more than 700,000 in 1979, but it then declined to under 500,000 under Conservative governments of the 1980s and 1990s.

The importance of the permanent higher civil service is not unique to Britain, though perhaps it has been most fully institutionalized there. In France, too, the higher civil service is filled with powerful generalists who can bring long tenure, experience, and technical knowledge to their particular tasks. In the United States, many top positions go to presidential appointees rather than to permanent civil servants. Despite this difference and a greater emphasis on technical specialization, there are permanent civil servants in the key positions just below the top appointees in such agencies as the Internal Revenue Service, the Federal Bureau of Investigation, the Central Intelligence Agency, the National Institutes of Health, and all the cabinet departments. These people tend to be specialists—such as military officers, diplomats, doctors, scientists, economists, and engineers—who exert great influence on policy formulation and execution in their specialties. Below these specialists and administrators are the vast numbers of ordinary government employees, postal workers, teachers, welfare case agents, and so forth, who see that governmental policies are put into practice. In 2004, the United States had 22 million public employees of all kinds, federal, state, and local, or about 17 percent of the total labor force. In many European countries, that proportion is even higher, approaching a third of the labor force in Norway, Denmark, and Sweden.

The Functions of the Bureaucracy

Bureaucracies have great significance in most contemporary societies. One reason is that the bureaucracy is almost alone in implementing and enforcing laws and regulations. In so doing, they may have quite a bit of discretion. Most modern legislation is general and can be effectively enforced only if administrative officials work out its detail and implementation. Policy implementation and enforcement usually depend on bureaucrats' interpretations and on the spirit and effectiveness with which they put policies into practice. But the power of bureaucracies is not restricted to their implementation and enforcement of rules made by others. In Chapters 4 and 5 we discussed how bureaucratic agencies may articulate and aggregate interests. Departments like those for agriculture, labor, defense, welfare, and education may be among the most important voices of interest groups. Moreover, administrative agencies in modern political systems do a lot of adjudication. Tax authorities, for example, routinely determine whether citizens have faithfully reported their income and paid their taxes, and these authorities assess penalties accordingly. While citizens may in principle be able to appeal such rulings to the courts, relatively few actually do.

Finally, bureaucracies are involved in communication. Political elites, whether executives or legislators, base many of their decisions on the information they obtain from the public administration. Similarly, interest groups, political parties, the business elites, and the public depend on such information. Most major agencies in modern governments have spokespersons whose job it is to inform and influence the media. With the increasing media power in modern societies, top government executives are eager to present their versions of events. Increasingly, however, large parts of the journalistic professions refuse to recognize any limits on the publication of private as well as political information. Leaks of secret or confidential information and intelligence have become a veritable flood. Thus political executives and bureaucracies can no longer control information in the ways that they formerly did. In dealing with the media, top administrators now must have more complex strategies and professional assistance. The art of "spin control" has replaced their reliance on classification and "executive privilege."

Bureaucracy and Performance

We commonly use the term "bureaucracy" to refer to all systems of public administration. Strictly speaking, however, bureaucracy refers to a particular way of organizing such agencies, a practice that gained favor in the latter part of the nineteenth century and the beginning of the twentieth century. According to the classical German sociologist Max Weber, bureaucracies have the following features:

1. Decisionmaking is based on fixed and official jurisdictions, rules, and regulations.
2. There are formal and specialized educational or training requirements for each position.
3. There is a hierarchical command structure: a firmly ordered system of super- and subordination, in which information flows upward and decisions downward.
4. Decisions are made on the basis of standard operating procedures, which include extensive written records.
5. Officials hold career positions, are appointed and promoted on the basis of merit, and have protection against political interference, notably in the form of permanent job tenure.[16]

No organization is perfectly bureaucratic in this sense, but professional armies come reasonably close, as do tax revenue departments.

These features of bureaucracies have a number of desirable effects. They promote competence, consistency, fair treatment, and freedom from political manipulation. Imagine what life could be like without bureaucracies. Before the advent of modern bureaucracy, public officials were often a sorry lot. Some of them inherited their jobs; others got them through family or political connections. Yet others bought their posts and used them either to enrich themselves or gain social status (or both). Many saw their jobs strictly as a sideline and devoted little time to their duties. No wonder, then, that public officials were often incompetent, uninterested in their jobs, corrupt, or all of the above. They often used their powers arbitrarily, to favor friends and neighbors, and to the disadvantage of others. Given the lack of rules and records, aggrieved citizens typically had few recourses.

But the negative connotations that the word "bureaucracy" has taken on suggest that such organizations have liabilities as well. Bureaucratic organizations can become stodgy, rule-bound, inflexible, and insensitive to the needs of their clients. In many cases, bureaucrats also have few incentives to be innovative and efficient, or even to work very hard. Although bureaucracies are supposed to be politically and ideologically neutral, in fact they tend to be influenced by the dominant ideologies of the time, to have conservative propensities, and to pursue institutional interests of their own.[17] Many citizens are exasperated with bureaucracy and its propensities for inefficiency and lack of responsiveness. This frustration is reflected in popular cynicism as well as in periodic attempts to reform government.

Mark Nadel and Francis Rourke suggest a variety of ways that government and societal agencies may influence and control bureaucracies, externally or internally.[18] The major external government control is the political executive. Although presidents, prime ministers, and ministers formally command subordinate officials and may have the power to remove them for nonperformance of duty, executives and bureaucracies actually depend on one another. Top executives typically try to persuade; rarely do they go to the extreme of dismissing or transferring civil servants. Centralized budgeting and administrative reorganization are other means of executive control. The threat to take away resources or authority may bring bureaucratic implementation into greater conformity with the aims of the political executive.

Modern authoritarian systems discovered that the bureaucracy was an essential tool of government control. Thus, recruitment of the bureaucracy was part of a larger pattern of control. Bureaucratic selection in the former Soviet Union, as in China today, was controlled through a device called *nomenklatura*. Under this procedure important positions were kept under the direct supervision of a party agency whose officials had the final word on recruitment. Moreover, the party offered a complicated set of inducements to control the behavior of the chosen officials. These inducements made it difficult for any but the topmost officials to have much freedom of action. Soviet leaders used normative incentives (such as appeals to party, ideology, and national idealism), financial incentives (such as better salaries, access to finer food and clothing, better housing, and freedom to travel), and coercive control (such as reporting by police, party, and bureaucrats). They used demotion or imprisonment, even execution, as penalties. To avoid a coup by police or military forces, the varied layers of command and inducement structures were interwoven, so that no layer could act independently.

In democracies, assemblies and courts also help control the bureaucracy. Legislative committee hearings or judicial investigations may bring bureaucratic performance into line with political desires. Sweden invented the institution of the **ombudsman** to prevent bureaucrats from doing injury or injustice to individuals.[19] This invention has been copied by other states. In the Scandinavian countries, Britain, Germany, and elsewhere ombudsmen now investigate citizen claims that they have suffered injury or damage as a result of government action. Ombudsmen typically have no power of their own, but report to the legislature for remedial action. Their cases rarely lead to criminal conviction, but often government officials change their policies as a result of embarrassing publicity. Thus, ombudsmen offer a more expeditious and less costly procedure than court action. Among the extragovernmental forces that constrain bureaucracies are public opinion and the mass media, as well as interest groups of various kinds.

All such controls on civil servants tend to be less effective outside the advanced industrial democracies. Authoritarian systems lack many of these controls, particularly external ones, such as elected political executives and legislators, independent courts, free mass media, and interest groups. Therefore, authoritarian regimes are particularly prone to bureaucratic inefficiency and inertia. Moreover, in many nonindustrial countries, mass media are neither independent nor influential, few citizens participate in politics, and lower level government employees are poorly trained and paid—all conditions that encourage bribery, extortion, and bureaucratic mismanagement.[20]

Successful democracy requires that public policies made by national assemblies and chief executives be implemented fairly and effectively; democracy depends on the rule of law. When ruling parties demand kickbacks of public money from construction firms seeking public works contracts, the democratic process is subverted by rent-seeking politicians. (See Chapter 1 and Box 1.2.) Similarly, when tax officials and border authorities are open to cash payments to overlook tax deficiencies and customs violations, democratic law making is undermined. Citizens who must bribe teachers to get education for their children or health officials to get immunizations are deprived of the benefits of democratic public policies. Such practices are all too common in the poorer nations of the world.

Failure of the rule of law is difficult to study systematically, but some comparative insight into corruption in public bureaucracies is provided by the surveys of perceptions of corruption on the part of businesspeople, academics, and analysts in different countries. These have been combined into the Corruption Perceptions Index, which rates about one hundred countries each year on a scale from 0 ("highly corrupt") to 10 ("highly clean"). Figure 6.3 shows on the vertical dimension the ratings for 2005 (based on a three-year moving average) of the twelve countries studied in this book.

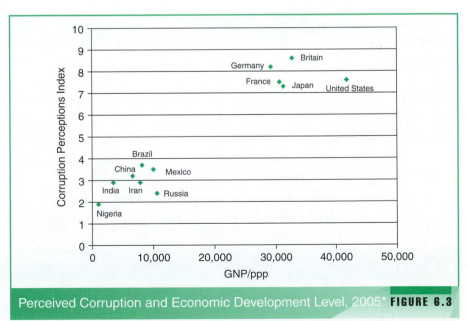

Perceived Corruption and Economic Development Level, 2005* **FIGURE 6.3**

*Economic development level from World Bank, downloaded from www.worldbank.org/data on July 6, 2006; Corruption Perception, Index from Transparency International, downloaded from www. transparency. org/ cpi/ index on July 6, 2006.

As we see, all of the countries experience some levels of corruption. The world's top-rated country in 2005 was Iceland at 9.7. But Britain, Germany, the United States, France, and Japan (despite individually notorious cases in each), rated in the top half of the scale. Brazil, Mexico, China, Iran, and India are far more corrupt, with scores in the low range of the scale. Russia, plagued by many problems of its dual economic and political transitions, scores even worse. Nigeria, despite its recent efforts at democratic transition, is perceived as one of the world's most corrupt countries.

We can compare the perceived corruption scores with the purchasing power parity (PPP) measure of economic wealth and productivity on the horizontal dimension of Figure 6.3. This comparison shows that corruption and the failure of the rule of law are very strongly associated with poverty and underdevelopment, as well as with direct indicators of widespread misery (see also Table 1.3 in Chapter 1).[21] However, some individual countries do better or worse than we might expect. For example, Russia is somewhat more corrupt than we would expect from its middle-level income.

The ills of bureaucracy, including inefficiency and inertia, are pandemic. This is truly a dilemma because we are unlikely to invent any schemes for carrying out large-scale social tasks without the organization, division of labor, and professionalism that bureaucracy provides. Its pathologies can only be mitigated. The art of modern political leadership consists not only of defining and communicating appropriate goals and policies, but also of getting them implemented by a massive and complex bureaucracy—how and when to press and coerce it, reorganize it, reward it, teach it, or be taught by it.

REVIEW QUESTIONS

- What are the advantages of more inclusive decision rules in making policies? What are the disadvantages?
- Why is the confidence relationship so important in parliamentary democracies?
- In what different ways can policymaking power be dispersed and limited by constitutional arrangements?
- What are the advantages and disadvantages of assembly representation that mirrors the characteristics of citizens?
- How are cabinets formed after national elections in parliamentary systems?
- Why are bureaucracies necessary but sometimes liabilities in policymaking?

KEY TERMS

assemblies
authoritarian regimes
bicameralism
bureaucracies
cabinet
chief executives
civil service
confidence relationship
constitutional regimes
decision rules
democracy

democratic presidential regime

federal systems

higher civil service

impeachment

judicial review

ombudsman

parliamentary regimes

policymaking

semipresidential regime

separation of powers

SUGGESTED READINGS

Aberbach, Joel, Robert D. Putnam, and Bert A. Rockman. *Bureaucrats and Politicians in Western Democracies.* Cambridge: Harvard University Press, 1981.

Döring, Herbert, ed. *Parliaments and Majority Rule in Western Europe.* New York: St. Martin's Press, 1995.

Huber, John D. *Rationalizing Parliament.* Cambridge: Cambridge University Press, 1996.

Laver, Michael, and Norman Schofield. *Multiparty Government: The Politics of Coalition in Europe.* Ann Arbor: University of Michigan Press, 1998.

Lijphart, Arend. *Democracy in Plural Societies.* New Haven, CT: Yale University Press, 1977.

———. *Patterns of Democracy: Government Forms and Performance in Thirty-Six Countries.* New Haven, CT: Yale University Press, 1999.

Linz, Juan, and Arturo Valenzuela, eds. *The Failure of Presidential Democracy: Comparative Perspectives.* Baltimore: Johns Hopkins University Press, 1994.

Mainwaring, Scott, and Matthew Shugart, eds. *Presidentialism and Democracy in Latin America.* New York: Cambridge University Press, 1997.

North, Douglass. *Institutions, Institutional Change, and Economic Performance.* Cambridge: Cambridge University Press, 1990.

Powell, G. Bingham. *Contemporary Democracies.* Cambridge: Harvard University Press, 1982.

Riker, William H. *Federalism: Origin, Operation, and Significance.* Boston: Little, Brown, 1964.

Sartori, Giovanni. *Comparative Constitutional Engineering.* New York: New York University Press, 1997.

Secondat, Charles de, Baron de Montesquieu. *The Spirit of the Laws.* London: Hafner, 1960.

Shugart, Matthew, and John Carey. *Presidents and Assemblies: Constitutional Design and Electoral Dynamics.* Cambridge: Cambridge University Press, 1992.

Stone-Sweet, Alec. *Governing With Judges: Constitutional Politics in Europe.* Oxford: Oxford University Press, 2002.

Strøm, Kaare. *Minority Government and Majority Rule.* Cambridge: Cambridge University Press, 1990.

Tsebelis, George. *Veto Players: How Political Institutions Work.* Princeton, NJ: Princeton University Press, 2002.

Weaver, Kent, and Bert Rockman, eds. *Do Institutions Matter? Government Capabilities in the United States and Abroad.* Washington, DC: Brookings Institution, 1993.

Weber, Max. "Bureaucracy." In H. H. Gerth and C. Wright Mills, eds. *From Max Weber.* New York: Oxford University Press, 1976, pp. 196–244.

Weingast, Barry R. "Political Foundations of Democracy and the Rule of Law." *American Political Science Review* 91, no. 2 (June 1997): 245–63.

ENDNOTES

1. For a skeptical view of constitutional design, see James G. March and Johan P. Olsen, *Rediscovering Institutions: The Organizational Basis of Politics* (New York: Free Press, 1989), 171–72. For a more sanguine argument, see Giovanni Sartori, *Comparative Constitutional Engineering* (New York: New York University Press, 1995).

2. John Locke, *Two Treatises of Government*, ed. Peter Laslett (Cambridge: Cambridge University Press, 1960); and Charles de Secondat, Baron de Montesquieu, *The Spirit of the Laws* (London: Hafner, 1960).

3. *The Federalist: A Commentary on the Constitution of the United States* (Washington: National Home Library Foundation, 1937).

4. On presidential decree powers, see John M. Carey and Matthew S. Shugart, *Executive Decree Authority* (New York: Cambridge University Press, 1998); for more general discussions of presidential powers, see Matthew S. Shugart and John M. Carey, *Presidents and Assemblies: Constitutional Design and Electoral Dynamics* (Cambridge: Cambridge University Press, 1992); and Scott Mainwaring and Matthew S. Shugart, eds., *Presidentialism and Democracy in Latin America* (New York: Cambridge University Press, 1997).

5. It is important to avoid confusion between the formal titles of government officials and the source of their selection and bases of their powers—which determine the type of political system. For example, Germany is a parliamentary system, whose executive is headed by a prime minister, although his official title is chancellor; and as in many parliamentary systems the German head of state is a ceremonial president, chosen by the legislature, with little policymaking power. See also Table 6.3.

6. Arend Lijphart, *Democracy in Plural Societies* (New Haven, CT: Yale University Press, 1977); G. Bingham Powell, *Contemporary Democracies* (Cambridge: Harvard University Press, 1982); and Arend Lijphart, *Patterns of Democracy: Government Forms and Performance in Thirty-Six Countries* (New Haven, CT: Yale University Press, 1999).

7. Donald Horowitz, "Comparing Democratic Systems," in Larry Diamond and Mark F. Plattner, eds., *The Global Resurgence of Democracy* (Baltimore: Johns Hopkins University Press, 1993), 127 ff.

8. Arend Lijphart, *Patterns of Democracy*, 226.

9. George H. Gadbois, Jr., "The Institutionalization of the Supreme Court of India," in John R. Schmidhauser, ed., *Comparative Judicial Systems* (London: Butterworth Enterprises, 1987), 111–42.

10. A major trend in the division and limitation of policymaking powers in recent years has been the growth of independent central banks. Central banks, such as the Federal Reserve in the United States, have the critical task of regulating the supply of money and the interest rates, as well as many financial transactions for government and society. In most countries, such bank policy was long controlled by the chief executive as part of the government bureaucracy. But in the last 20 years, and especially since the early 1990s, many countries have given their central banks substantial independence and set for them the primary task of using monetary policy to maintain price stability and limit inflation. Their independence from the executive is encouraged by giving bank governors long terms of office free from the possibility of dismissal, as well as stipulated policy objectives and responsibilities. Such independence reassures investors, domestic and foreign, and seems to constrain inflation, but it limits the economic policy alternatives of the chief executive and cabinet.

11. For a survey of parliamentary committees in Europe, see Ingvar Mattson and Kaare Strøm, "Parliamentary Committees," in Herbert Doring, ed., *Parliaments and Majority Rule in Western Europe* (New York: St. Martin's Press, 1995), 249–307.

12. Senator Roman Houska quoted in *Time* magazine March 30, 1970.

13. See Pippa Norris, "Legislative Recruitment," in Lawrence LeDuc, Richard G. Niemi, and Pippa Norris, eds., *Comparing Democracies* (London: Sage, 1996), 184–215; and Richard E. Matland, "Women's Representation in National Legislatures: Developed and Developing Countries," *Legislative Studies Quarterly* 23, no. 1 (February 1998): 109–25.

14. Adam Przeworski, et al., *Democracy and Development* (New York: Cambridge University Press, 2000).

15. See the relevant chapters in Michael Laver and Kenneth A. Shepsle, *Cabinet Ministers and Parliamentary Government* (New York: Cambridge University Press, 1994).

16. See the discussion in Julien Freund, *The Sociology of Max Weber* (NY: Random House, 1969), 234–35.

17. See Joel Aberbach, Robert D. Putnam, and Bert A. Rockman, *Bureaucrats and Politicians in Western Democracies* (Cambridge: Harvard University Press, 1981).

18. Mark V. Nadel and Francis E. Rourke, "Bureaucracies," in Fred Greenstein and Nelson Polsby, eds., *Handbook of Political Science*, vol. 5 (Reading, MA: Addison-Wesley, 1975), 373–440.

19. See Frank Stacey, *The British Ombudsman* (Oxford: Clarendon Press, 1971); and Roy Gregory and Peter Hutchesson, *The Parliamentary Ombudsman: A Study in the Control of Administrative Action* (London: Allen & Unwin, 1975).

20. On the difficulties involved in reducing administrative corruption in developing countries, see Robert Klitgard, *Controlling Corruption* (Berkeley: University of California Press, 1989).

21. For a statistical analysis explaining scores on the Corruption Perceptions Index, see Daniel Triesman, "The Causes of Corruption: A Cross-National Study," *Journal of Public Economics* 76 (June 2000): 399–457, who suggests lower levels of economic development, shorter exposure to democracy, and federalism to be among the factors encouraging more perceived corruption.

PUBLIC POLICY

Public policy consists of all the authoritative public decisions that governments make—the outputs of the political system. Policies or outputs are normally chosen for a purpose: they are meant to promote end results that we refer to as political outcomes. Different policies may be more or less efficient ways to reach the outcomes that policymakers want. But whether a particular outcome is good or bad ultimately depends on political goods and values. And whatever values and goals policymakers and citizens have will surely affect their evaluation of the political outcomes they actually reach. Since politicians and citizens often disagree over political goods and values, it is important to keep these goals in mind when we study public policy. In this chapter, we shall discuss these aspects of public policy in order, but we begin by considering what governments actually do.

GOVERNMENT AND WHAT IT DOES

Governments do many things. Some things they do are timeless. In the days of the Roman Empire, for example, defense against external and internal enemies was a major government responsibility. It continues to be so in most societies today. In other ways, governments today do things that were unthinkable in the past. For example, contemporary governments regulate telecommunications and air traffic, policy areas that were unknown until the twentieth century.

Governments produce many goods and services, though exactly which ones vary a great deal from country to country. In most societies, governments provide law enforcement, roads, and postal services, and in many countries they do much more. In the former Soviet Union and other communist states, governments owned and operated most major industries and produced everything from military equipment to such consumer goods as clothing and shoes. In a capitalist society, such as the United States, most consumer goods are produced in the private sector. In much of Europe, the government produces more than in the United States, but far less than in the former Soviet Union. In some developing countries, the government produces very few goods or services.

The range of government involvement varies not just among countries, but also among different economic sectors within the same country. For example, one study showed that the U.S. government employed only 1 percent of the poeple engaged in mining and manufacturing, but 28 percent of those working for the utilities that supply gas, water, and electrical power; in France, the corresponding figures were 8 percent and 71 percent, respectively. Compared with socialist countries, governments in capitalist free-market societies tend to leave more production to private firms. Yet, there is no society in which the government produces no goods or services, and conversely no state in which all industries are run by the government. Even in the former Soviet Union, part of the agricultural sector was private, as were many simple consumer services, such as baby-sitting. Other ostensibly communist societies, such as China today, feature a lot of private enterprise, particularly in the consumer goods sector.

Public Policies

The importance of governments goes far beyond their role as producers of goods and services. Indeed, this may not even be their most important role in most contemporary states. Governments also engage in various forms of public policy. In Chapter 1; we discussed three important challenges facing contemporary states: building community, fostering development, and securing democracy and human rights. Many **public policies** are wholly or in part directed at these challenges. Public policies are designed to strengthen national identity and community by reinforcing a common language or culture, or by promoting allegiance to a shared political heritage. A host of economic policies aims to promote economic and social development and to make its benefits broadly accessible. Finally, government policies establish or enhance democratic institutions that enable citizens to control political decisions. In the past century, most Western nations have been transformed from authoritarian, or oligarchic (systems ruled by the few), regimes to democracies. Government policy has increasingly been used to meet popular needs and demands. Even so, we cannot always assume that what democratic governments do is what is in the best interest of their citizens.

Public policies may be summarized and compared according to outputs—the actions that governments take to accomplish their purposes. We classify these actions or outputs under four headings:

1. **distribution**—of money, goods, and services—to citizens, residents, and clients of the state;
2. **extraction** of resources—money, goods, persons, and services—from the domestic and international environments;
3. **regulation** of human behavior—the use of compulsion and inducement to bring about desired behavior; and
4. **symbolic outputs**—political speeches, holidays, rites, public monuments and statues, and the like—used to exhort citizens to engage in desired forms of behavior, build community, or celebrate exemplary conduct (see Chapter 1).

Political systems have different policy profiles. Some governments produce a lot of goods and services but regulate little. Elsewhere, the government may be heavily engaged in extraction and distribution, but rely on the private sector to produce most goods and services. In the next sections, we shall discuss these four types of policies, beginning with distribution.

DISTRIBUTION

The famous political scientist Harold D. Lasswell argued that the essence of government is deciding "who gets what, when, and how." Politics, he thought, is essentially about distribution. Whether or not we agree with Lasswell's point of view, there is no question that distributive policies are very important in contemporary societies. Whether or not they are democratic, all governments have to distribute resources in order to survive. Distributive policies include transfers of money, goods, services, honors, and opportunities to individuals and groups in the society. Such policies generally consume more government resources and employ more government officials than anything else that modern governments do.

Distributive Policy Profiles

Health, education, and national defense are among the policy areas that consume the largest proportions of government spending worldwide. Figure 7.1 reports central governmental expenditures in these policy areas as a percentage of gross domestic product (GDP). Clearly, central government expenditures depend heavily on economic development. Developed countries generally allocate from one-half to two-thirds of their central government expenditures to education, health, and welfare. France, Germany, and Britain spend more than two-thirds of their budgets in these areas, compared with just under one-half in the United States, where a larger share of health care spending is in the private sector. Before 1989, the Soviet Union and the communist countries of Eastern Europe spent less on education, health, and welfare than the democracies of Western Europe. But as these Eastern European countries have introduced market economies, their expenditure patterns have become more similar to the West.

Since World War II especially, governments have greatly expanded their spending on education. Developing societies have made large efforts to provide at least primary education for all their citizens, while most of the richer societies have also experienced a huge increase in secondary and university (tertiary) enrollments. A few decades ago, fewer than 5 percent of young adults in most European countries were able to get a college education. Today, those numbers have risen to 40 percent or more (see Table 7.4). Since most of these colleges and universities are public, government spending on secondary and higher education has risen substantially.

Public health is another major spending category. Some developing countries, such as India and Nigeria, typically spend less on health than on education. The government

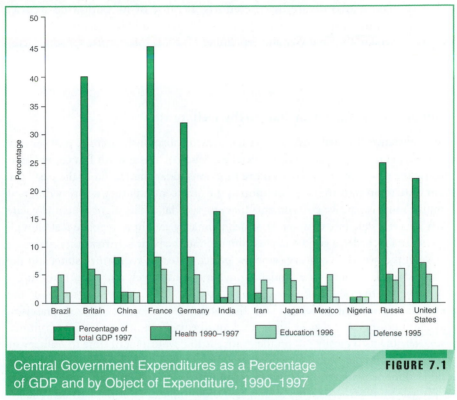

Central Government Expenditures as a Percentage
of GDP and by Object of Expenditure, 1990–1997

FIGURE 7.1

Source: World Bank, *World Development Report: 1999–2000* (New York: Oxford University Press, 2000),
Table 14, 256–57; Table 7, 242–43; Table 6, 240–41; Table 17, 262–63.

in Nigeria seems to have little impact on its people in these areas. India's efforts
are only slightly better. Sadly, the countries that need them most have the least to spend
on education and health. Poor nations, with limited budgets and many pressing
demands, cannot easily spare the resources for health and education. Also, social security expenditure in poor nations tends to be low, because shorter life expectancies
and high birth rates mean that there are comparatively few older people. But part of
the explanation of the low social expenditures in poor countries may also have to do
with poor measures. Just as our GDP measures fail to include the subsistence economy
and therefore underreport the wealth of the poorest countries (see Chapter 1), our
measures of health expenditures may similarly underreport the efforts of the poorest
states. In these societies the aged and the infirm typically receive some care through
the extended family, and these services go unreported in our statistics.

National security spending shows a different pattern. Particularly among less-
developed countries, spending varies as much with the international environment
as with overall economic means. Some states that are locked in tense international confrontations (such as those in the Middle East), or that are trying to exert international

influence make extraordinary defense efforts. Because of its worldwide security commitments, the United States is by far the heaviest military spender, although between the end of the Cold War and September 11, 2001, U.S. defense spending actually decreased. Japan, which spends as much as most Western countries on health and education, has spent relatively little on defense since World War II.

From the Night Watchman State to the Welfare State

The importance of distributive policies has grown enormously over the past century or so, particularly in industrialized societies. Much of this growth has come about because the government performs more functions today than it did in the past. The **night watchman state** that was common in the nineteenth century was very different from the more expansive governments that emerged later. The night watchman state was a Lockean state (see Chapter 1), which primarily sought to regulate just enough to preserve law, order, a good business climate, and the basic security of its citizens.

With the twentieth century came the **police state,** the **regulatory state,** and the **welfare state.** The police state regulates much more intrusively and extracts resources more severely than the night watchman state. The most oppressive forms of the police state have been associated with the totalitarian ideologies (Nazism, fascism, and communism) that also left their mark on the past century. Fascist and communist governments typically call on their citizens to devote a lot of time to military or other community service and try to control their lives. But the twentieth century also produced more benign forms of big government. The regulatory state has evolved in all advanced industrial societies as they face the complexities of modern life. Finally, the welfare state, which is found particularly in prosperous and democratic societies, distributes resources extensively to provide for the health, education, employment, housing, and income support of its citizens.

The main reason that distribution has become such a dominant concern in modern governments lies in the welfare state. The welfare state refers to a set of government, and sometimes private, policies involving old age pensions (known in the United States as social security), health, sickness, and accident insurance, unemployment benefits, and the like. Over time, welfare state policies have also come to include public education, housing subsidies, child and childcare benefits, and other distributive policies.

The first modern welfare state programs were introduced in Germany in the 1880s. In response to rapid industrialization and urbanization, the German government under Chancellor Bismarck began offering social insurance programs that protected workers against unemployment, accidents, sickness, and poverty during old age. During the twentieth century, and particularly from the Great Depression of the 1930s until the 1970s, most industrialized states adopted and greatly expanded such welfare state policies. As developing countries become wealthier, they also tend to spend more of their resources on welfare state services.

Figure 7.2 shows that the welfare state in advanced capitalist—**Organization for Economic Cooperation and Development (OECD)**—countries has continued to

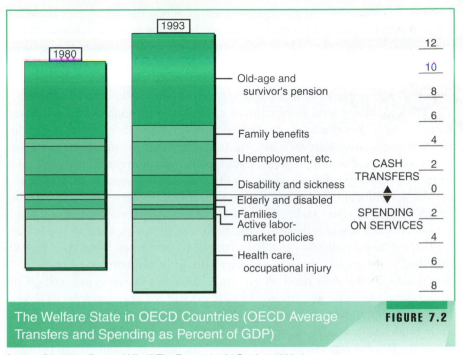

1993

1980

Old-age and
survivor's pension

Family benefits

Unemployment, etc.

Disability and sickness

Elderly and disabled
Families
Active labor-
market policies

Health care,
occupational injury

12
10
8
6
4
CASH   2
TRANSFERS
▲   0
▼
SPENDING 2
ON SERVICES
4
6
8

**The Welfare State in OECD Countries (OECD Average
Transfers and Spending as Percent of GDP)**   **FIGURE 7.2**

Source: "Privatising Peace of Mind," *The Economist,* 24 October, 1998, 4.

grow during the 1980s and 1990s, albeit at a somewhat slower rate. As the figure
shows, welfare state spending consists of two major categories: cash transfers to individuals and families, and direct government spending on services. Though both categories have grown, the transfer programs remain the largest. Among the individual
programs that make up the welfare state, old-age pensions (social security) and health
care loom particularly large. In many European countries with jobless rates of up to 10 or
15 percent, unemployment benefits are another major government outlay.

The welfare state is a mixture combining a social insurance scheme and a program of social redistribution. It is in part paternalistic (forcing people to put away
money for their old age and potential illnesses) and in part Robin Hood (taking from
the rich and giving to the poor). The balance between these two functions depends in
part on which programs a particular country emphasizes and in part on how it
finances them. Thus, not all welfare states are alike. Even among the advanced industrial countries, some welfare states are larger than others, and different political systems emphasize different benefits. All the wealthier nations try to assist the aged, the
disabled, and the unemployed; but differences in expenditures reflect contrasts in
priorities and historical experiences.

Because welfare benefits can be expensive and governments have limited funds,
three principles govern most welfare state provisions. One is *need:* help and services
are provided to those who need them the most. Social assistance is most commonly

based on this idea. A second principle is *contribution*: benefits should go to those that have contributed to the program, for example, by paying taxes or insurance premiums. This is the basic idea behind social security in the United States, though other criteria also enter in. A third principle is *entitlement*, or *universalism*: everyone should have the benefit, regardless of specific circumstances. This is the principle that most countries apply to primary education or to treatment for life-threatening diseases.

The U.S. model stresses equality of opportunity through public education. Especially in higher education, the United States made a much greater and earlier effort than did most European nations. In contrast, on the European continent, social security and health programs traditionally took precedence over education. Americans began spending on social security and welfare programs much later, and the U.S. government still does less in these areas than the governments of most other advanced democracies. And in many areas of welfare provision, U.S. programs are needs-based, whereas those in some European countries, such as Sweden, are entitlement-based (universalistic). For example, in the United States child benefits ("welfare") are given only to needy recipients for a limited period of time. In Scandinavia, on the other hand, all parents, (billionaires as well as paupers) get the same payment from the government. In addition, they get generous parental leave at close to full pay. In sum, compared with Europeans, Americans have historically put more emphasis on equality of opportunity and less on welfare obligations. This may reflect the U.S. heritage as a nation of immigrants, many of whom arrived poor and have been expected to prosper by their own efforts.

Also, it is important to keep in mind that many welfare services in the United States are provided by private foundations, churches and other religious organizations, and individuals. In recent years, multibillionaires, such as Warren Buffett and Bill and Melinda Gates, have made huge donations to charitable causes in the United States and abroad. And they are not alone. In 2005 Americans gave $260 billion to charitable organizations. More than three-fourths of these gifts came from living individuals, many of them people of very limited means. The nonprofit sector of the U.S. economy now accounts for 9 percent of the GDP, more than twice as much as in 1960. It employs close to 10 percent of the American workforce, more than the federal and state governments combined. This nonprofit sector exists in other developed states as well, but generally on a much smaller scale.

Challenges to the Welfare State

Welfare states have many beneficial consequences. The Western European countries that pioneered these programs have virtually eradicated dire poverty, and they have created a much more "level playing field" for their citizens. Crime rates tend to be low in countries with extensive welfare states, and most of the programs are popular with ordinary citizens. Yet, the welfare state is also expensive. As government expenditures have grown to between one-third and one-half of GDP in most industrial democracies, they have caused serious concern about the ability of future generations to pay. One of the most serious problems is that at the same time that senior citizens are qualifying for greater pension benefits and health care costs are rising rapidly, the ranks of the elderly are swelling relative to those in the workforce. This is reflected in the dependency ratio, which is the proportion of those outside the workforce (because they are too young or too old) to those in the working-age population. Over the next decades, dependency ratios will increase in all advanced industrial societies, and particularly in such countries as Japan where the fertility rate is low and life expectancy high. Therefore, fewer working people will have to pay higher taxes just to support existing health and welfare programs. In the United States, Medicare and Social Security may incur large deficits in the future. In other countries, social welfare programs are already costing more than their designated taxes are bringing in.

Another problem is that some welfare state policies give citizens few incentives to work. Norway and Sweden are among the leading countries in the world in life expectancy and public health statistics. Yet, workers in these countries are on sick leave about twice as often as those elsewhere in Europe, as the average Swedish worker misses about five or six weeks of work per year. In Norway, more than 10 percent of the working-age population is on disability pensions, partly because generous sick leave benefits let workers keep virtually their entire pay from the first day they miss work, and because it is fairly easy to qualify for disability benefits. But these policies are costly. In Sweden, sick pay and disability benefits account for more than 10 percent of the government's total spending.

These problems with the welfare state have stirred efforts to prevent further increases in spending obligations (entitlements) and to contain the costs of those already in effect. Thus the gradual expansion of welfare benefits that characterized most of the twentieth century can no longer be taken for granted.

EXTRACTION

Since distribution means that governments spend, there must also be ways for governments to collect money and other resources. All political systems *extract* resources from their environments and inhabitants. When simple societies go to war, for example, individuals of specific age groups (most commonly young men) may be called on to fight. Anthropologists have estimated that in some hunter-gatherer societies, such obligations have been so onerous that about half of all males have died in warfare. (Thomas Hobbes would not have been surprised.) Such direct extraction of services is still found in modern states, in the form of compulsory military service, jury duty, or compulsory labor imposed on those convicted of crime.

The most common contemporary forms of resource extraction, however, are taxation and borrowing. *Taxation* is the extraction for governmental purposes of money or goods from members of a political system, for which they receive no immediate or direct benefit. Tax policies are designed to meet many different objectives, which sometimes conflict. On the one hand, governments often want to collect as much tax revenue as possible from their citizens in order to finance various services. On the other hand, they do not want to kill the goose that lays the golden egg. The more governments tax their citizens, the less these people are inclined to work, and if the tax burden becomes too onerous, they may try to evade taxes or even leave the country altogether. Another common trade-off in tax policies is between efficiency and equity. *Efficiency* means extracting the most tax revenue possible at the lowest cost to economic production. *Equity* means taxing in such a way that, as much as possible, no one is unfairly burdened, and particularly so that those who have the least are spared. In most societies, the tax system is designed to redistribute wealth in favor of the less well-off. Therefore, income taxes are generally progressive, which means that citizens with greater incomes are taxed at higher rates than those who earn less. Yet, there is a limit to how progressive income taxes can be. Highly progressive income taxes can reduce people's incentive to work and thus hurt capital formation. Therefore, they are often inefficient.

Personal and corporate income taxes and taxes on capital gains and wealth are called **direct taxes,** since they are directly levied on persons and corporations. Such taxes, as well as property taxes, tend to be progressive. But although corporate income taxes are meant to be progressive, corporations often avoid them through creative accounting or by moving their operations to countries where taxes are lower. If personal income taxes become too high, similar things can happen. **Indirect taxes** include sales and value-added taxes, excise taxes, and customs duties. Their distributive effects depend on who purchases the relevant commodities and services. Since the poor spend more of their income on food and clothing than do those who are better off, sales (or value-added) taxes on such necessities are regressive (which means that the poor pay relatively more than the rich). But indirect taxes on luxury goods may be progressive, since the poor rarely purchase yachts, fine jewelry, or private planes. Payroll taxes, which are often used to finance pensions (for example, social security in the United States), tend to hit the middle class, since the wealthy often receive a larger share of their income from dividends, interest, or capital gains. Taxes on wages also penalize people in the labor force relative to retirees and homemakers and can therefore hurt employment or drive businesses into the "underground economy" in which they do not report their incomes.

Political systems that rely heavily on sales and payroll taxes are less likely to attain a progressive tax structure overall. On the other hand, such taxes are less "visible" than income taxes and seem to generate less resentment and tax avoidance. In many countries, particularly where the government does not have good financial records, indirect taxes are easier to collect. Finally, the more mobile a tax object is, the more difficult it is to tax. Financial investments tend to be highly mobile, which makes them difficult to tax. Land and buildings, on the other hand, are not very mobile, and many states tax them substantially.

Besides redistribution and efficiency, tax policies are often designed to promote such values as charity, energy conservation, or home ownership. For example, many countries stimulate home ownership by making mortgage interest payments tax deductible. The rationale is that home ownership promotes stable families who take an active interest in their neighborhoods. If such tax incentives are too generous, however, they can cause economic distortions. Families may put all their savings into housing, so that businesses are starved of capital. Moreover, mortgage deductions are primarily a middle-class benefit of little use to the truly poor, who rarely own their own homes.

Figure 7.3 shows the central government revenues as a percentage of **gross domestic product (GDP),** the total value of goods and services produced by a country's residents in a year. For the average country, about a fifth of the GDP is extracted by the central government's taxes, but in some countries the proportion is much higher. Regional and local taxes add to the tax burden. In federal systems—such as Brazil, Germany, India, Russia, and the United States—these taxes can increase the total tax burden by a third or more.[1] Governments also derive revenues from nontax sources (the lighter columns in Figure 7.3), such as administrative fees and income from business enterprises that they run.

The tax profiles of different countries vary both in their overall tax burdens and in their reliance on different types of taxes. Sweden has the highest tax rates overall, as it extracts more than 50 percent of its GDP in taxes. France comes close to the 50-percent mark. Britain and Germany are among a number of advanced industrial societies that collect about 40 percent of GDP, while the United States and Russia

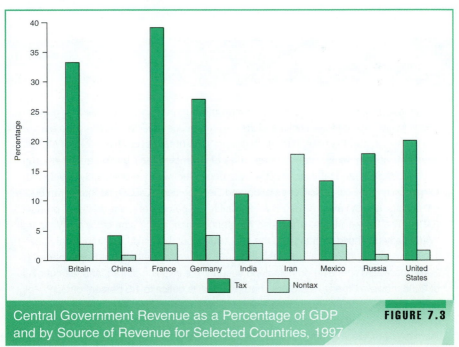

Central Government Revenue as a Percentage of GDP and by Source of Revenue for Selected Countries, 1997

FIGURE 7.3

Source: World Bank, *World Development Report, 1999–2000* (New York: Oxford University Press, 2000), Table 14, 256–57.

extract about a third. Outside the European and North American areas, central government revenue rarely exceeds 20 percent of GDP. The central government revenue of India is under 15 percent, or about 20 percent more if we add state and local governments.

Countries also differ in how they collect their revenues. Some advanced industrial countries (including Germany and France) rely heavily on social security taxes imposed on both employers and employees. In both Germany and Britain, most of the revenue comes from social security and income taxes, but whereas Germany relies far more heavily on social security payments, Britain relies more on income taxes. The United States and Japan, which fall below average in total tax burden, depend to a large extent on direct income taxes rather than on sales and consumption taxes.[2] Poorer countries, such as Iran, India, and Mexico, receive most of their revenue from indirect taxes.

Although overall tax burdens continue to grow, income tax rates have decreased in Western countries since the early 1980s, as there has been a shift from direct income taxes to less visible indirect consumption taxes. Growing tax burdens led to taxpayer revolts and some scaling back of government extraction. From 1975 to 1990, British top marginal income tax rates declined by 43 percentage points, Swedish rates by 35 points, and Japanese rates by 25 points. During the same time period in the United States, federal rates declined by 42 points (although they then rose by about 13 points by the end of the Clinton administration, but have come

Balancing the Books

BOX 7.1

In the long run, governments cannot spend more money than they raise. If governments fail to balance their books and instead run budget deficits, they have to borrow money, which creates debt that future generations of taxpayers have to pay off. Yet, even rich governments are notoriously bad at balancing their books, and many run budget deficits year after year. In 2004, nineteen of the twenty-eight (highly developed) Organization for Economic Cooperation and Development (OECD) countries ran budget deficits, and the average deficit was equal to 3.5 percent of gross domestic product (GDP). The United States, which had run deficits most of the time since the Vietnam War, briefly balanced its budget in the late 1990s, but then slid back into fiscal imbalance due to the stock market crash in 2000, the terrorist attacks of September 11, 2001, increased spending on homeland security, the invasion of Iraq, and tax cuts. As of 2006, however, the United States had reduced its deficit to 1.9 percent of GDP, well below European countries such as France, Germany, and Italy. When these countries in the 1990s decided to adopt a common currency, the Euro, they also committed themselves to keeping their respective national deficits smaller than 3 percent of GDP. In practice, however, they have often been unable to keep that promise.

down by about 4.5 points under President George W. Bush). The average decline in top tax rates for all OECD countries was 18 percent.[3] In Russia, President Putin cut income taxes drastically shortly after he came to power. Tax rates have come down because of the spread of economic views that stress the importance of entrepreneurial incentives for productivity. Lower marginal income tax rates stimulate economic activity and lessen incentives for tax evasion, but they may cause income inequalities to grow.

REGULATION

Regulation is the exercise of political control over the behavior of individuals and groups in the society. Most contemporary governments are not only welfare states, they are also regulatory states. Governments regulate for many reasons, as we discussed in Chapter 1. As social contract theorists such as Hobbes and Locke realized, regulation can facilitate many beneficial activities. Economic production and commerce, for example, rely on government regulation to establish and protect property rights and to enforce contracts. There need to be rules to keep traffic moving smoothly on the freeways, in the air, and on the airwaves. Citizens and consumers often demand protections against fraud, manipulation, and obnoxious externalities, such as toxic waste and pollution. And governments are increasingly involved in setting product standards, particularly for pharmaceuticals and food, to make sure that these products are safe. Governments also regulate to shield their citizens, and often particularly children and women, from physical and other abuse, and to some extent they protect animals and plants against cruelty and environmental degradation.

Government regulation has proliferated enormously over the last century. Industrialization and urbanization have caused problems in traffic, health, and public order. Industrial growth has also generated concerns about industrial safety, labor exploitation, and pollution. Moreover, the growth of science and the belief that humanity can harness and control nature have led to increased demands for government action. Finally, changes in citizen values have led to demands for new kinds of regulation. Thus, government regulation in the United States has extended to include gun control, protection of voting rights, prohibition of discrimination in employment, pollution abatement, and the like. At the same time, however, at least most Western societies have lessened their regulation of birth control, abortion, divorce, blasphemy, obscenity, and sexual conduct.

Governments regulate the lives of their citizens in many ways. Although we often associate regulation with legal means, there are other ways to regulate as well. Governments may control behavior by offering material or financial inducements or by persuasion or moral exhortation. For example, many governments try to reduce tobacco use by a combination of methods: bans on smoking, tobacco sales, or advertising; sales ("sin") taxes; and information campaigns to convince people of the hazards of smoking.

Regulation and Development

BOX 7.2

In the advanced industrial countries of North America, Japan, and Western Europe, regulation has grown enormously along with their industrial and postindustrial economies. It is easy to think, therefore, that there is more regulation in wealthy countries than in poor ones. But this is not always true. In fact, low-income countries sometimes regulate more than rich ones. This is particularly true of regulations of business entry and competition. In many less developed countries, it is cumbersome and time-consuming, for example, to get the permits necessary to start a new business. Such regulations often mainly serve to create *rents* that government officials can exploit for their own benefit (see Chapter 1). They protect existing businesses by giving them monopolies or other protections. Many politicians expect the business-people who benefit from these regulations (often their family members, friends, or business associates) to show their gratitude through kickbacks and other favors. Or business owners pay off politicians or civil servants to get around onerous regulations or to avoid long delays in handling their applications. Overregulation of this kind tends to hurt economic productivity and keep out foreign investment.

The Peruvian economist Hernando de Soto reports a sobering experience with abusive government regulation. As an experiment, he registered a small clothing factory in Lima, Peru, and decided in advance not to pay bribes. While he was waiting for his business to be registered, government officials asked him for bribes no fewer than ten times. Twice he broke his own rule and paid the bribe so that he would not be forced to give up his experiment. After ten months, his factory was finally registered. In New York, a similar procedure takes four hours.

Source: World Bank, *World Development Report 2005*, Chapter 5; William Easterly, *The Elusive Quest for Growth: The Economists' Adventures and Misadventures in the Tropics* (Cambridge: MIT Press, 2001) 233.

But even though there are many similarities in regulative policies across the world, states often differ substantially in their policy profiles. Patterns of regulation vary not only with industrialization and urbanization, for example, but also with cultural values. In the study of public policy, we describe and explain such differences among political systems by asking the following questions:

1. What aspects of human behavior and interaction are regulated and to what degree? Does the government regulate such domains as family relations, economic activity, religious activity, political activity, geographic mobility, professional and occupational qualifications, and protection of person and property? These questions have to do with the *domain* of government regulation.
2. What social groups are regulated, with what procedural limitations on enforcement, and what rights? Are these sanctions applied uniformly, or do they affect different individuals or groups differently? Are there rights of appeal? Such questions help us identify the *subjects* of regulation.

3. What sanctions are used to compel or induce citizens to comply? Does the government use exhortation and moral persuasion, financial rewards and penalties, licensing of some types of actions, physical confinement or punishment, or other forms of coercion? These questions help us map the *instruments* or *mechanisms*, of regulation.

    Although all modern states use sanctions, they vary in their goals and strategies. Yet, one aspect of regulation is particularly important politically: government control over political participation and communication. Recall from earlier chapters that democracy requires political competition. Governments in authoritarian systems often suppress political competition by prohibiting party organization, voluntary associations, and political communication. Government regulation in this area therefore has a crucial effect on democracy. Yet, governmental regulation is not always negative. Our civilization and amenities depend on regulation. Government regulation commonly promotes such values as the safety of persons and property, sanitation, prevention of environmental pollution, safe disposal of toxic wastes, maintenance of occupational safety, and equal access to housing and education.

    Table 7.1 shows the political rights and civil liberties ratings for the countries included in this book, based on expert judgments. Political rights refers to citizen opportunities to participate in the choice of political leaders—voting rights, the right

TABLE 7.1

Political and Economic Rights and Liberties, 2004–2005

Country	Political Rights	Civil Liberties	Economic Freedom
Brazil	2	3	5.9
Britain	1	1	8.1
China	7	6	5.7
France	1	1	7.3
Germany	1	1	7.6
India	2	3	6.7
Iran	6	6	6.1
Japan	1	2	7.5
Mexico	2	2	6.6
Nigeria	3	3	5.6
Russia	6	5	5.6
United States	1	1	8.2

Note: Expert ratings of political rights and civil liberties for each country on 1 (highest) to 7 (lowest) scale. Economic Freedom scored on summary scale from 0 (low) to 10 (high).

Source: Freedom House website, www.freedomhouse.org (downloaded February 3, 2006); James Gwartney and Robert Lawson with William Easterly, *Economic Freedom of the World: 2006 Annual Report.* (Vancouver: Fraser Institute, 2006), 13.

to run for office, and the like. Civil liberties refers to protections in such areas as freedom of speech, press, assembly, and religion, as well as to procedural rights, such as trial by a jury of peers and bans on arbitrary or cruel treatment. The rich democratic countries all have ratings of 1 or 2 for both political and civil rights. India, Brazil, and Mexico, which have improved significantly in recent years, follow next. At the other extreme, China, Iran, and most recently Russia substantially suppress both political rights and civil liberties. China in particular has tried to control the media comprehensively and sets few limits on government regulation vis-à-vis the individual. Nigeria is rated in the middle. These rankings, of course, vary over time. Rights and liberties in the United States have improved since the civil rights movement of the 1960s. Nigeria's military governments of the 1990s were repressive and frequently brutal, but things have improved there since power was turned over to an elected civilian president in 1999.

There is a strong correlation between political and civil rights. No country that scores high on participatory rights also scores very low on civil liberties, and no country low on participatory rights is high on civil liberties. This suggests a strong relationship between popular participation and the rule of law and equitable procedure. In a study of governmental repression in 153 countries during the 1980s, Steven C. Poe and C. Neal Tate found that positive civil and political rights records were best explained by democratic political institutions and conditions of peace and social order. Authoritarian states and those involved in internal or international war were the most frequent civil rights violators. A high level of economic development also helps explain a strong rights record.[4]

Table 7.1 also reports the level of economic freedom in each country. It is not always true that countries that are politically free also foster economic freedom, or vice versa. For example, China provides a lot less political freedom than Nigeria, but the level of economic freedom in the two countries is about the same. And even though Britain and France score the same on political rights and liberties, Britain has a higher level of economic freedom. On the whole, though, political and economic freedoms tend to go together.

COMMUNITY-BUILDING AND SYMBOLIC OUTPUTS

A fourth type of output is symbolic policies. Much communication by political leaders takes the form of appeals to the courage, wisdom, and magnanimity embodied in the nation's past; or appeals to values and ideologies, such as equality, liberty, community, democracy, communism, liberalism, or religious tradition; or promises of future accomplishment and rewards. Political leaders appeal to such values for different reasons—for example, to win elections or to push their own pet projects. But at the same time many symbolic appeals and policies have the purpose of building community—for example, by boosting people's national identity, civic pride, or trust in government.

Symbolic outputs are also intended to enhance other aspects of performance: to make people pay their taxes more readily and honestly; comply with the law more faithfully; or accept sacrifice, danger, and hardship; Such appeals may be especially important in times of crisis. Some of the most magnificent examples are the speeches of Pericles in the Athenian Assembly during the Peloponnesian War, or those of Franklin D. Roosevelt in the depths of the Great Depression, or of Winston Churchill during Britain's darkest hours in World War II. But symbolic policies are important even in less extreme circumstances. Public buildings, plazas, monuments, holiday parades, and civic and patriotic indoctrination in schools all attempt to contribute to the population's sense of governmental legitimacy and its willingness to comply with public policy.

OUTCOMES: DOMESTIC WELFARE

While we can describe different government policies, it is not always clear what their consequences will be. How do extractive, distributive, regulative, and symbolic policies affect the lives of citizens? Unexpected economic, international, or social events may frustrate the purpose of political leaders. Thus a tax rebate to stimulate the economy may be nullified by a rise in the price of oil. Increases in health expenditures may have no effect because of unexpected epidemics or rising health costs, or health services may not reach those most in need. Sometimes policies have unintended and undesirable consequences, as when the introduction of benefits for troubled social groups lead others to simulate the same troubles to get the same favors. Consequently, to estimate the effectiveness of public policy, we have to examine actual welfare outcomes as well as governmental policies and their implementation.

Table 7.2 compares a number of welfare indicators. The first two columns report measures of economic well-being or its lack: growth in private consumption and the share of the population living on less than $2 per day. The severe problems of Nigeria and India are particularly notable: the vast majority of those populations live on less than $2 a day. The latter columns report the availability of critical public facilities: safe water and sanitation. While most of the people of the developed world have access to safe water, this is true for less than half of the population of many less-advantaged countries. In Nigeria, for example, only 49 percent of the population had access to safe water in 1990, though by 2002 this percentage had risen to 60. The good news is that most of the poorer countries in our sample experienced solid progress over the past decade or so, although that progress may be more secure in China and India than in oil-dependent Nigeria.

In Chapter 1, we saw how income distribution tends to be most unequal in medium-income developing societies, such as Brazil, and more equal in advanced market societies as well as in low-income developing societies, such as India (see Table 1.4 in Chapter 1). In his studies of European economic history, Simon Kuznets showed that in the early stages of industrialization income distribution became more unequal, whereas in later stages of industrialization income distribution again came closer to equality.[5] This "Kuznets curve" reflects the fact that in the early stages of modernization, traditional farmers tend to be left behind as industry and commercial agriculture begin to grow. At higher levels of economic attainment, however, the number of poor farmers is reduced compared with the industrial and service sectors. In addition, when trade unions and democratic political parties emerge, they tend to

	Private Household Consumption Annual Growth (%) 1990–2003	Population Below $2 per Day %, ca. 2000	Access to Safe Water (%) 1990/2002	Access to Sanitation (%) 1990/2002
Country				
Brazil	3.4	22.4	83/89	70/75
Britain	3.1	ND	100/100	100/100
China	8.5	46.7	70/77	23/44
France	1.6	ND	100/100	96/ND
Germany	1.5	ND	100/100	ND/ND
India	4.9	80.6	68/86	12/30
Iran	3.5	7.3	91/93	83/84
Japan	.4	ND	100/100	100/100
Mexico	2.8	26.3	80/91	66/77
Nigeria	3.7	90.8	49/60	39/38
Russia	.9	7.5	94/96	87/87
United States	3.7	ND	100/100	100/100

TABLE 7.2 Welfare Outcomes, 1990–2005

Source: World Bank, *World Development Indicators 2005*, Tables 2.5, 2.15, 4.10 (downloaded February 3, 2006), from http://devdata.worldbank.org/wdipdfs/tab2_5.pdf,2_15.pdf, from http://devdata.worldbank.org/wdi2005/Table4_10.htm and previous editions.

make the income distribution more equal through taxation, wage policy, and welfare state policies.

Table 7.3 (page 187) reports on health outcomes. During the 1990s, the average public health expenditure per capita for the economically developed countries was $2,505, compared with $182 for the developing countries. The average number of physicians per 1,000 people in the developed world was 2.8, compared with 1.3 in the developing world. But in Nigeria the number was only 0.2 in 1990 and 0.3 in 2004. The country has a high birth rate, but almost one out of ten infants fails to survive the first year of life; and more than one-third of Nigerian children under age 5 suffer from malnutrition. Nigerian citizens have a life expectancy at birth of just 45 years (compared with 75–80 years in advanced industrial countries).

Nigeria demonstrates the ills of poverty, but some poor countries cope more successfully than others. Consider the difference between China and India. With similar levels of GDP per capita, Chinese average life expectancy is 71 years and infant mortality is 30 per 1,000 live births, while those of India are 63 years and 63 per 1,000, respectively. China has three times as many physicians as India relative to its population. Almost half of India's children under age 5 are undernourished, compared with a sixth of those in China. Fortunately, however, health conditions are improving in most of the poor countries, including India.

BOX 7.3

Government and the Rural Poor

Visitors from rich countries are often shocked and appalled at the poverty they see in the fast-growing cities of the developing world. Poverty in these teeming metropolises is often exacerbated by crime, violence, homelessness, and pollution. Yet, poverty is even more of a problem in the countryside than in the cities. The poorest countries in the world are overwhelmingly rural, and in most poor countries poverty rates in the countryside are much higher than in the cities. In Brazil, for example, only 15 percent of the urban population fell below the country's (modest) poverty line in 1998, whereas 51 percent of the rural population did so. There are many reasons that rural poverty is often so dire. In rural areas, there is often less investment in education and infrastructure. Farmers in poor countries often find it difficult to obtain title to their land or credit (see Box 7.4). And rural-dwellers are more susceptible than city-dwellers to the vagaries of the climate.

But part of the problem of rural poverty can also result from government policy. In many African states, for example, the rulers tend to favor the urban population because they want the country to modernize and industrialize. Sometimes politicians also worry that a starving urban population might riot and bring down the government. For these reasons, governments tend to keep food prices artificially low, which hurts farmers. Governments also tend to prefer targeted government agricultural programs (often subsidies), which help particular groups of farmers (often wealthy ones). Such targeted programs help governments gain political supporters but are often wasteful. Even in democratic countries where the majority of voters are poor farmers, government policies often do little for them. Many voters do not trust politicians who promise to deliver broad public goods (such as health care and education), but instead support candidates who promise targeted private goods (such as jobs and subsidies). Thus, even spending on schools becomes a way to create jobs rather than to educate children. In India, teachers' salaries account for 96 percent of recurrent expenditures in primary education. Even so, teacher absenteeism is rampant. When inspectors made unannounced visits to rural schools, about two-thirds of the teachers were absent.

Sources: Robert H. Bates, *Markets and States in Tropical Africa.* (Berkeley: University of California Press, 1981); Philip Keefer and Stuti Khemani, "Why Do the Poor Receive Poor Services?" *Economic and Political Weekly*, 28 February, 2004, 935–43; World Bank, *World Development Report 2002*, 31–32.

While the incidence of infant mortality and malnutrition is much lower in advanced economies, these problems are still serious among the poor in advanced industrial countries, such as the United States. The United States spends the largest proportion of its GDP on health care (approximately 15 percent) of any country. At the same time, however, the United States has a somewhat higher infant death rate than Japan and Western Europe due to more widespread poverty, drug abuse, and unequal access to health care. As Table 7.3 shows, Japan has an exceptional health

BOX 7.4

Microcredit

One of the greatest obstacles to economic growth in many poor areas is the difficulty of obtaining credit. In advanced industrial countries, property owners (for example, farmers or home owners) typically have a recognized title to their property. If they want to invest to expand their business or start a new one, they can borrow against this collateral. People in poor countries rarely have this opportunity, and it is especially difficult for poor farmers and women to obtain loans. As a result, they often cannot get the funds they need to tide them over hard times or to take advantage of promising business opportunities.

Muhammad Yunus, a U.S.-educated professor of economics, had noticed these problems in his native country of Bangladesh. In 1974, he began extending small loans to poor people to help them out of these circumstances. His first loan amounted to $27 from his own pockets, which he lent to forty-two people, including a woman who made bamboo furniture, which she sold to support herself and her family. In 1976, Yunus founded Grameen Bank to make loans to poor Bangladeshis. The bank has since then given out more than $5 billion in loans. To secure its loans, the bank sets up a system of "solidarity groups," which meet on a weekly basis and support each other's efforts. As of May 2006, Grameen Bank had almost 7 million borrowers, 97 percent of whom were women. Their repayment rate is 98 percent. In 2006, Muhammad Yunus and the Grameen Bank received the Nobel Peace Prize for these efforts to help poor people improve their lives.

record. It has the longest life expectancy and the lowest infant mortality rate among all the study countries in this book. But its fertility rate of 1.3 means a declining population. (With no net migration, a fertility rate of approximately 2.1 results in a steady-state population.)

Table 7.4 (page 188) tells us about access to education and information technologies, such as newspapers and personal computers. As we can see, many more people are reached by newspapers in rich and well-educated countries, such as Japan, than in the developing world. Yet even in poorer countries, communications have become much easier. Television has become widely available even in countries at middling development levels (e.g., Brazil and Mexico). Personal computers, however, are much rarer outside the advanced industrial economies. Compared with people in Brazil, people in the United States are three times more likely to own a television, but ten times more likely to own a personal computer. In the developed countries, most adults and many children have a cell phone, but in India and Nigeria there are about twenty-five people to a phone. Even so, the advent of cellular phones has made it much easier to connect the rural population in developing countries where there are often very few land lines.

Table 7.4 also provides a picture of educational attainment. The first column, showing public education expenditure as a percentage of GDP, gives a rough measure

	TABLE 7.3
Health Outcomes, 1990–2004	

Country	Total Health Expenditure as % of GDP, 2002	Physicians per 1000 Citizens, 1990/2004	Life Expectancy at Birth 2003	Infant Mortality per 1,000 Live Births 2003	Fertility Rate, 2003
Brazil	7.9	1.3/2.1	69	33	2.1
Britain	7.7	1.4/1.7	78	5	1.6
China	5.8	1.5/1.6	71	30	1.9
France	9.7	2.6/3.3	79	4	1.9
Germany	10.9	3.1/3.6	78	4	1.3
India	6.1	0.5/0.5	63	63	2.9
Iran	6.0	0.3/1.0	69	33	2.0
Japan	7.9	1.7/2.0	82	3	1.3
Mexico	6.1	1.1/1.7	74	23	2.2
Nigeria	4.7	0.2/0.3	45	98	5.6
Russia	6.2	4.1/4.2	66	16	1.3
United States	14.6	2.4/5.5	77	7	2.0

Source: World Bank, *World Development Indicators 2005*, Tables 2.14, 2.16, 2.17, 2.19 (downloaded February 7, 2006), from http://devdata.worldbank.org/wdi2005/Table2_14.htm,Table2_16.htm,Table2_17.htm,Table2_19.htm.

of the "priority" given to education. Remember, however, that private schools, which in some countries are very common, are not counted here. There are differences in educational requirements: Nigeria requires only children from ages 6 to 12 to attend school. And the differences in dollar expenditures per student are very large. The outcomes are predictable enough. At the high end in educational outcomes, France, Germany, Japan, and Britain have virtually all of their primary and secondary school-age children in schools, and about half of the college-age population is in some form of advanced education. In the United States, college education is even more common. Nigeria has only 8 percent of the appropriate age cohort in tertiary education, by far the poorest record of these countries. India's figure is 11 percent.

The payoffs of development and education are clearly reflected in literacy rates: 30 to 40 percent of all adult Indians and Nigerians are unable to read or write. Yet China has less than 10 percent illiteracy. But because they are often based on the number of school years completed, not on actual reading ability, literacy figures are a crude measure of skill and competence and must be treated with caution. The high official literacy figures in the United States, for example, conflict with studies showing substantial functional illiteracy among American adults.

Women in developing countries often lag behind in literacy. For example, fewer than half of all adult females in India are reported to be literate. The discrepancy between male and female literacy rates tells us something of the status of women. Where women make up a smaller proportion of the labor force, female illiteracy also

TABLE 7.4

Education and Information

Country	Public Education Expenditure as Percent of Gov't Spending, 2002–03	Gross Percentage of Relevant Age Group Enrolled, Tertiary, 2002–03	Percentage 15 Years and Above Illiterate, Male/ Female, 2002	Female Share of Labor Force, 1998	Newspapers per 1,000 Inhabitants, 2000	Personal Computers per 1,000 Inhabitants, 2003
Brazil	12	18	14/13	35	46	75
Britain	11	64	ND	44	326	406
China	ND	13	5/13	45	59	28
France	11	54	ND	45	143	347
Germany	10	49	ND	42	291	485
India	13	11	32/55	32	60	7
Iran	18	21	16/30	ND	28	91
Japan	11	49	ND	41	566	382
Mexico	24	21	7/11	33	94	82
Nigeria	ND	8	26/41	36	25	7
Russia	12	70	0/1	49	105	89
United States	17	81	ND	46	215	659

Source: World Bank, *World Development Indicators 2005*, Tables 2.10, 2.11, 2.13; 5.10, 5.11 (downloaded February 7, 2006), from http://devdata.worldbank.org/wdi2005/ Table2_10.htm,Table2_11.htm,Table2_13.htm, Table5_10.htm, Table5_11.htm, also World Bank, *World Development Indicators 2000* (for data on female labor force participation).

Women and the Informal Economy

BOX 7.5

Parmila is an Indian widow in her thirties with two young children. Although she comes from a wealthy family, her husband's death forced her to take various part-time jobs. She collects wood from local forests, dries it, and then twice a week walks five miles to sell it at a local market. In the winter (November to January), she works on farms dehusking rice. She gets to keep some of the rice she produces. Outside of the rainy season, she also works as a laborer on a construction site, where her boss pays her about half of the Indian minimum wage. Parmila's total income is very low by Western standards, but it is enough to allow her to send her two children to school. Parmila does not ask for sympathy or for financial support from her relatives. "Even in times of acute crisis, I held my nerves and did not give in to circumstances," she says. "My God has always stood with me."

Women make up an increasing share of the world's workers. In most non-Islamic countries, they now make up 40 percent or more of the labor force. But in many parts of the world, most women work in the informal economy, where their work is often poorly paid. It commonly also escapes taxation and regulation. In India and in many African countries, for example, more than four out of five women who work outside of agriculture are in the informal economy. Many women choose such jobs voluntarily. They may do childcare for others or produce arts and crafts, often for local consumption. These jobs may be attractive because they can be performed at home while the women also take care of their own children or relatives. But many women also work in the informal sector because they face discrimination elsewhere. And some are enticed or forced into exhausting, dangerous, or degrading work in sweatshops or in the sex industry. While the informal economy can offer job flexibility, it can also be a place where there is little protection against abusive working conditions.

Source: William Easterly, *The Elusive Quest for Growth: The Economists' Adventures and Misadventures in the Tropics* (Cambridge: MIT Press, 2001), 45.

tends to be higher. Faced with poverty, disease, and the absence of a social safety net, parents in poor countries traditionally want to have many children, to ensure that some survive and can support them in old age. But in large families mothers usually have few opportunities to educate themselves or hold jobs outside the home. Modernizing the status of women generally makes them better informed and more capable of making choices that lead to a more stable and healthy population. As women are educated and/or enter the labor force, they recognize the advantages of smaller families and become more aware of the importance of education and adequate health care.

Table 7.4 also reveals the sobering difficulties of trying to change societies, even in an area such as literacy, where modern technologies are available. It is hard for a poor country to spend a high percentage of its GDP on education, because it must then make sacrifices elsewhere. And the effects are limited if much of the country's productive effort has to go into feeding a rapidly growing population. No matter how large the educational effort may be, it does not translate into much per child, because the resource base is small and the population is growing rapidly. Moreover, since most older people are illiterate, the net effect on literacy is slow. And in many poorer countries, their best-educated young people often leave the country to take jobs in the big cities of the rich countries.

All of these data show how governmental and private efforts, in societies at different levels of economic development and of differing social structures and cultures, affect human life chances. Economic development affects economic prosperity; public health provisions, such as sanitation and the availability of potable water; and access to the outside world through telephone and television, roads, and other infrastructure. But although natural resources and socioeconomic structure constrain these outcomes, government and private efforts can make a big difference.

OUTCOMES: DOMESTIC SECURITY

As Thomas Hobbes would have reminded us, maintaining domestic law and order and protecting persons and property are among the most basic government responsibilities. Without them the conduct of personal, economic, and civic life are impossible. It is therefore worrisome that until recently crime rates have been on the increase in many advanced industrial countries, as well as in the developing world. Thus in the United States the crime rate increased by almost 15 percent between 1982 and 1991. In France the 1990 incidence of crimes against persons and property was almost twice that of 1975. In Russia the crime rate doubled between 1985 and 1993, as the moral and legal order collapsed. The country now has a murder rate almost five times as high as the United States. Brazil and Mexico also have considerably higher murder rates than the United States, while those of such European countries as England, France, and Germany are a small fraction of the U.S. numbers. China has similarly low murder rates, whereas Japan is even lower.

High crime rates are primarily a problem of the larger urban areas where much of the population of modern countries resides. The causes of urban crime are complex. Rapidly increasing migration into the major cities, from the domestic countryside or from poorer foreign countries, increases diversity and often conflict. The pace of urbanization is particularly explosive in many developing countries, such as Brazil and Nigeria, where there are severe problems of poverty and infrastructure. The newly arrived city-dwellers often find themselves uprooted from their cultures, unwelcome, without a job, and living in squalor far apart from their families and traditional communities. Also, inequality of income and wealth, unemployment, and drug abuse, lie behind this general decline in public order and safety. In some former communist countries, the situation is compounded by the fact that traditional authorities and law enforcement have collapsed.

Yet, crime rates have recently come down significantly in the United States and some other countries. The number of murders per 100,000 inhabitants in the United States peaked at 9.4 in 1994, and declined to 5.7 in 2003 (see Figure 7.4). There are

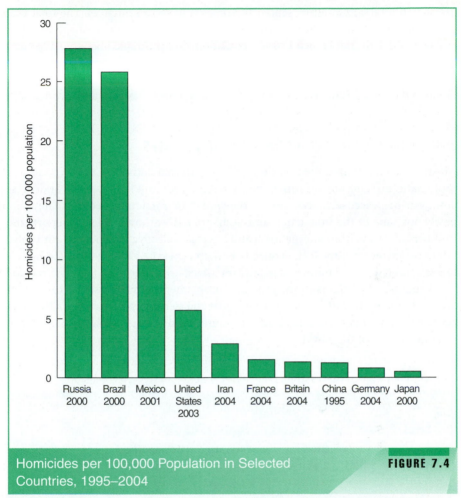

Homicides per 100,000 Population in Selected Countries, 1995–2004

FIGURE 7.4

Source: *United Nations Demographic Yearbook, 2002* (New York: United Nations, 2002) and "United Nations Surveys on Crime Trends and the Operations of Criminal Justice Systems" downloaded from http://www.unodc.org/unodc/en/crime_cicp_surveys.html.

several reasons that crime rates have recently come down in the United States and elsewhere. One is a strong economy, in which more young people have been able to find jobs. A second reason is stricter law enforcement. This is reflected in part in the number of police officers relative to total population, which ranges from one police officer for every 350 persons in the United States, to 820 in India, and 1,140 in Nigeria. In the United States, both federal and state governments have also sought to reduce crime by increasing the length of imprisonment. By removing the criminally prone from the streets, these authorities have succeeded in cutting the crime rate, but at the cost of an exploding prison population. The United States now imprisons more people than any other country, including communist China. The total prison population in the United States in 2004 was around 2.2 million, including 1.3 million in state prisons, and

700,000 in local jails awaiting sentencing or serving short sentences. The total U.S. prison population has for the past ten years been increasing at a rate of about 50,000 per year. Similarly, the French prison population almost doubled between 1983 and 1990.[6] A third cause of lower crime rates has been a decrease in the number of youth at the age at which most crimes are committed. Yet, as the 15- to 25-year-old male population in the United States is now on the rise, violent crime may increase once again.

INTERNATIONAL OUTPUTS AND OUTCOMES

Most states engage in a great variety of international activities. Such economic, diplomatic, military, and informational activities may result in prosperity or depression, war or peace, secularization or the spread of particular beliefs.[7] The most costly outcome of the interaction among nations is warfare. Table 7.5 reports the numbers of deaths from international and internal collective violence for our twelve study countries for almost the entire twentieth century (1900–1995). The figures are mostly civilian and military deaths from interstate warfare, but they also include the slaughter of civilians in the efforts to implement communism in the Soviet Union, the holocaust of European Jews under the German Nazis (Hitler's National Socialist Party), many "ethnic cleansing" episodes in Europe and Africa, and civil wars in all parts of the world.

TABLE 7.5

Deaths from Collective Civilian-Military Violence, 1900–1995

Country	Civilian Deaths	Military Deaths	Unspecified Deaths	Total Deaths
Brazil	—	1,000	2,000	3,000
Britain	131,000	1,350,000	—	1,481,000
China	4,047,000	2,671,000	818,000	7,536,000
France	490,000	1,830,000	—	2,320,000
Germany	2,232,000	7,150,000	—	9,382,000
India	889,000	71,000	37,000	997,000
Iran	120,000	468,000	1,000	589,000
Japan	510,000	1,502,000	—	2,012,000
Mexico	125,000	125,000	10,000	260,000
Nigeria	1,005,000	1,000,000	6,000	2,011,000
Soviet Union/Russia	12,028,000	11,901,000	96,000	24,025,000
United States	—	524,000	—	524,000
TOTALS	21,577,000	28,593,000	970,000	51,140,000

Source: Adapted from Ruth Leger Sivard, "Wars and War Related Deaths, 1900–1995," *World Military and Social Expenditures 1996* (Washington, DC: World Priorities, 1996), 18–19. U.S. deaths add Korean and Vietnam war totals, from U.S. Department of State figures, to Sivard report of World War I and II deaths.

Over the long haul, the deadly costs of international warfare have gradually escalated. One authority estimates that more than 90 percent of the war deaths since 1700 occurred in the twentieth century. Civilian deaths caused by war have increased even more rapidly than military ones. In the last decades of the twentieth century, more than three-quarters of the war deaths were civilian.[8]

Table 7.5 shows that the people of USSR/Russia, by a margin of more than two-to-one, were the most numerous victims of the tormented history of the twentieth century. The enormous Russian casualties during World War I destroyed the czarist regime. Its collapse was followed by the 1917 Bolshevik Revolution, the Civil War (1918–1921), and Stalin's Great Terror (particularly in the 1930s), each of which cost the lives of millions. Soviet suffering climaxed in World War II with a total of 17 million civilian and military dead. All told, the USSR/Russia suffered more than 24 million civilian and military deaths in the wars and political horrors of the twentieth century.

Germany suffered the second-largest number of deaths from twentieth-century collective violence. More than 3 million deaths, mostly military, occurred in World War I. In World War II, Germany suffered almost 5 million military and another 1.75 million civilian deaths. Other countries with huge losses include China (7 to 8 million) and Japan, whose more than 2 million deaths include half a million civilians, notably many residents of Hiroshima and Nagasaki. French and British sufferings were of roughly similar magnitude. Both countries took horrendous military casualties in the trench warfare of World War I. Since the Civil War, the United States has largely avoided the horrors of large-scale fighting on its own soil, but it still suffered over 120,000 deaths in World War I and close to half a million in World War II. While in the Korean and Vietnam wars, America suffered only moderate losses by these terrible standards, Korean and Vietnamese casualties were in the millions.

After World War II, the most devastating conflicts have occurred in the Third World. The partition of formerly British India into India, Pakistan, and Bangladesh has been associated with numerous deadly conflicts within and between the three countries. Some two million lives, mostly civilian, have been lost. In recent years, much of the world's media focus has been on conflicts in the Middle East, but conflicts in Africa have in fact been more frequent and devastating. Many African countries, newly independent from about 1960, but with borders arbitrarily drawn by colonial powers, have serious problems of national cohesion and have suffered from chronic civil war. Large-scale civil war in Nigeria (1967–1970) cost perhaps more than a million lives, and more sporadic conflict has continued to the present time. In 2002, for example, when the country hosted an international beauty contest, violent clashes erupted between Muslims and Christians that resulted in hundreds of deaths.

The end of the Cold War around 1990 witnessed a wave of instability and conflict in Eastern Europe and Central Asia. The breakup of the Soviet Union and Yugoslavia resulted in bloody border wars and secessional conflicts (for example, in Bosnia and Kosovo in the former Yugoslavia, and Chechnya in Russia). These conflicts brought another wave of ethnic slaughter, religious clashes, and struggles for power among different warlords. But since 1992, the number of wars and casualties has gradually and steadily declined. And although recent years have seen horrific acts of terrorism, its annual human toll has not changed much. Some students of international conflict see hope in what they call the "democratic peace," the fact that democratic countries hardly ever fight wars against one another. As more countries become democratic, will the world also become more peaceful?

The Uppsala Conflict Data Project reports of 118 armed worldwide conflicts (defined as involving at least twenty-five battle deaths) from 1989 through 2004. In 2004, there were thirty ongoing conflicts, of which seven involved more than 1,000 deaths.[9] Each was a civil war occurring within state boundaries, although a few were internationalized in that foreign powers were also involved. In every year since the end of World War II in 1945, there have been more civil wars than interstate conflicts (wars between countries), and the civil wars have also caused more casualties than interstate wars. There are many reasons for the high incidence of civil war. Some are related to ethnic or religious conflicts. But others seem mainly due to struggles between warlords over lootable resources, such as diamonds, gold, or oil. External actors—such as the United Nation (UN), the United States, NATO, or strong regional powers—can sometimes help end civil wars, but in some cases (such as Angola) civil wars have been prolonged because foreign powers have been engaged on both sides of the conflict.

The UN in the post–Cold War world has intervened in some of these conflicts by providing peacekeeping missions when the parties to conflicts are ready to accept these mediations. More rarely the UN intervenes as a peacemaker, as in Bosnia and later in neighboring Kosovo in the 1990s, or when the peace-keeping mission in Sierra Leone (West Africa) was converted into a peacemaking effort. The UN's effectiveness in controlling domestic and international collective violence depends on consensus among the great powers. How tenuous this consensus can become is illustrated in the troubled efforts of the UN to disarm Iraq after the Gulf War of 1990–1991 and later to prevent Saddam Hussein's government there from producing weapons of mass destruction, leading to the U.S.-led invasion of 2003.

The economic costs of national security can be high. Many countries face a massive national debt that often includes large deferred costs of borrowing for earlier wars and the maintenance of national defense. Many states, particularly in conflict-prone regions, feel that they need to spend significantly on national defense because of the "security dilemma"—they have to "take out insurance" against the possibility that their neighbors might be aggressive. While military expenditures in the world have declined since the collapse of the Soviet Union, the horrors of September 11, 2001, have led to a new costly mobilization of resources against international terrorism.

POLITICAL GOODS AND VALUES

If we are to compare and evaluate public policy in different political systems, we need to consider the political goods that motivate different policies. That leads us back to the issues we discussed in Chapters 1 and 2, to the functions and purposes that governments serve. This book is organized around the concepts of system, process, and policy. We can think about values as "political goods" related to each of those levels of analysis.

At the system level, there is a long tradition in political analysis that emphasizes order, predictability, and stability. Citizens are most free and most able to act purposefully when their environment is stable, transparent, and predictable. We call these conditions **system goods,** since they reflect the functioning and effectiveness of the whole political system. While people generally want some measure of change and new opportunities, most prefer stability to abrupt and unforeseeable change. Political instability—constitutional breakdowns, frequent leadership changes, riots, demonstrations, and the like—upsets most people's plans and can cost lives and cause material destruction. System goods have to do with the regularity and predictability with which political systems work, but also with their ability to adapt to environmental challenges.

Regularity and adaptability are typically somewhat in conflict. Sometimes order and stability are at the top of the agenda. In the United States, the administration of Warren Harding after World War I was such a period, called "a return to normalcy." There was a similar withdrawal from mobilization after World War II and the Korean War. On the other hand, the 1930s and the 1960s were periods of change and adaptation, in which the reach of governmental powers was extended. But the stress on change and adaptation can also be a call for reductions in the scope in government, as in the Thatcher administration in Britain or the Republican "Contract With America" of 1994–1995.

Another school of thought emphasizes goods associated with the political process—citizen participation and free political competition. Democracy is good and authoritarianism is bad, according to this school of thought, because of the way citizens are treated in the process, and not because democracy, for example, produces better economic results. Democratic procedures and various rights of due process, then, are **process goods.** Process goods include participation, compliance, and procedural justice. We value participation not merely as a means to responsive government, but for its own sake, since it enhances citizen competence and dignity. Compliance with authority can also be a good, as individuals respond to the impulse to serve others, which can be one of humanity's most gratifying experiences. U.S. President John F. Kennedy in his inaugural address called on such impulses to serve and sacrifice when he said, "Ask not what your country can do for you; ask what you can do for your country." Procedural justice (trial by jury, habeas corpus, no cruel and unusual punishment) is another crucial process value, without which citizens would have much greater reasons to fear their governments.

Procedural goods also include *effectiveness* and *efficiency.* A preference for effectiveness means that we prefer policies that actually lead to their desired purpose over policies that do not. Efficiency means that policies should attain their objectives at the lowest possible cost. If two alternative policies would lead to the same result but at very different costs, we would prefer the policy with the lower cost. In designing government agencies, most of us would prefer lean and inexpensive institutions to bloated agencies that produce no better results.

A third and final focus is on **policy goods,** such as economic welfare, quality of life, freedom, and personal security. We value a political system that improves welfare, decreases inequalities, enhances public safety, enables people to live lives they want for themselves, and cleans up its environment, whatever the political process that produces these results. Well-meaning people do not always agree which of these policy goods are most important. Yet, there are at least two important criteria that most of us would agree that government policy should meet. The first is *fairness.* The problem is that people often disagree over what is fair. In some situations, we believe that fairness requires all people to be treated equally (as when family members attempt to divide a tempting pie). In other situations, fairness demands that individuals be treated according to performance (as when grades are given in a college course). And in yet other situations, fairness means that people are treated according to their needs (for example, in cases of medical treatment). Thus fairness can imply *equal treatment* in some cases, *just desserts* (reward in proportion to merit or contribution) in others, and *treatment according to need* in yet others. Many distributive policies—for example, pension systems such as social security in the United States—rely on some combination of these criteria.

The debate over these various conceptions of fairness is never settled. In most cases, however, fairness would rule out practices that are *arbitrary* or *partial.* Few of us would find it fair if government officials threw dice to determine who would be imprisoned or be given pensions, or if they made such decisions solely on the basis of their personal prejudices or connections. We can think of fairness in this sense as reflected in the process good of *procedural justice.*

The second consideration is the promotion and preservation of *freedom.* As anarchists, libertarians, and other government skeptics would remind us, public policies should promote and protect freedom and basic human and political rights. If two policies are equally efficient and fair, then we would prefer the one that respects the rights and liberties of the citizens to the greater extent. But even in a democratic society, freedom is not always chosen over other political goods. The right to bear arms, protected in the Second Amendment to the U.S. Constitution, is a hotly contested issue, as many Americans would like to prevent those most likely to cause harm from carrying lethal weapons. Similarly, freedom of speech is a constitutional guarantee, but many people want to prohibit speech that is insulting, blasphemous, or offensive.

Liberty is sometimes viewed only as freedom from governmental regulation and harassment. Freedom is more than inhibition of government action, however, because even private individuals and organizations may violate the liberty and privacy of others. In such cases, liberty may be fostered by government intervention. Much legislation against racial segregation and discrimination generally has been impelled by this purpose. Liberty to act, organize, obtain information, and protest is an indispensable part of effective political participation. Nor is it irrelevant to social, political, and economic equality. Prior to the breakdown of communism in Eastern Europe and the Soviet Union, it was a common view that the communist countries were trading liberty for equality. In contrast, capitalism was said to trade off equality for liberty. But one important thing that came to light after the collapse of communism was the extent of corruption and privilege in communist societies. While they had surely traded off liberty for a basic security of employment, it was not clear that the communists had otherwise gained much in the way of equality.

Table 7.6 draws on our three-level analysis of political systems to present a checklist of political goods or values. There is no simple way to say which value should prevail when they conflict. In fact, different preferences among such values as freedom, fairness, and efficiency set different cultures, parties, and political philosophies apart. One society or group of citizens may value fairness over liberty; another may make the opposite choice, as in Patrick Henry's famous exclamation, "Give me liberty or give me death!"

Political Goods

TABLE 7.6

Levels of Political Goods	Classes of Goods	Content and Examples
System level	System maintenance	The political system features regular, stable, and predictable decision-making process.
	System adaptation	The political system adapts to environmental change and challenges.
Process level	Participation in political inputs	The political system is open and responsive to many forms of political speech and action.
	Compliance and support	Citizens fulfill their obligations (e.g., military service and tax obligations) to the system and comply with public law and policy.
	Procedural justice	Legal and political procedures are orderly and fair (due process) and there is equality before the law.
	Effectiveness and efficiency	Political processes have their intended effects and are no more cumbersome, expensive, or intrusive than necessary.
Policy level	Welfare	Citizens have access to health care, learning, and material goods, which the government seeks to distribute broadly.
	Security	The government provides safety of person and property, public order, and national security.
	Fairness	Government policy is not discriminatory and recognizes individuals from different ethnic, linguistic, or religious groups; vulnerable or disadvantaged citizens are protected.
	Liberty	Citizens enjoy freedom from excessive regulation, protection of their privacy, and respect for their autonomy.

TRADE-OFFS AND OPPORTUNITY COSTS

One of the hard facts about political goods is that we cannot always have them all simultaneously. A political system often has to **trade off** one value to obtain another. Spending funds on education is giving up the opportunity to spend them on welfare, or to leave them in the hands of those who earned them. **Opportunity costs** are what you lose in one area by committing your resources to a different good. They often arise when politicians have to decide how much to invest for the future rather than spend today (for example, when they determine future retirement benefits). Even more difficult are the trade-offs between security and liberty. Extreme liberty, as Hobbes would tell us, would give us a highly insecure world where the strong might bully the weak and where collective action would be difficult. Yet, without liberty, security may be little more than servitude or imprisonment. The trade-offs between political goods are not the same under all circumstances. Sometimes increasing liberty will also increase security (for example, because riots against censorship will end). And under some conditions investment in education will be paid back many times in health and welfare, because trained citizens can better care for themselves and work more productively. These are positive trade-offs in which there may be no opportunity costs. But often you cannot "have your cake and eat it, too." One of the important tasks of social science is to discover the conditions under which positive and negative trade-offs occur.

Regrettably, political science has no way of converting units of liberty into units of safety or welfare. And we can never calculate the value of a political outcome gained at the cost of human life. Political decisionmakers often have to make such conversions, but as political scientists we can only point to value judgments that they are willing to make. The weight given to various goods differs across cultures and contexts. A religious faith or a political ideology may tell us how one value should be traded against another, and thus offer an orderly basis for choice. Such schemes may be invaluable for those pressed into action in the terrible circumstances of war, revolution, and famine. But when people do not share these underlying schemes and values, there may be serious conflicts. Sadly, there is no ideology, just as there is no political science, that can solve all these problems objectively.

REVIEW QUESTIONS

- What explains the growth of the welfare state?
- What are the advantages and disadvantages of different types of taxes?
- Do some governments tend to promote political rights and others civil rights, or do civil and political rights tend to go together?
- How is the welfare outcome for women changing in developing countries today?
- What sorts of armed conflicts are most common in today's world, and what problems do they cause?

KEY TERMS

direct taxes

distribution

extraction

gross domestic product (GDP)

indirect taxes

night watchman state

opportunity costs

Organization for Economic Cooperation and Development (OECD)

outcomes

police state

policy goods

political goods and values

process goods

public policies

regulation

regulatory state

symbolic outputs

system goods

trade off

welfare state

SUGGESTED READINGS

Bates, Robert H. *Markets and States in Tropical Africa.* Berkeley: University of California Press, 1981.

Bratton, Michael, and Nicholas van de Walle. *Democratic Experiments in Africa: Regime Transitions in Comparative Perspective.* New York: Cambridge University Press, 1997.

Castles, Francis G., ed. *The Comparative History of Public Policy.* Cambridge, UK: Polity Press, 1989.

Dahl, Robert. *Democracy and Its Critics.* New Haven, CT: Yale University Press, 1989.

Diamond, Larry, ed. *Democracy in Developing Countries.* Boulder, CO: Lynne Rienner, 1992.

Easterly, William. *The Elusive Quest for Growth: The Economists' Adventures and Misadventures in the Tropics.* Cambridge: MIT Press, 2001.

Flora, Peter, and Arnold Heidenheimer. *The Development of Welfare States in Europe and America.* New Brunswick, NJ: Transaction Books, 1981.

Gourevitch, Peter. *Politics in Hard Times.* Ithaca, NY: Cornell University Press, 1986.

Harbom, Lotta, and Peter Wallensteen. "Armed Conflict and Its International Dimensions, 1946–2004." *Journal of Peace Research* 42, no. 5, (2005): 623–35.

Jackson, Robert, and Carl Rosberg. *Personal Rule in Black Africa.* Berkeley: University of California Press, 1982.

Keefer, Philip, and Stuti Khemani. "Why Do the Poor Receive Poor Services?" *Economic and Political Weekly*, 28 February, 2004, 935–43.

Lijphart, Arend. *Patterns of Democracy.* New Haven, CT: Yale University Press, 1999.

Lindblom, Charles E. *Politics and Markets.* New Haven, CT: Yale University Press, 1978.

Olson, Mancur. *The Rise and Decline of Nations.* New Haven, CT: Yale University Press, 1982.

———. *Power and Prosperity.* New York: Basic Books, 2000.

Putnam, Robert D. *Making Democracy Work.* Princeton, NJ: Princeton University Press, 1993.

Tsebelis, George. *Veto Players: An Introduction to Institutional Analysis.* Princeton, NJ: Princeton University Press, 2002.

Wilensky, Harold, *Rich Democracies: Political Economy, Public Policy, and Performance.* Berkeley: University of California Press, 2002.

Wilson, James G. *The Politics of Regulation in the United States.* New York: Basic Books, 1980.

ENDNOTES

1. See World Bank, *Entering the 21st Century: World Development Report 1999–2000* (New York: Oxford University Press, 2000), Table A.1, 216–17.

2. Peter Flora and Arnold Heidenheimer, *The Development of Welfare States in Europe and America* (New Brunswick, NJ: Transaction Books, 1981); and Arnold Heidenheimer, Hugh Heclo, and Carolyn Teich Adams, *Comparative Public Policy*, 3rd ed. (New York: St. Martin's Press, 1990).

3. Heidenheimer, Heclo, and Adams. *Comparative Public Policy*, 211–19.

4. Steven C. Poe and C. Neal Tate, "Repression of Human Rights to Personal Integrity in the 1980s: A Global Analysis," *American Political Science Review* 88, no. 4 (December 1994): 853–72.

5. Simon Kuznets, "Economic Growth and Income Equality," *American Economic Review* 45 (1955):1–28.

6. World Bank, *World Development Report: Infrastructure for Development* (New York: Oxford University Press, 1994), Overview, 1 ff.

7. Peter Gourevitch, in his book *Politics in Hard Times* (Ithaca, NY: Cornell University Press, 1986), analyzes the policy responses of five Western industrial nations—Britain, France, Germany, Sweden, and the United States—to the three world depressions of 1870–1890, 1930–1940, and 1975–1985. Gourevitch shows how these crises affected business, labor, and agriculture differently in each country; consequences for political structure and policy varied greatly. Thus the world depression of the 1930s resulted in a conservative reaction in Britain (the formation of a "National" government), a moderate left reaction in the United States (the "New Deal"), a polarization and paralysis of public policy in France ("Immobilisme"), a moderate social democratic reaction in Sweden, and a radical right and left polarization in Germany, leading to a breakdown of democracy and the emergence of National Socialism. While the causes of World War II were complex, the pacifism of Britain, the demoralization and defeatism in France, the isolationism of the United States, and the nihilism and aggression of Germany were all fed by the devastating worldwide economic depression of the 1930s.

8. Ruth Leger Sivard, *World Military and Social Indicators* (Washington, DC: World Priorities, 1993), 20.

9. See Lotta Harbom and Peter Wallensteen, "Armed Conflict and Its International Dimension, 1946–2004," *Journal of Peace Research*, 42, no. 5 (2005), 623–35.